PRAISE FOR *SECRETS OF THE SPRAKKAR*

"Riveting."

—*New York Times*

"*Secrets of the Sprakkar* is a fascinating window into what a more gender-equal world could look like and why it's worth striving for. Iceland is doing a lot to level the playing field: paid parental leave, affordable childcare, and broad support for gender equality as a core value. Reid takes us on an exploration not only around this fascinating island but also through the triumphs and stumbles of a country as it journeys toward gender equality."

—Hillary Rodham Clinton

"With warmth, wit, and insight, First Lady Eliza Reid explores the reasons why Iceland is one of the best places on earth for women, as well as the challenges still ahead in achieving full gender equity. *Secrets of the Sprakkar* is an illuminating, inspiring, and absorbing book about how a more equitable society could elevate us all."

—Cheryl Strayed, #1 *New York Times* bestselling author of *Wild*

"What a world of possibilities Eliza Reid unveils in this warm and wonderful book! It made me want to pack my bags and move to Iceland."

—Ruth Reichl, *New York Times* bestselling author of *Save Me the Plums*

"The fact that the Icelandic language includes the word 'sprakkar'—an ancient term that translates to mean 'extraordinary women'—in its lexicon tells you a great deal about the country of Iceland. And in her marvelous memoir, Eliza Reid tells us a great deal more: not only about her life in Iceland but also about gender equality in action, and the sense of purpose that all of us seek. This is a charming and necessary book."

—Meg Wolitzer, *New York Times* bestselling author

"A warm and intimate exploration of what one small country can teach the world about gender equality. Eliza Reid charts her personal journey from a Canadian farm to Iceland's presidential residence and along the way proves to be the best possible guide to the historical, geographical and cultural factors that helped women thrive and built a vibrant modern society."

—Geraldine Brooks, Pulitzer Prize–winning author

"Everyone who visits Iceland quickly learns that the little country contains some of the world's most extraordinary women, their lives rooted in a social and political culture that nurtures equality between men and women without ignoring the pleasures and complexities of family life. It's a pleasure to see that culture marked out for us through the sometimes wry but always beautifully personal and perceptive lens of the remarkable Eliza Reid."

—Adam Gopnik, *New Yorker* staff writer

"A breath of fresh Icelandic air! Eliza Reid crafts a highly original, warm, and honest journey into the heart of the small Nordic island nation and its rich culture and history, creating an empowering read on how striving for equality can improve everyone's lives."

—Katja Pantzar, author of *The Finnish Way*

"Charting her own love of the nation and her journey to becoming its First Lady, alongside histories of other formidable women, Eliza Reid's *Secrets of the Sprakkar* sheds light on Iceland's unique approach to gender equity—an emblematic look at what's possible in the fight for women's rights worldwide. A fascinating, hopeful, and inspiring read."

—Esi Edugyan, bestselling author of *Washington Black*

"Reading *Secrets of the Sprakkar* is like sitting down with your favorite, smartest, warmest girlfriend and hearing all about the extraordinary women, history, and culture of her tiny adopted country. Reid celebrates Iceland and its attitudes toward women while also discussing where it has some room for improvement. By the time I finished this book, I felt I had traveled to Iceland and gotten to know its beauty and quirks and, most importantly, its *sprakkar*."

—Ann Hood, bestselling author

"Laced with frank discussions of domestic abuse, intersectionality, and other complex issues, this is a winning portrait of a country at the forefront of the fight for gender equality."

—*Publishers Weekly*

"Reid... is uniquely placed to observe the country which leads the world in gender equality, providing generous parenting leave, abundant childcare, and free prenatal services... The tiny country of Iceland should serve as an inspiration to the rest of the world."

—*Booklist*

"Reid's style is amusing, her thoughts are honest, and the issues she discusses are becoming more important by the day."

—*Washington Post*

"Reid artfully weaves incisive, relatable observations into her impressive new book on gender equality... an accessible, highly personal read."

—*StarTribune*

"Eliza Reid has compiled here a daring, insightful, often humorous and often fascinating look at women in Iceland... A real page turner and one that everyone should read, regardless of gender."

—*Reykjavik Grapevine*

"The sometimes funny, always insightful episodes really put you in touch with Icelandic culture and its attitude towards women—an uplifting and inspiring memoir that reads like a novel."

—*Conde Nast Traveler*

"Insightful and encouraging."

—Maria Shriver's *Sunday Paper*

"Her debut is a wonderful read. "

—Lögberg Heimskringla

"The book is peppered with lively personal anecdotes about Reid's life as first lady, interviews with notable local women, and observations about daily life in the beautiful country… It's interesting to hear so directly and unguardedly from an active first lady."

—*The Kit*

"[A] delightful love letter to [Reid's] adopted nation, in which she employs an engaging blend of reportage and memoir."

—*Quill & Quire*

SECRETS

OF THE

SPRAKKAR

Iceland's Extraordinary Women and
How They Are Changing the World

ELIZA REID

Copyright © 2022, 2023 by Eliza Reid
Cover and internal design © 2022, 2023 by Sourcebooks
Cover design and illustration © Kimberly Glyder
Energy rune by Alrún Nordic Design
Internal design by Holli Roach/Sourcebooks
Internal map by Jillian Rahn/Sourcebooks
Internal images © Getty Images, redchocolatte/Getty Images, Vectorios2016/iStock

Sourcebooks and the colophon are registered trademarks of Sourcebooks.

All rights reserved. No part of this book may be reproduced in any form or by
any electronic or mechanical means including information storage and retrieval
systems—except in the case of brief quotations embodied in critical articles or
reviews—without permission in writing from its publisher, Sourcebooks.

This publication is designed to provide accurate and authoritative information in regard
to the subject matter covered. It is sold with the understanding that the publisher is not
engaged in rendering legal, accounting, or other professional service. If legal advice
or other expert assistance is required, the services of a competent professional person
should be sought.—*From a Declaration of Principles Jointly Adopted by a Committee
of the American Bar Association and a Committee of Publishers and Associations*

This book is a memoir. It reflects the author's present recollections of experiences
over a period of time. Some names and characteristics have been changed, some
events have been compressed, and some dialogue has been re-created.

Published by Sourcebooks
P.O. Box 4410, Naperville, Illinois 60567-4410
(630) 961-3900
sourcebooks.com

Cataloging-in-Publication Data for the hardcover edition
is on file with the Library of Congress.

Printed and bound in Canada.
MBP 10 9 8 7 6 5 4 3 2 1

SPRAKKAR *(plural noun):*

An ancient Icelandic word meaning extraordinary
or outstanding women
Pronounced: SPRAH-car
(singular: sprakki)

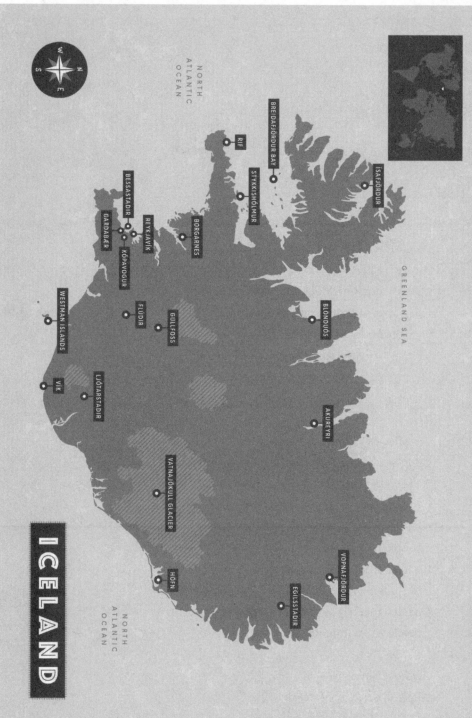

CONTENTS

FOREWORD

WHEN I READ ELIZA REID'S op-ed in the New York Times in 2019, I didn't feel like what she had to say about the arm-candy duties of first ladies had much to do with me, but the first thing I noticed about her book *Secrets of the Sprakkar* when I reviewed it for the *Washington Post* in January of 2022 was how amusing it is, and the second thing I noticed was how observant Eliza Reid is. Reid comes from Ontario, Canada. She has lived in Iceland since August of 2003, when she was twenty-seven, and is evidently something of an explorer (before she moved to Iceland, she was a rower for her college at Oxford, and crossed Russia and Central Asia on the Trans-Siberian Express. She also went for a solo backpacking trip to southeast Asia). She writes like an explorer, too, which is one of the charms of this book. This is a book about a place that is simultaneously a popular tourist destination and one of the most unusual places on Earth. Reid begins with the issues and skills that she was interested in but needed to figure out, and then she spreads her narrative outward and lets the reader follow her as she observes, understands, and analyzes what she needs to learn about, beginning with giving birth and raising small children in the capital area.

One of the most fascinating things about Iceland is that since the first years of Norse colonization, in the 9th century, every group of inhabitants has had to adapt to the landscape and the climate (one of my favorite Icelandic authors, Halldór Laxness, has written about this). Reid, who already had a successful career in her twenties, knows this, but as she explores, she is self-effacing, and the reader feels like he or she is coming along for a very pleasant ride.

Even though she is the First Lady of Iceland (her husband, Gudni Thorlacius Jóhannesson, was elected in 2016 and re-elected in 2020) she knows that her job in this book is not to do some sort of PR—it is to let readers in the States know what they can learn from Iceland (and readers in other English-speaking countries, too). In her discussion of the representation of women in Icelandic business, she is honest— although more women in Iceland are CEOs, the percentage is still not what it could be. But it is not wealth and corporate life that really interests her. After that chapter, she investigates other issues that are more controversial or even dangerous. How do women successfully express their sexuality? How to they work their way into the media? And how do they take care of the ecosystem? Eliza Reid visits a woman who not only owns the large family farm, but also understands for historical and geographical reasons that she could lose her farm to a volcanic eruption at any time (and she could have been a fashion model). And then Reid visits the women who work in the fishing industry, which is difficult and can be dangerous. *Secrets of the Sprakkar* is as much a travel guide as it is a socio-political exploration and analysis.

Maybe the chapter American readers should pay the closest attention to is the one on immigrants (when I lived there, immigrants were few and far between). Reid's interviews include two very interesting women—one who came from Mexico and now lives in a remote Icelandic village, and another, who came from Jamaica, and is now a lawyer.

Reid understands that politics is a fine line, even in Iceland, where a few members of the Althing (the Icelandic legislature) went to a nearly empty bar one evening in November of 2018 and downed a few, then started ranting about some female members, using denigrating expressions to describe their colleagues. Their conversation was recorded by another customer and put online. It caused quite an uproar.

Reid does not advocate violence, though she does cite one of the most famous women in Medieval Iceland, Ólöf "the rich" Loftsdóttir, who not only amassed a fortune, but also revenged herself on British pirates who killed her husband, Björn and seven other men in 1467 by enslaving, exiling, and killing many of the British pirates (and there is more to the story). Reid advocates education, solidarity, peaceful but vocal political action. She also understands that within Iceland, the United States, and most countries in the world, things can always get worse. The key is to not give up. And to maintain your sense of humor.

Jane Smiley

September 2022

AUTHOR'S NOTE

I AM AN ENTREPRENEUR, AUTHOR, speaker, mother, feminist, and immigrant, and I am married to the president of Iceland. Although there is no formal role titled "First Lady," certain duties and functions are expected, if not required, of a spouse of the head of state. As such, my public statements are often analyzed, praised, and critiqued. I have been cognizant of this in the writing of this book.

In Iceland, the role of president is largely, but not exclusively, symbolic. The president is the head of state of Iceland. It is an elected position, and the president has veto power over legislation and can play an influential role in steering the formation of coalition governments. However, it is the prime minister who is the head of the government, and political decision-making from day to day resides within government and parliament. The president (and I, therefore, as a vocal spouse) does not have a political platform or make public statements on budgets, laws, or political strategy for the nation.

In many countries, the issue of gender equality is steeped in politics, affecting legislation that encompasses issues from health care to education. Here in Iceland, however, the debate is no longer *whether* gender equality is an important objective but how best to achieve it. To paraphrase former American First Lady Hillary Rodham Clinton, gender equality is a human rights issue, not a political one. I therefore do not see this book as espousing political views. I leave that to the politicians.

This book is a modern portrait of a country and its people using interviews combined with my own fallible memories and impressions. It is neither fully comprehensive nor unbiased. It has not been fed through focus groups, stripped of substance by PR consultants, or varnished to a vapid sheen worthy of what cynics might expect from someone who bears the moniker "First Lady." It is, I hope, a testament to the type of society we can build when we are vigilant about creating and ensuring equal opportunities, experiences, and rewards for people of all genders.

A note on spellings: The Icelandic alphabet considers vowels with accents (á, í, ý, etc.) as distinct letters, with distinct pronunciations, and I have kept these in the book. Additionally, Icelandic has three letters that are unknown in English: æ, pronounced "aye," which I have kept in this book; ð, pronounced like the "th" in *although*, which I have often replaced with "d," as per custom; and þ, pronounced like the "th" in *think*, which I have often replaced with "th," as per custom. For example, while I have written Gudni for my husband's name and Thóra for the name of the journalist, in Icelandic, these are written Guðni and Þóra.

1

AN IMMIGRANT IN ICELAND

A guest's eyes see more clearly

IN ICELAND, IT'S CONSIDERED BAD luck to start a new job on a Monday. A Friday is acceptable, the first day of the calendar month (if it does not fall on a Monday, of course) even better, but if you really want to make a success of your career, avoid starting on a Monday.

My working life on this North Atlantic island therefore began on a Tuesday in October, one that was cloudy with a stiff breeze, as so many October days here are. Having been a resident of Iceland for not quite six weeks, I was unaware of the Monday rule. I was keen to start my new job, but when the CEO of the small software start-up where I had been hired as a marketing specialist gave me the starting date, I felt in no position to suggest an alternative. After all, I was lucky. I had landed a job that related to my previous experience in a country where I did not speak the language and knew practically no one aside from my fiancé and his family.

I moved to Iceland for love in 2003 when I was twenty-seven years old. Before I met my future husband, Gudni Jóhannesson, in the autumn of 1998, my entire knowledge of the country consisted of being able to recognize its flag and its location on the map and identify its capital city as Reykjavík (thanks to hours playing *Where in the World Is*

---

*   *Glöggt er gests augað*: "A guest's eyes see more clearly" is an Icelandic idiom that means that those who are new to an environment or who are guests see things in clearer focus than those who have always been there.

Carmen Sandiego? on a Commodore 64 in the 1980s). I did not know that, even then, Iceland was considered one of the best places in the world to be a woman. That a unique alchemy of history, people, policies, and luck have produced a country that is arguably closer than any other to clutching the golden ring of gender equality.

Gudni and I met in graduate school at Oxford University in England, two foreigners among many at one of Oxford's colleges, St. Antony's, that specialized in international studies. Gudni was the first Icelander to attend St. Antony's and one of only a handful who were studying at the entire university. To me, a twenty-two-year-old Canadian woman who grew up on a hobby farm in the Ottawa Valley, his obscure nationality was alluring. He was quiet, owned many books and few other possessions, and didn't drink as enthusiastically as the other students (I assumed that was what all Icelanders were like). He was also tall and easygoing, and he sparingly but devastatingly deployed a bone-dry, self-deprecating humor to match that of the British.

I had moved across the ocean to England just a couple of months after completing my bachelor of arts degree in Canada, using the excuse of graduate school to experience a new country, get further into debt, and postpone making any decisions about what I actually wanted to do with my life. My cohort fell broadly into two groups. On one hand, there were those who, like me, had been in school all our lives, were hardworking enough to have been accepted at one of the world's most prestigious institutions, but prioritized our time in an arguably less constructive way (I never missed a pub or poker night and didn't bother to hear then Czech president Václav Havel deliver a sought-after keynote talk because I knew I would not be tested on it). On the other hand, some students had more maturity. Many had sacrificed much to be at Oxford, quitting jobs, painstakingly saving money, upending families. They were there to get the most they could out of the experience.

Gudni, of course, not only attended the talk of the aforementioned Cold War dissident but also volunteered as an usher at the event. He read the index of every book first, no matter the topic, in case there was an entry for Iceland. He clipped out articles in the newspaper on topics as diverse as historiography and sporting heroes and filed them meticulously by subject in a series of binders, on the chance that sometime in the distant future, he could use them in an article or speech (a more prescient activity than the future president knew at the time).

From this behavior and the smattering of gray hairs around his temples, I suspected he was marginally older than I, perhaps as wizened as twenty-six. Once, at midnight during a house party in a smoke-filled, cramped basement flat, when I was trying to get to know this intriguing but quiet man a little better, he casually mentioned being an undergraduate student when the Berlin Wall fell. I was in Grade Eight in 1989.

"How old *are* you?" I asked when I realized that my estimate of his age might be overly optimistic.

"I am thirrrty," he said and smiled, rolling the *r* just a moment too long, as one would do if speaking Icelandic.

This can't be possible, I remember thinking. It was midnight. Two revelers who quite likely did not know each other's names were making out in the corner. Cigarette smoke was thick in the air. No one as old as "thirrrty" would ever want to stay out that late in this environment, surely. I nodded, sipped my beer, and changed the subject.

"What are you up to over the holidays?"

It was only mid-November, but people were already booking flights home for when term ended.

"I'll be visiting my daughter," he replied nonchalantly, as if it was so obvious that I needn't have asked.

I nearly spit out my beer. *Of course you are. If the world is suddenly so topsy-turvy that I am flirting at midnight with a man who has just entered his fourth decade, then it would be perfectly natural that he also has a child and a handsome, r-rolling, Nordic family back in Iceland whom he has never mentioned in the two months I've known him.* This rather put a spanner (I was in the UK now, so it was not a wrench) in the works for my flirtation with the Viking. *Game off,* I thought, as if this conversation were a weekend road hockey pickup game and his personal life were a passing car.

"Oh, of course. What about her mother?" I ventured.

"I'm not visiting her," he replied, maintaining eye contact with me. *Game on.*

Gudni was the first divorcé I counted among my friends. He had not mentioned his four-year-old daughter before because in the gamut of small talk when students first meet, no one thinks to ask about children, and he was not the type to offer up more detail than necessary. In that key developmental decade of one's twenties, he had completed his first master's degree, fathered a child, gotten married then amicably divorced, and finally relocated to England. He was eight years older than I, at that time more than one-third of my life, yet somehow the fact that we were both students put us on a level playing field. And he made me laugh.

By the end of the academic year, we were a couple. Eighteen months later, we were living together in a small flat in Hampshire as he completed his PhD in history and I worked in sales and marketing for a rather posh two-hundred-year-old company that had only recently stopped addressing people as Mrs. or Miss instead of by first name (Ms. being, it seemed to me, a title they unofficially reserved for divorcées and lesbians). On weekdays, Gudni often made the two-and-a-half-hour, one-way trip via train and Underground to the Public Record Office (now National Archives) near Kew just outside London to pore over records of British-Icelandic relations. I helped write marketing brochures on how to identify counterfeit pharmaceuticals or luxury goods and corrected people who asked on a virtually daily basis where in the States I was from. In the evenings, I worked on learning a few phrases of Icelandic, a Norse language that has changed little in the eleven hundred or so years since the island was settled. My CD-ROM taught me such helpful phrases as *Where is the train station?* (there are no trains in Iceland) and *Where is the beach?* (a small part of the country straddles the Arctic Circle).

I had a plan...of sorts. Gudni was finishing up his degree, completing a one-hundred-thousand-word dissertation on twentieth-century fishing disputes in the North Atlantic, and he understandably wanted to return to the island where he was missing so much of his daughter Rut's childhood (although she visited us regularly and he spent most summers with her in Iceland). If we wanted to be together, it would be in Iceland or nowhere, at least while she was still growing up. And if I was going to move there with Gudni, it would be to stay. I'd need to make a life for myself there, outside of being his partner. It could not be a dress rehearsal; I didn't want it to be easy for me to give up on the partnership when I despaired at the 10:00 a.m. darkness in December or if I were unable to understand conversation in Icelandic at dinner parties. If this was going to be the main performance of my life, I thought it was just as well to be married, to be legally committed to each other until death do us part.

Therefore, one sunny March weekend, just a couple of months after we had decided we'd soon be leaving the UK and beginning a new adventure together in Iceland, when we escaped our routines to walk along the sea in north Cornwall, I proposed to him, and he accepted. I had smuggled a bottle of champagne into my suitcase, and we drank it in the Fawlty Towers–esque B and B where we were staying before celebrating our engagement with some takeaway fish and chips in a seaside village. On the phone the next day, Gudni's pleased mother said to him, "I hope you did it properly!" He confessed the true circumstances of the betrothal only months later.

I figured if I was about to move to this remote island where I did not speak the language and did not have a job, then I might as well be broke too and make a truly fresh start. I cashed in my share options from the company where I'd been working and planned a one-hundred-day solo trip. I'd begin on the Trans-Siberian Railway through Russia and Central Asia and end with six weeks backpacking around Southeast Asia.

I arrived in Iceland to live on August 21, 2003, almost ten years to the day before my fourth child would be born. While I had been living out of a thirty-pound backpack, drinking mango lassies, riding camels, and sleeping under mosquito nets, Gudni had submitted his doctoral thesis and found a small one-bedroom apartment for us to rent in a four-story building near the University of Iceland in central Reykjavík. Rut, who was now nine, stayed with us on a pullout sofa every second weekend.

A few days after my move, Gudni noticed an ad in the local paper for a marketing specialist at a company where English was the working language. I got the job, and my first day was that windy Tuesday in October. After only six weeks in the country, I was fortunate to have found a good position that could support us financially while Gudni began a postdoc research role at the university. I also started eight hours a week of intensive Icelandic lessons. I had learned that I could pack away for good my umbrella, that vital accessory of the UK; it was no match for Icelandic wind. I bought a bus pass to ferry me to and from work (generally with other immigrants, senior citizens, middle-school kids, or those who had no driver's license for one reason or another). I marveled at autumn's lingering sunsets over Faxaflói Bay and waking up to see snowfall on Mount Esja, which towered over the city.

I was in the midst of the high that constitutes the first blush of culture shock, when everything is new and exhilarating. I had moved for love, yes, but here I was earning an income *and* learning the language, beginning to create my own raison d'être for life in Iceland. I could already see there would be moments that called for patience and persistence but that I would like it here.

Starts-ups are often male dominated, those in the software industry especially so. When I joined the company that autumn almost two decades ago, I was the fifteenth employee and the fourth woman. The company was founded by former Icelandair employees, and it designed software for airlines. It was the perfect environment in which to undergo the initial steps of the transition from foreigner to Icelander. I progressed from milky tea to strong black coffee, from business suits and heels to khaki pants and cotton tops. With every day growing shorter, my colleagues tolerated my grumbling about the impending winter darkness. As lifetime residents of the world's northernmost capital city, where the latitude causes extreme shifts in daylight hours, from virtually twenty-four-hour light in June to an official sunrise of 11:22 a.m. and sunset of 3:29 p.m. on December 21, they were aware of how much worse it was going to get (both the darkness and the grumbling!). Despite not knowing much of the language yet, I was considered one of the team, welcomed as one of a group of people who were doing something fun, exciting, and new. I was nerdy enough to fit in with the programmers, casual enough to fit in with the guys, and young enough to want to go out for drinks on a Friday night. There was a small kitchen where we could prepare our own lunches and a room with throw pillows and a DVD player where employees could leave their children on a day when school was closed. I would never have seen that at my British workplace.

Our CEO was one of the four women at the company. She had a background in banking but here acted as CEO, CFO, and HR director and had a host of other responsibilities, including apprising the company's board of directors about all developments. The board met in our office's single conference room every few months at the tail end of the workday, about five people sipping strong coffee and indulging in local pastries ordered for the occasion.

The board's chair was a woman in her late thirties called Halla Tómasdóttir. She had spent several years in the corporate world in the United States, returning to Iceland to work on various opportunities in business and finance and start a family. I first met her as I passed by one of those board meetings. She had just returned from maternity leave with her second child and was chairing the meeting as she nursed the baby. In this testosterone-laden environment, no one batted an eye, no one made a "joke," and at least one male board member later bounced the wee one on his lap while Halla addressed a point on the agenda.

Almost two decades later, this snapshot stays with me. I could withstand dark winters, windy weather, and a poor selection of fresh vegetables in the shops if this interaction between a mother and her child was considered a natural, healthy, and completely unremarkable moment of a business meeting. I was still in my twenties, childless, carefree, satisfied and so very fortunate in my life, but I also knew that looming ahead was societal pressure to have a family, to advance in my career, to contribute or at the very least conform to a norm on what middle-class, educated women like me should achieve. But was it possible that I had landed in a country where, with a bit of luck, women could just maybe have it all?

At the end of an August day almost a year later—it could well have been a blasted Monday—I was asked into the office of the CEO and told the company had to reduce its budget. And there I was left blindsided, laid off. In the coming months, Halla was one of many people I contacted as I tried to cultivate my self-esteem and find new employment, a challenge that proved much more difficult my second time around in Iceland. We stayed in touch occasionally over the years. I profiled her when I changed career directions and worked as a journalist for *Iceland Review* magazine and sought her advice when a friend and I launched our own project, the Iceland Writers Retreat. She was always encouraging and helpful. Our paths would continue to cross.

When I was memorizing flags and capital cities as a geeky child, I assumed that because the flag of Iceland and those of its Nordic cousins (Denmark, Norway, Sweden, and Finland) were similar, its population must also be. Likely a few million or maybe up to ten million? In fact, Iceland has one of the smallest populations of any independent nation. On New Year's Day 2021, it was a mere 368,590,[1] small enough that rounding to even the nearest thousand seems to do our society a disservice. In the time that I have lived in this country, the population has grown by more than a quarter.

Countries with fewer people than Cleveland, Ohio, or Bristol in the UK are forgiven for possessing a Small Nation Complex. (I grew up in Canada, which, despite its size and population also has SNC due to its proximity to a massively larger neighbor to the south, so I bear a rather natural affection for this affliction.) In Iceland, SNC manifests itself in a healthy interest in the frequency with which the country is mentioned in foreign media or what even the most minor celebrity thinks of his or her experience in visiting the country ("How do you like Iceland?"

is the most loaded question any visitor can answer and should be dealt with in the same vein as "Do I look fat in this?").

It's hard to top many global charts if you're small. In fact, Iceland is often left off global rankings simply because the data available are not extensive enough to include. If reaching a seven-figure population is still decades, if not centuries, away, the best (and most frequent) way to show a bit of national pride in a global context is to invoke the per capita statistic. We have a high GDP and extensive investment in the arts and are major contributors to international development—per capita. In 1955, when Halldór Laxness won the Nobel Prize for Literature, Iceland became the nation with the most Nobel Prize for Literature recipients—per capita.* (If you have never heard of Halldór Laxness, please don't upset a native-born Icelander by admitting that to them.) We cannot wait until we win our first ever Olympic gold medal to leap ahead in that event's per capita stats. Surely, we have the most per capita statistics of any nation—per capita.

There are, however, a few areas in which Iceland leads the world in real, unconditional terms. Even better, these are the areas that actually count. I live in one of the happiest nations on earth. Iceland has the highest rate of acceptance of homosexuality among OECD countries.[2] It is the world's most peaceful country, helped no doubt by the fact that it has no military.

With these and other broad standard of living indices, we Icelanders remain in perpetual and friendly competition with the other Nordic countries. For example, all five nations appear in the top ten list for happiness (the United States, United Kingdom, and Canada are not in that upper tier, though they are all in the top twenty). Although each of the five Nordic countries has a distinct culture, history, and language,

---

* In 1992, Iceland lost this claim after St. Lucia's Derek Walcott became that year's literary recipient. But we are always happy for other nations to perform well in the per capita games.

we share enough common values and connections that we often stick together on the international stage.[†] Iceland in particular often creates its own legislation based on preexisting laws in other Nordic states or the European Union. Once we're talking sports, though, all bets are off. There are few things more thrilling for an Icelander than watching one of our national teams defeat Denmark (which ruled Iceland from the fourteenth century until 1944[3]) in a competition.

Perhaps what has garnered this island the most proverbial column inches as far as quality of life is concerned, however, is the state of gender equality. One of the United Nations Sustainable Development Goals, that of gender equality and women's empowerment, aims to end discrimination, eliminate gender-based violence and harmful practices, and ensure women's participation in the workforce and access to health and reproductive care. Study after study, time after time, proves that the more gender-equal a society is, the happier, longer living, and more economically prosperous it is for *all* its citizens.[4] And according to the World Economic Forum at least, for the past thirteen years in a row, Iceland has taken home the trophy for the nation closest to achieving this ideal.[5] The index ranks countries on how well they have succeeded in closing the gender gap in the areas of employment, education, health, and politics. The other Nordic countries are nipping at our heels or are ahead by some measures.[6] But simply put, when judged by these matrices, Iceland is the planet's finest country for women, and so, if any country is finally to achieve gender equality, Iceland has an excellent head start.

As a society, in Iceland, we have passed the tipping point of *whether* gender equality is important or valuable and have progressed to debate

---

[†] Don't make the mistake of referring to Iceland as part of Scandinavia, though. For various reasons that include language, history, and geography, both Iceland and Finland should never be considered Scandinavian nations.

how to achieve it. Accordingly, Iceland has the highest level of female participation in the workforce. There is little to no social stigma regarding single parents or young mothers. There is a female chief of police and bishop of the national church. Famously, in 1980, the country voted in the world's first democratically elected female head of state and had the world's first openly lesbian head of government in 2009. For several years, the Icelandic chapter of UN Women has made the largest national contribution of any country to the global fund—in real, not per capita, terms—thanks largely to the number of regular monthly donors and numerous creative fundraising campaigns.

Icelanders, and I count myself among them, are justifiably proud of these achievements, but we all know there is a lot of work that remains to be done. This sub-Arctic island is not a paradise for women; the patriarchy is powerful and ingrained. For example, despite a law on gender quotas on corporate boards, at the time of writing, the country has no female CEOs among companies that trade on the Iceland Stock Exchange. The women's shelter in Reykjavík is often fully booked, and reports of domestic violence increased during the COVID-19 pandemic. So when we praise success to date, there is strength to be found in that word *but*. Being aware of ongoing challenges is the first step in eliminating them, and it does not diminish the significant advances that we have accomplished together. It is this normalization of the value of gender equality throughout all facets of society that is so remarkable to me as an immigrant—as an Icelandic saying goes, my "guest's eyes see more clearly."

After I was laid off from my job, my "guest's eyes," which had so blissfully observed a woman nursing her infant during a board meeting, had trouble focusing on the positive again. I was filling out as many job applications as I could, but without a full grasp of the language yet, it was challenging to get full-time employment. To keep busy, I pitched story ideas to a new English-language newspaper, the *Reykjavík Grapevine*, and covered such topics as the Eurovision Song Contest, where to get a haircut in the capital, and eventually various restaurant reviews (these were my favorite assignments, because I could eat for free at upscale establishments). This led to a part-time but regular gig as a staff writer for *Iceland Review*, the country's oldest English-language publication, whose team also put together *Atlantica*, then the in-flight magazine for Icelandair. On my days off, I took on various freelance projects that were usually linked with writing or proofreading English copy. Within a couple of years of my professional nadir, I was my own boss, doing projects I loved, travelling regularly around Iceland and to Icelandair destinations in Europe and North America. By late 2008, I was busy enough that I decided to incorporate my growing business as a company and registered it during the last week of September that year.

Ten days later, Iceland's three major banks had collapsed, its currency had plummeted in value, and the nation became embroiled in its worst-ever economic recession to date, dubbed simply the Crash. Iceland was one of the first and most visible casualties in the world of that year's great economic downturn. Although I lost my job, as did tens of thousands of others around the country, my freelance work increased as companies shifted from permanent employees to contractors for vital assignments.

Iceland's recovery from financial disaster was remarkably swift, aided in no small part by a dramatic increase in tourism to the country. By 2015, the International Monetary Fund's emergency loan to the Icelandic state had been fully paid off, bilateral relations mended with nations that had been hurt by our banks' bankruptcies, and the country garnered somewhat ill-placed praise for jailing some bankers, overall a remarkable evolution from near catastrophe to economic growth. My professional recovery continued too; I was asked to begin editing the new, more Iceland-focused, in-flight magazine that Icelandair was producing, and a few years later, a friend and I created a retreat for those who love the written word, the Iceland Writers Retreat, which has become an annual feature on Iceland's cultural calendar.

I felt equally fortunate in my personal life, due in no small part to family-friendly policies that are the norm in Iceland. Gudni and I married in 2004 and moved into a tiny, nearly hundred-year-old yellow wooden house in the western part of central Reykjavík, just a stone's throw from the sea (admittedly, one is never much farther than that in the city, much of which is located on a peninsula). He got a job teaching at Reykjavik University, lost it in the Crash, and eventually found a permanent tenure-track position in the History Department at the University of Iceland, penning several critically acclaimed books in the same period. I worked on my travel writing skills, spending seven weeks on a solo backpacking trip in West Africa in 2006 and publishing a multipart series in the local newspaper on my travels.

Within a month of returning from that adventure, I was pregnant. I would spend almost the entire next eight years pregnant with or breast-feeding four babies who arrived at almost exact two-year intervals. It would barely have been feasible, and not even desirable, were it not for generous parental leave benefits to which Gudni and I were both entitled, even as freelancers, and for heavily subsidized child care from the time the parental leave expired. When my youngest child, and first girl, was sent to the 8:00 a.m. to 4:00 p.m. care of a licensed childminder at about one year old, we paid the full fee for her, about $400 a month, including two hot meals and snacks. Thanks to the city's "sibling discount," the preschool for her three-year-old brother was 75 percent off the regular, already subsidized price, and free—except for the cost of meals—for our five-year-old and for the after-school care of our oldest, who was in Grade Two by then.

Happily, sleepily, Gudni and I stumbled through those years of early parenthood in a haze of pureed foods and washable diapers and broken household objects. After a few years of regular but unreliable incomes, he had secured his dream job at the university, and I was thrilled to be running the Iceland Writers Retreat and writing regularly. We eventually reconciled ourselves to the fact that our twelve-hundred-square-foot little yellow house would soon become rather a tight fit for our rambunctious brood, and we took out a second mortgage on a larger fixer-upper just a ten-minute walk away. After the stress and hassle of moving and shifting all four children to different schools and preschools, we were settled—and swore we'd never move again until our old age.

Presidential elections in Iceland are held every four years on the last Saturday in June. In 2016, with the expectation that the then president, seventy-three-year-old Ólafur Ragnar Grímsson, would not seek a record sixth term in office, the number of individuals who announced their intention to replace him was significant. Reykjavík's chattering classes spent extensive time pontificating on the would-be job seekers' varying merits and predicting who might be next to enter the race. Gudni was in the process of writing a book on the history of the presidency in Iceland and was often asked to appear as a neutral pundit on current affairs programs to discuss ongoing political issues of the day. Perhaps, he mused hopefully, he'd even be called upon to analyze the results on election night itself.

As it turned out, his television moment arrived a little earlier. On April 3, 2016, a conglomerate of international news outlets released what became known as the Panama Papers, which implicated various political and business leaders in offshore tax havens. One person identified in the papers was Iceland's prime minister, Sigmundur Davíd Gunnlaugsson, who once owned a company that was registered in the British Virgin Islands with his wife. While not illegal under Icelandic law, with the memory of Iceland's economic disruption still fresh in people's minds, protestors gathered outside Iceland's parliament, the Althing, the next day to demand change.

Local television stations interrupted their regular programming to cover the protests and their significance. Would the prime minister resign? Would other public figures who were implicated in the scandal resign? Was there other recourse under Iceland's constitution? Could the president play a role in demanding the prime minister's resignation? The debate called for an expert to deconstruct the issues in a digestible way that would not show deference to one political party or another.

On April 4, Gudni Jóhannesson, pundit, history professor, father of five, and expert on the presidency, appeared on television, alongside others, for six hours, commenting on the ongoing situation.

Then our phone started ringing.

Although several accomplished individuals had declared their intention to run for president, at a time when it suddenly became clear that the role, while largely ceremonial, held with it certain powers under the constitution and these powers needed to be well understood, many watched this thoughtfully spoken, insightful man and believed he might just be the right person at the right time for the job. Within a couple of days, the number of emails, Facebook messages, and phone calls from strangers grew from a trickle to a steady stream, all of them encouraging Gudni to take a step he had never seriously considered before—running for public office.

Six weeks before the election, on my fortieth birthday, with me and his five children by his side, Gudni announced to a packed concert hall that he was putting his name forward for president of Iceland.

With no incumbent in the race, more individuals than ever sought the post; nine made it past the stage of collecting nominations from around the country to have their names listed on the ballot. Of the nine, four were men, three of whom consistently polled over 10 percent of likely voters. All the women but one claimed less than 1 percent support in polls. The exception, who was little known nationally when she declared her intention to seek the office in late March that year (the election was scheduled for June 25) but who progressed steadily in the polls until finishing in second place to Gudni, was none other than Halla Tómasdóttir, former chair of the board of the company where I had worked my first year in Iceland. The young daughter she had been nursing during the meeting was now a teenager.

Halla and I encountered each other several times in person during those frantic weeks, always in a friendly way, despite the ongoing competition. (Incidentally, Gudni and I were also well acquainted with a third leading candidate, the writer Andri Snær Magnason.) At times, living in Iceland can feel like living in a dispersed, naturally stunning village. Campaigning for the highest office in the land alongside candidates even a newbie such as me had known for several years seemed only fitting.

My life changed irrevocably on June 25, 2016, when Gudni won the presidential election with 39.1 percent of the vote to Halla's second place 27.9 percent; he took office on August 1. As we had been travelling around the country during the campaign, holding rallies, shaking hands, sampling cream cakes and strong coffee, I had had an inkling of what might come.

In a whirlwind five weeks between the election and the inauguration, we were in a limbo of sorts, leaving behind our old jobs (his at least), our home, and our anonymity for a future we had only ever glimpsed on television and read about in newspaper articles. Our election team had finished their job of getting their guy the most votes, and the staff of the office of the president, who would stay on into the new administration, were not yet working for us. During that time, we navigated dozens of interviews and other media requests, put our house up for rent, found new schools for the children, decided if we needed new furniture for the private part of the large presidential residence, and tried to prepare the kids for the change to come.

Then, as now, I continued my own work. I am called *forsetafrú* in Icelandic, which translates as "wife of the president." No one suggested I use the word *forsetamaki*—"spouse of the president." In English, I am generally called First Lady, because it's an easily recognizable term, and even though it's implied, it does not explicitly use the words "wife of."

The fact is, though, that being First Lady is not a job. It comes with no salary, no dedicated staff, no clothing allowance, no pension. I was not elected to a position. Yet the presidential office helps to arrange flights and meetings in which I take part (in my capacity as First Lady only). I have my own business cards and letterhead and access to a small office at the presidential headquarters, had I chosen to work there. It is an immense honor and privilege, and every day, I do my best to serve my adopted country in this capacity.

The role does come with expectations, many of them more appropriate to an era when men exclusively claimed the spotlight and the women "standing behind them" supported their husbands' caprices. I am only the sixth First Lady since the country's independence from Denmark in 1944. The first three, who served until 1980, were all well-respected women who took on a very traditional spousal role for the era, usually staying away from the public eye and stepping forward only to act as well-coiffed cohosts during large social receptions or state visits. During the sixteen-year tenure of Iceland's only female president to date, there was no consort.

When Ólafur Ragnar Grímsson became president in 1996, his popular wife, Gudrún Katrín Thorbergsdóttir, took on various issues, such as drug addiction prevention among youth, and earned much praise in doing so. Gudrún Katrín succumbed to cancer only two years after her husband took office.

Ólafur Ragnar married his second wife, Dorrit Moussaieff, five years later. Dorrit, who like me was born and raised abroad, had a spontaneous and friendly nature that was popular with Icelanders. During her time as First Lady, she continued to work for her family's London-based jewelry business, and in her husband's later years as president, she spent much of her time outside Iceland.

I have also continued my own projects, including writing this book and running my company. After all, why should I get a new job because my husband was elected to one? This choice has led to some public discussion, but the overwhelming feedback is positive: in progressive Iceland, where the ambition for gender equality has been normalized, of course a spouse of the head of state should pursue her or his own endeavors.

From those early memories of seeing women smoothly operate in what I had experienced as male-dominated fields to giving birth to four children in under six years and founding my own business on the eve of a devastating economic collapse, I've had the privilege of enjoying what it's like to be a woman living in arguably the world's most gender-equal country. More recently, I have learned to use my unexpected platform as First Lady to help modernize expectations of an outdated role and to add another immigrant's voice and perspective to the equality fight.

Really, in many ways, this book is my love letter to Iceland—an appealingly imperfect country, a society that is constantly working to improve, where debate thrives but solidarity and empathy envelop us when crises occur. A nation where women persist in seeking equality and where most of us feel supported in that ambition most of the time. A country I am proud to call my home, where I have succeeded as an entrepreneur and learned to use my voice when fate handed me a platform, and one where I believe our achievements today will lead to even more equal futures for the generations to come as well as serve as inspiration to people around the world.

But my story alone does not paint a complete picture of the joys and challenges of female existence on this North Atlantic island. I wanted to explore what it is about Icelandic society that makes it so conducive to improving life for girls and women—and therefore men, boys, and nonbinary people too. Because surely these lessons can be applied elsewhere, to inspire people in Vancouver and Vermont, in Dundee and Dallas.

Do the ingredients for success stretch back to the time of the epic family feuds that were chronicled in the centuries-old tales collectively known as the sagas, which featured numerous tenacious women, or more recently to the 1980 election of Vigdís Finnbogadóttir, the world's first democratically elected female head of state? Is it a matter of crediting government-imposed policies, such as heavily subsidized child care and government paid parental leave for both parents, or should we look more to why this society pushes for new laws to be created, like the recent legal amendments to codify the rights of trans and nonbinary individuals? How about the liberal attitude toward single parenthood and sexuality in general, or a broader definition of masculinity? How much can we attribute to the small, cohesive, family-centric society where everyone needs to wear a lot of professional hats in order to have a thriving country? And what can we learn from the recent influx of immigrants, who bring new experiences and backgrounds to Iceland but who face their own unique challenges once here?

Certainly, the independent, stalwart, determined women who have left their marks on this society over the centuries have inspired their descendants today, not least through a confidence and belief that we can each play a role in improving our communities. Iceland is a storytelling nation, and many living Icelanders have been raised on a diet of the heroics of women in the sagas, the gumption of those who avenged wrongs, and the grit of those who fought against the odds for their principles.

For this book, I spoke to dozens of extraordinary women in Iceland. These *sprakkar*, to use an ancient Icelandic term, come from all ages and walks of life and regions of the country. Many of them fly under the radar, but their lived experiences nevertheless help portray a society that values the ambition of gender equality and is endeavoring to elevate it. They are women like you and me and the women we know. Together, they form a portrait of life in a country where gender equality is within reach—tantalizingly close to an unfixed finish line—yet also where frequently demoralizing and damaging challenges persist. Whether First Lady, sheep farmer, immigrant, soccer star, comedian, mayor, or sex advisor, we are all Icelanders sharing our stories and insights about what makes this land so equal for so many. And we are revealing the secrets about how we can nurture, support, and elevate the *sprakkar* who live within us and in our communities so we can all do our part to achieve gender equality, no matter where we live.

2

HELPING PARENTS HELPS US ALL

The raisin at the end of the hot dog*

WHEN I BECAME FIRST LADY of Iceland in 2016, I accepted a lot of interview requests from my native Canada. It was unlikely, to say the least, for a Canuck who grew up in rural Ontario to become spouse to the head of state of a nation thousands of kilometers away. I was so excited (and still am!) to take on the role and enthusiastic to brag about my adopted homeland to viewers and listeners back across the Pond.

Inevitably, similar themes arose among the various interviews. But the strangest question I was asked with alarming regularity was "Growing up on a hobby farm in the Ottawa Valley, did you ever imagine that you would one day become First Lady of Iceland?" It took a few interviews to realize that the questioners were never being rhetorical.

In my youth, I had no long-term plan per se, much less one that involved marrying the future head of state of a country I knew almost nothing about. I figured I would go to university, study something related to the social sciences or humanities, try to see a bit of the world, get a challenging job, and enjoy myself along the way. Marriage and children were not an integral part of my life's ambition.

I was not opposed to the idea of having a family, but I felt that getting married would depend on whether I actually met someone I

---

* *Rúsínan í pylsuendanum* means a pleasant surprise, the icing on the cake as it were (though, as elsewhere, raisins and hot dogs are never served together in Iceland).

wanted to spend the rest of my life with and having children on whether said partner was of the same mind and all systems were go.

Just like moving to Iceland and becoming First Lady, I never thought I would give birth to four children in less than six years and become a stepmother to another. Such is the beautiful unpredictability of life.

Had I stayed in Canada, I doubt I would have been so prolific in offspring. But in Iceland, somehow, it just seemed so easy to have a child—and then another, and another, and another. Here, comprehensive, midwife-led prenatal care is free of charge; even the nominal fees that usually accompany medical appointments and procedures in Iceland are waived. My husband and I each took several months of parental leave, during which we received payments from the government. When we returned to work full-time, our children were first cared for by a licensed childminder and then at a preschool a five-minute walk from our house, both of which were heavily subsidized by the city of Reykjavík. With these supportive systems in place, we didn't need to prioritize financial considerations when deciding the size of our family.

It's no wonder, then, that Iceland's fertility rate is one of the highest in Europe, at 1.97 children per woman, a figure that has only recently dipped below 2. Fertility rates were even higher in previous generations, due to a combination of lack of access to birth control, high infant mortality, and a need to populate the country with new generations to farm the land and fish the oceans. Indeed, when Icelanders say someone is "rich," they are often referring to offspring and not finances. With the increase in living standards and affluence, family sizes have shrunk, but children are still considered one of life's greatest joys, and I am by no means thought of as unusual for having a brood of four.

Despite the nation's reputation as tolerant of many lifestyles, women do still face strong societal pressure to have kids, albeit not necessarily as part of a 1950s *Leave It to Beaver*–style nuclear family. Those who have elected to defy this convention are approached with an almost scientific curiosity, and not always with understanding. Gudni and I had been a couple for five years when I moved to Iceland in my late twenties. From the outset, there were nudges, winks, and often outright questions from well-meaning in-laws and new Icelandic friends about when we would get on with it (since Gudni already had a daughter, it was clear to them that any delay in our procreation must be entirely of my doing). When we got married a year later, the pressure only increased. A large majority of first babies are born to unwed parents in Iceland (weddings are expensive, and there are no moral hang-ups about people "living in sin"), but because I was a foreigner, some people thought maybe we wanted to be old-fashioned about it. After the wedding, though, that excuse evaporated. Someone asked me if perhaps I was simply scared of having children.

The expense of children, for the big-ticket items such as child care and university, is relatively low in Iceland, freeing parents from investing in special bank accounts for future education or factoring pricey summer camp into the annual budget. It also somewhat eases the pain of buying packs of diapers or other costly but necessary imported goods that are twice the price as advertised on Amazon. The government pays single parents who are primary caregivers for their children (usually mothers) the minimum child support payments and takes those payments from the other paying parent, avoiding the potential for charged interactions with an ex-partner about finances and the stress of wondering whether the next month's proverbial check will even arrive.[7]

That policy helps remove some mental strain, but the logistics of managing a family remain universal. Most days seem like endless balancing acts between paid and unpaid work commitments and the everyday demands of parenthood, like shuttling children between after-school activities, reminding them to complete their homework and take their bathing suits to school on swim days, wiping noses, bandaging scraped knees, and all the other minutiae of managing a household. Even strong social support systems cannot alleviate this feeling of being pulled in many directions at once.

I am one of those lucky women who got pregnant quickly once deciding to try. When the faint blue line materialized on the pregnancy test one dark December morning in 2006, I didn't feel any different and had no sixth sense of my impending motherhood. But I had googled a lot—crucially in English, which inevitably led me to websites based in the United States, Britain, or Canada (and sometimes farther afield) and therefore the prenatal care protocols of those nations. I did as instructed by the websites and called my local healthcare facility, explained I was pregnant, and scheduled an appointment with a doctor, where, I assumed, I would have blood taken to confirm the pregnancy and be presented with a detailed schedule of upcoming appointments and advice.

I duly showed up a few days later, paid the 700 krónur (about U.S. $5.00) fee to see a doctor, and explained my situation. Even though that nominal amount is clearly not the actual cost to the system of my visit, as a Canadian, I still found it strange to cough up anything at all to see a doctor (only adults between eighteen and sixty-seven who are not on social benefits need to pay such fees themselves, and only up to a maximum amount per year). The regular visits with midwives, however, are free of charge, as is everything directly related to pregnancy and childbirth, the costs being covered through my taxes, part of which goes to Iceland's universal healthcare system.

"Congratulations!" The doctor smiled when I told him my news. "Don't forget to take some prenatal vitamins."

And that was that. No warnings about listeria, changing cat litter, or avoiding certain exercises at the gym, let alone any tests to prove my condition. Unbeknownst to me then, all prenatal care in Iceland is managed by midwives rather than doctors. That first visit to the doctor was superfluous, and I left with instructions to call the local midwife.

Little did I know that first phone call with midwife Gígja Sveinsdóttir would be the beginning of a long and intimate relationship. Gígja repeated the doctor's reminder about prenatal vitamins, adding a folic acid recommendation to the mix, and after hearing that I felt generally well and had no underlying medical conditions, told me to pay her a visit when I thought I was just about three months pregnant.

Thus was my introduction to what is a quintessentially Nordic, hands-off approach to pregnancy and childbirth, which I needed to adjust to at first but ultimately came to find very positive. Pregnancy, after all, is a normal and natural state, and extensive research indicates that in low-risk pregnancies, there are fewer medical interventions during midwife-led births than those directed by a physician. Iceland also has one of the lowest C-section rates of higher income countries, at about 16 percent of all births (in the United States, the comparable figure is almost one-third), and some of the best overall birth outcomes in the world.[8]

During my pregnancy, Gudni and I did what so many other expectant parents do. We painted the baby's room and bought baby clothes, and I signed up for a prenatal swimming class. Gudni and I attended the only birthing class that was taught in English; it was composed mostly of practical information on where to park outside the hospital and featured a graphic and dubbed Swedish video of "Lina and Lars" and their birth journey. Breathing techniques were not part of the preparation. Neither was a baby shower; there is no local tradition for this, and gifts for the baby are usually delivered when someone visits the newborn for the first time.

Gígja was practical and easygoing with her advice. I avoided sushi and other raw foods, but this being the aquatic wonderland that is Iceland, she knew it would be futile to advise expectant moms to avoid our ubiquitous hot tubs. "Just don't go in the ones that are 44°C [111°F]," she advised.

At work, I continued to fly abroad to write travel features for *Atlantica* magazine, indulging in exaggerated self-sympathy when I had a backache or morning sickness. Remarkably, the wondrous miracle I was gestating in my belly did not attract the same awe or sympathy that I felt I deserved! I was accorded no extra credit for my condition— though if and when I specifically requested help with something like lifting a heavy object, such assistance was easy to come by.

Iceland is not a country where chivalry is a guiding value. At a class on breastfeeding, all the seats in the waiting area were taken by some heavily pregnant women *and their partners*, leaving numerous other moms-to-be standing. I remarked to Gudni that one would never have seen that in the UK, where we used to live, but then he retorted that there simply wouldn't be as many expectant fathers attending such a class there in the first place.

That first pregnancy was an easy, carefree journey, full of anticipation and excitement of what was to come.

Then I actually had to give birth.

"When I was in labor, I thought all women who had more than one baby were insane. And after I gave birth, I was just angry with all men for a while. I wondered why we women weren't all carried around on golden thrones everywhere we went," comedian Saga Gardarsdóttir jokingly confessed to me. As one of only a few female stand-up comedians in Iceland, thirty-three-year-old Saga has been vocal about the humor behind one of life's most common, painful, and joyous experiences.

Saga and I were speaking about pregnancy, labor, and motherhood while soaking in the barely chlorinated waters of my local outdoor swimming pool, one of seventeen in the capital region. Thanks to its abundance of natural hot water piped from deep underground and filtered through porous lava rock, Iceland probably has more outdoor swimming pools per capita (naturally) than any other nation. While the trope of how to meet locals has one visiting a pub in the UK or a café in France, in Iceland, the greatest chance of a meaningful encounter with residents is while sitting outside in a hot tub (known as a "hot pot"). Soaking in water while barely clothed erases life's hierarchies and epitomizes the egalitarianism that Icelandic society does its best to uphold. You can't tell the difference between a plumber and a politician (or a First Lady and a comedian, for that matter) in the hot pot, but given that soaks can last a long time, you do have the chance to talk about much more than the weather or the dismal results of the local sports team.

So it was only appropriate for Saga and me to recall some of the most personal moments of our lives within earshot of others. And many women who have given birth find a sort of macabre appeal in hearing the agony of others' labor and delivery stories. In any case, I was familiar with her candor. In the changing room for the obligatory prepool nude shower, Saga warned me one thing might appear a little unusual. "I've put tape over my nipples," she confessed. "It's a last-ditch effort to discourage my daughter from breastfeeding."

Saga's daughter, Edda Kristín, was born two and a half years earlier. "Like all women who fixate on the fleeting nature of life, I was convinced I was infertile," joked Saga about how she became pregnant by accident and found out after a night out in New York City with her improv friends. "So it happened by a mixture of carelessness and a que será, será mentality."

It may have been an unplanned event, but her partner, Snorri Helgason, whom she had met years earlier at the swimming pool (of course), was thrilled. When we chatted, Saga mentioned that she and her now husband, Snorri, had just celebrated their six-year anniversary with a romantic dinner at a dimly lit restaurant. Not their wedding anniversary, which was just over two years before, but the anniversary "of when we first went home together."

Glossing over talk of Icelandic dating norms, Saga and I compared labor trials and tribulations.

Iceland does a lot of things well when it comes to having babies. There is an emphasis on the natural process of birth, from soft lighting in the delivery rooms to plenty of pain relief options before an epidural is (sometimes grudgingly) approved.

When I was in my baby-making phase, the gold standard of birthing locations in Iceland was the Nest.* A separate wing at the hospital in Reykjavík, think private room with king-size bed, La-Z-Boy chair, hot tub for laboring mothers, and a space for both labor and postpartum recovery. New mothers spoke reverentially about the Nest as the most comfortable, serene, and relaxing location for this most important of events. Any pregnancies deemed high risk were not permitted to labor in the Nest, nor were new babies or mothers with any complications allowed to spend their recovery time there. For everyone else, it was an aspiration and highly deserved reward.

When Saga went into labor, her folk musician boyfriend, Snorri, showed up with his guitar. "We thought it would be so relaxing," she

---

* The Nest closed in 2014 due to budget cuts; there is now, however, a small, midwife-led birthing center that has since opened in Reykjavík and has proven very popular because women receive continuous care and know their midwives well.

told me. "He was supposed to play all this soothing music, but he started with Nick Drake, and I just found it so irritating that he was singing songs by some *guy* who felt sorry for himself.

"I had a straightforward, six-hour birth," Saga continued as we sat in the 38°C (100°F) pool. "But at the time, I remember thinking I must be particularly bad at this. Surely it's not normal to find it *so* painful and difficult?"

An epidural was not in the cards for her, though.

"It turns out my ex-boyfriend, whom I dated for seven years, was the anesthesiologist on duty," admitted Saga. "He's a great guy who has no doubt soothed the suffering of many women, but he was just not the person I wanted to make polite small talk with in my state, sweaty and naked."

Fortunately, I had no Icelandic ex-boyfriends whom I could encounter under awkward circumstances.

By the time I was about eight months pregnant with my first child, I was confident I would end up in the Nest for both the birth and recovery. The pregnancy had gone well and was deemed low risk, and more importantly, I had a *positive attitude and outlook on life.* Those women who scream and moan and shout and swear while in labor on television? They must be glass-is-half-empty folks, I thought. They didn't take vitamins every day or diligently practice Kegels.

Like so many first-time parents, I had devoured week-by-week pregnancy guides and online sites, following whether my little guy was the size of an apricot or a grapefruit. I had particularly paid attention to the sections on birthing plans and duly made notes to the effect that I wanted to be able to eat and drink during my labor, was open to the idea of a water birth, and wanted the baby placed directly on my chest before swaddling.

Reality hit me about forty-five minutes after the third prostaglandin tablet had been administered to me at the maternity ward of the Landspítali National Hospital—most emphatically *not* the Nest—to induce my labor after my pregnancy had dragged two weeks past its due date, with no natural indication that my son had any interest in making an appearance.

In any case, my carefully prepared plan encompassed what was essentially the standard of care in Iceland, where a request for needles might more likely refer to acupuncture than to an epidural. (During our prenatal class, the midwife instructor claimed that only 20 percent of women in Iceland used one, probably because there were so many other, noninvasive pain relief options available, while she said the rate was 85 percent in Canada, where her children were born.) Some of the midwives in the ward are trained in aromatherapy, and many birthing rooms, not just those in the Nest, have their own hot tubs. And as it turns out, swaddling is not even a thing in Iceland. In the most straight-forward births, no one is in a rush to remove the baby to record details like length and weight, leaving the infant instead to rest and warm up on its mother's chest.

I was one of the 20 percent who shamelessly pleaded for an epidural during all four of my labors—though those pain-relieving meds only worked during two of them. With the exception of my first, whose birth required some medical intervention from a doctor, all my children were delivered exclusively by midwives, though not the reliable Gígja whom I had visited regularly. The healthcare service distinguishes between midwives such as Gígja, who are responsible for prenatal care, and those who work on shift at the hospital. The midwives who delivered my babies were women whom I had never met before and just happened to be on duty at the time.

After two of my four deliveries, I did also enjoy what I had dubbed the unofficial business class wing of the hospital and spent the recovery period in the Nest. The midwife settled me and my newborn in a soft king-size bed, gave me some pamphlets on breastfeeding, and left a buzzer with instructions to press it if I needed anything. Otherwise, I was left undisturbed to gaze adoringly at the new little one and try to catch a few winks.

After bringing baby home—unnamed, because in Iceland, it's rare to announce a name for the baby until its christening, and certainly not while still in the throes of recent delivery—reassuring Gígja visited me almost daily for a week to weigh the baby using a handheld scale and a tea towel in which to support the little one, and probably to assure herself that my home situation was not dire. Aside from a brief, five-day-old wellness checkup at the hospital, neither mother nor babe had to visit the health clinic until the wee one was six weeks old.

Becoming a mother was more of a shock to my system than I had anticipated. I thought my experience as a stepmother to a post-toddler girl every other weekend, copious reading of pregnancy and newborn books, and the positive attitude that had failed me in labor would be sufficient. The lack of sleep, the difficulty of learning to breastfeed (as it turned out, that positive attitude was also no defense for cracked nipples and milk duct infections), and the challenge of finding some sort of routine in my changed world were all more difficult than I expected. I thought I deserved an award for getting out of my pajamas by noon, though my son Duncan, whom I could not stop gawking at, was as perfect as the motherhood clichés could predict. Like so many other women, it took time for me to nurture my confidence as a mother (something that was significantly easier to channel with my next three babies). Fortunately, time was something I had in abundance because of Iceland's generous parental leave program.

Before Duncan was born, half my working days were spent at a magazine and half on a variety of projects. As a self-employed individual for the latter assignments, I was obliged to pay extra taxes into a social security system that an employer would normally cover, but that also meant I was entitled to a full parental leave despite not being employed full-time by a company.

Iceland's parental leave program is one of the cornerstones of the nation's approach to equality. One of its crucial provisions is a "use it or lose it" stipulation. At the time I took my maternity leave, one parent was entitled to three months' paid leave, the other parent an additional three months, and a third three-month segment could be paid to either parent or divided between them.* This allocation encouraged both parents to take time off from work or risk "losing" those months of leave and at the time was a novel innovation on the standard practice of paid leave that almost exclusively mothers used the majority of.

Saga and I continued comparing details of our transitions into motherhood as we soaked in the balmy 14°C (57°F) August summer evening weather. Naturally, being self-employed did not prevent her from receiving her mandated maternity payments. And when her leave finished, she returned to the stand-up comedy circuit with plenty of new fodder for her routines.

"I used to do a lot of gigs for large groups of men, and they loved all the racy humor," she told me. "When I went back to work and had incorporated a lot of jokes about parenthood into the routine, their eyes would just glaze over. On the other hand, I got so much good feedback from women who could identify with so much of what was being said. So many topics in stand-up are 'male' ideas because that's how we've

---

* The program has since been expanded to twelve months in total, with each parent having five months and the remaining two to be split as desired.

been trained to identify something as interesting or funny. But when I speak about something more feminine, people are so thankful."

Many of Saga's most popular jokes come from the self-doubt and guilt that so many new mothers—but fewer fathers—feel, despite all the societal supports the country provides. "If I turn on the TV, will she become a video game addict who shits in pizza cartons, or if I ban it, will she end up some hapless poet?" or "She's two and a half years old. Am I too late to send her to a shrink?"

I asked Saga what her daughter might think of all this humor at her expense in fifteen or twenty years' time.

"Well, I'll always pay for that shrink," she replied with a smile.

There are obvious benefits of Iceland's groundbreaking parental leave program. Since young men are just as likely to take parental leave and the government rather than private companies covers the cost, women face less prejudice in the workplace. A further result is that fathers are more involved in the childcare routine from the outset.

In Reykjavík, fathers are often spotted pushing landscape strollers with sleeping infants around town. These strollers also double as beds, since the prevailing wisdom is that fresh air is vital to a baby's development. When a baby is ready for a nap, he or she is bundled up in clothing (it never gets very warm in Iceland, even in summer), snuggled into a sleeping bag, and placed into the stroller, which is then left on a balcony, back porch, or yard with a monitor to alert the parent when the baby wakes. It's not uncommon for parents who live on, say, the fourth floor of an apartment building to leave their infant on the front lawn of the building or for a harried parent to sneak into the local café and grab a cuppa while the stroller and its invaluable contents remain outside on the sidewalk. If the little one wakes, a passerby will generally act as a human baby monitor, popping inside to call out, "Whose baby is crying?"

Gudni took four months of parental leave with each of our children, facilitating the forging of a strong bond with them all that exists to this day. He geeked out at the national archives, one of his favorite haunts, while they slept in the stroller outside. He attended the weekly parents' meetings at the local church and would return home to ask me details about new motherhood so he could take part in the discussion with the exclusively female attendees. ("Are you also losing your hair now?" he asked me earnestly after one such meeting.) He never seemed to question where other members of his sex were at those gatherings, even though so many of them also took parental leave. They certainly weren't at the national archives either.

Like so many Icelanders, he had his own, laid-back approach to parenthood. One day, I saw him getting ready for what he announced was to be a full-day trip to the library, the parents' group at the church, and perhaps a stop at a friend's. Gudni had *nothing* with him but the baby—no diaper bag, clean diapers, food, drinks, wet wipes, cloths, or any of the extensive list of items that I couldn't leave home without. Failing to resist the urge to comment—after all, he had begun his journey as a parent before I did—I asked if there was really *nothing* he would need all day.

"Oh," he casually replied. "I'm going to stop for a banana at the store on the way."

Had the roles been reversed, there would have been whispers behind my back, glances exchanged that surely I should have had the foresight to prepare for the day during which the baby could spit up, have a diaper blowout, not want a banana, soil his clothes, etc. For my husband, it was admirably quirky to head out on the town with our son, two carefree males ready to rule the world! No diaper changes!

A banana for lunch! Water straight from the tap of some public washroom! The old stereotypes of gender-based roles for each parent are hard to erase, even in Iceland.

But as our offspring multiplied and aged, Gudni's laid-back yet involved style of parenting presented a happy counterpoint to my obsessive planning and another adult on whom the kids could rely. More importantly, thanks to his parental leave, he was present. He knew their favorite foods, which onesies fit best, which Icelandic folk song made them giggle the most.

Research backs up my impressions from watching Gudni parent. Fathers who take parental leave are more likely to be involved in the care of their children later, including with household duties. They are less likely to separate from their partner. Boys whose fathers were actively and regularly engaged in their upbringing have fewer behavioral problems, and girls have fewer psychological problems. In fact, studies show children's relationships with their fathers are stronger and healthier in Iceland than in other countries. Although it's clearly possible to form strong bonds in locations where paternity leave is not available, time is a valuable commodity, and generous, affordable leave helps to give us that time to experience those moments that won't return.[9]

"Look," called my third son one spring evening when we saw a chick chirping mournfully by a pond in search of an adult duck. "That chick's missing its daddy!"

Unnur Brá Konrádsdóttir is one of tens of thousands of working mothers in Iceland, striving to stabilize the balance of work, motherhood, social life, and personal time that, despite social and official supports to encourage it, remains elusive. Unnur Brá grew up on a farm, the youngest of nine children, trained as a lawyer, worked in municipalities in the remote Westfjords region and in the south of the country, and was first elected to parliament in 2009.

An unexpectedly early parliamentary election that required active campaigning at the end of 2016 meant that Unnur Brá returned to work only six weeks after her youngest child, Hervör Úlfdís Gná, was born. But in child-friendly Iceland, she could be flexible. No one batted an eye when she brought Hervör along with her to meetings of the general committee, putting her to sleep in a stroller inside the room while Unnur Brá continued to chair those sessions.

The meetings, the campaigning, the responsibilities with her two other children, who were eight and twelve at the time—it was a lot to juggle, but politically, Unnur Brá couldn't really afford not to be there. She hadn't gotten a chance to campaign as much as she wanted during the primary season before the general election, which came earlier than expected and landed during the final few weeks of her pregnancy.* Now that parliament was again in session, Unnur Brá wanted to be as visible as possible. "I didn't think I had any other options," she said.

Then, on a fateful October day that began like any other, someone in parliament addressed a point of order on a bill that Unnur Brá's committee was dealing with. In the Althing, Iceland's sixty-three-member parliament, seating is chosen on a random basis at the beginning of each session, and each speaker stands at a pulpit at the front of the chamber to deliver speeches and remarks, all of which are televised.

* Iceland's elections are run on a party list system. The country is divided into six constituencies, each with a number of representatives based on the region's population. Parties submit a ranked list of individuals who run for parliament in that constituency, and this list is usually determined in a primary that can be even more competitive than the general election. Each election, voters generally vote for a specific party (though they have the option of striking out the names of any candidates they particularly dislike) rather than an individual who represents a party. When ballots are counted, seats are assigned proportionally to parties based on the percentage of votes they receive. To put it simply, if a party receives, for example, 30 percent of the votes in a ten-seat constituency, the first three people on its list will become members of parliament.

Parents are all familiar with Murphy's Law that if your child has a reliable routine, that one time you *need* them to follow the schedule will be the moment they won't. That is what happened to Unnur Brá in parliament on that October day. At the exact moment she needed to stand and address a point of order in the agenda, Hervör was not sleeping soundly in her stroller, as she usually was at that time of day, but was instead quietly being nursed by her mother.

"I had to decide between ripping her from my breast and handing her crying to my colleague to comfort or just taking her with me," Unnur Brá told me. She had to make a split-second decision, and perhaps maternal instinct pointed her to the latter option.

It seemed to come as no surprise to anyone in the room, as the televised proceedings show. The somewhat glazed stare accorded all speakers near the end of a bureaucratic day is apparent in the officials at the podium behind her. Unnur Brá spoke for forty-eight seconds, Hervör pressed against her chest, silent and content. After speaking, Unnur Brá took her seat.

"Then everything just went crazy," she remarked.

It turns out it was the first time in Iceland that someone had nursed her baby in parliament, and a lot of people noticed and sent Unnur Brá messages to the effect that she was unwittingly breaking new ground. The local news picked up the story, and then an English-language media outlet propelled Unnur Brá into her fifteen minutes of internet fame.

The moment was nothing special for Unnur Brá. "Of course you feed your child if it's hungry, whether that's breast milk or a sandwich. But it was interesting to experience how noteworthy others thought it was," she conceded. "That surprised me a bit, though after the fact, I had a chance to reflect on how beautiful it was."

Unnur Brá's experience garnered international attention, albeit fleetingly, but the extensive welfare policies in Iceland help facilitate and encourage a gentle transition back to work for all parents in the country. This is perhaps one reason why Iceland has one of the highest percentages of women working outside the home of any nation in the world.[10]

Many building blocks are already in place to encourage mothers to return to the workplace and to facilitate that transition. In a 2020 speech, American senator Elizabeth Warren described affordable child care as "infrastructure for families." It's clearly one of the most vital building blocks for gender equality.

Iceland's government knows this. By the time children reach the age of about one year, or whenever parents use up all their leave, subsidized childcare services take over from parental leave payments.[11] The childcare services are administered and financed by municipalities, which determine the fees, with additional discounts generally allocated for single parents, parents in full-time education, or those with disabilities. Siblings are usually also discounted, at a rate determined by each municipality.

The services themselves are generally excellent. Our childminder lived a five-minute walk from our house and was originally from Colombia. She and her mother cooked mouthwatering Colombian food for the kids and sang often to them, so they knew many words in Spanish before they had learned them in Icelandic or English. At the preschools, which they attended until compulsory elementary schooling started in the first grade, the emphasis was always on play and social interaction rather than intensive, academic learning.

By the time I had my fourth child (and first daughter) when the others were five, three, and two, it was no longer a challenge to be out of my pajamas by noon. The three older boys were at preschool and with a childminder, and I enjoyed my maternity leave to focus on only one child, yet with the confidence that came from having had three others.

"I am really proud of our parental leave system," Unnur Brá told me. "Although of course we can still improve and are improving. It's not easy to manage it all, but life isn't always easy. It makes a difference that your kids see that you're doing something that makes a difference, although of course you need to make sure you get quality time with the family too.

"I find it so interesting that there are societies that don't think this comprehensive parental leave is important," she continued. "Do those countries have the means to see that half of their citizens aren't working? That they are not contributing to the economy? Not developing ideas? Not founding companies? I don't understand it. Imagine if all the men in Iceland were just working at home; there would be so much missing in society."

Now Hervör is a happy and active four-year-old. "My daughter thinks there's nothing better than going to preschool in the morning to play with all her friends, though she's also happy to see me when I go to pick her up," said Unnur Brá. "She's learning about what it's like to live in society."

February 2014: My children are six, four, two, and six months old. I recorded an "average" night in my diary:

> 7:30 p.m.: Edda (6 months) to sleep.
> 7:50 p.m.: Sæthor (2) to sleep.
> 8:30 p.m.: Duncan (6) and Donnie (4) to sleep.
> 11:00 p.m.: Me to sleep.
> 11:40 p.m.: Edda wakes up.
> 11:40 p.m.–12:10 a.m.: Try to settle her with soother, walking, etc.

12:10 a.m.–12.40 a.m.: Feed Edda and put her back to bed.

1:45 a.m.: Sæthor wakes up. Gudni goes to settle him.

2:15 a.m.: Edda wakes up. Fall asleep feeding again.

3:00 a.m.: Stir and switch sides for Edda.

3:20 a.m.: Put Edda back into her crib.

3:30 a.m.: Sæthor wakes up. Gudni goes in to settle him.

3:35 a.m.: This wakes Edda up.

3:35 a.m.–3:55 a.m.: Edda babbles to herself (and us).

4:45 a.m.: Donnie wakes up. Comes into our bed.

5:30 a.m.: Edda wakes up. Move her to the bed to feed her.

5:45 a.m.: Sæthor wakes up. Gudni moves to spare bed with him.

6:00 a.m.: Move Edda to other side.

6:45 a.m.: Donnie wakes up for the day.

6.45 a.m.: Move Edda to crib.

6:50 a.m.: Edda wakes up for the day.

7:00 a.m.: Sæthor wakes up for the day.

Somehow, this routine worked for several years, as do variations on this sleep-deprived theme that play out the world over. I doubt it would have been possible without another parent, flexibility in my working hours, copious quantities of coffee, and a self-tolerance about how I was lax on so many other aspects of my life.

"I was at the end of my rope," confessed Unnur Brá when I enquired as to whether the women-having-it-all ideal might be possible in equality-focused Iceland. "To get ready for each day, with the stroller, diapers, everything else for the car, arrive at the right time, make sure the baby is fed at the right time so she sleeps when she should. Chairing committees and voting and then packing it all up again and going home to cook supper, clean the house, and get breakfast ready for the other two kids, get their school snacks for the next day, put the laundry on. I was exhausted."

Unnur Brá agreed that women in Iceland still bear the brunt of the mental load, acting as the acclaimed "household CEO" who keeps track of everything going on inside the home and among its family members. "I have friends who say at the end of the school year that their husbands still don't remember that gym class is on Tuesdays and Thursdays and the kids need to bring their sports clothes to school then. Until things like that improve, we won't have equality."

Despite general societal beliefs in gender equality in Iceland, studies show that, as in other countries, in heterosexual relationships, domestic responsibilities still fall disproportionately to the woman.[12]

And it works both ways. "My husband always remembers to change the oil in the car; I never think of that," Unnur Brá continued. "But if I were alone and the car broke, I would pay for that service. You can't buy the service of organizing a family, or if you buy the service to help with the kids, you're criticized, and then you have that guilt, that you're not doing it well enough."

Unnur Brá was one of relatively few mothers to hire an au pair when her children were young and she had a schedule with atypical working hours.

"I have met women who told me, 'Well, I have chosen to raise my children myself.' That is painful," admitted Unnur Brá. "My ex-husband was never spoken to like that, of course."

Families are the basis for a functional, prosperous society. To make it all work, we all need help. Free, regular, midwife-led prenatal care, generous paid parental leave for everyone, and subsidized, high-quality, accessible child care all provide a societal skeleton for what families work through together and level the playing field so people of all backgrounds and circumstances have more equal opportunities.

None of this guarantees that women can "have it all." And there is much we could improve in Iceland. Finland's day care is free from the age of eight months. Swedish day care facilities are open for at least twelve hours on weekdays and in some cases are available twenty-four hours a day. And while women take on more responsibility in the workplace, they still maintain the lion's share of household duties, including that time-consuming "mental load."

The point really isn't to try and have it all, though. It's to understand the art of compromise, that you can achieve more satisfaction by acknowledging the need to prioritize your time. I didn't have it all, but I was satisfied with the things I chose not to have, what I chose not to prioritize—exercising regularly at the gym, deep cleaning the house, and owning more than one outfit aside from jeans and my old maternity tops, many of which still fit distressingly well.

Somehow, by providing many tools to work with, Iceland has the infrastructure to maximize this potential by letting one try to puzzle it all together. Saga gets to be a freelancer who can rely on parental leave payments to spend valuable time with her daughter without losing face at work. Unnur Brá faces no churlish looks for doing what comes naturally as a mother. I could maintain my sanity by placing my children in excellent child care during working hours, including when I was taking maternity leave with a newborn.

The freedom of not letting finances be the primary driver for whether to have more children. The confidence in knowing that from womb through to childhood and beyond, a supportive healthcare system is in place. The knowledge that in the preschool years of a child's development, the education system emphasizes socialization over grades on standardized tests. These, for me, are the icing on the cake, the "raisin at the end of the hot dog" as we would illogically say here, and perhaps the largest reason that the people of Iceland are so tantalizingly close to achieving gender equality.

Yet hope is not lost for those who cannot rely on an "infrastructure for families" such as this. I am in no position to evangelize on how it's possible to juggle even more when I have been so fortunate as to rely heavily on Iceland's financial and practical support for parents. Even now, with all my privilege, strong organizational skills, and a healthy coffee habit, I drop many balls. But I maintain my sanity because I feel comfortable with what I have chosen to let tumble for a moment while I focus on keeping something else aloft. Everyone must create their own priorities and choose where to concentrate limited energies on any given day. Certainly, it's the greatest waste of energy to stare at all the fallen balls and worry we dropped the wrong ones. Accept imperfection. Ask for help. Offer it. No one is an island. If we have a smaller or no safety net to catch us, then it's all the more important to heed the advice piped over the loudspeakers every time we fly: Put the oxygen mask on yourself before assisting others. And breathe deeply.

THE SAGA-ERA SPRAKKI WHO DEFIED CONVENTION

"I AM VERY DEMANDING WHEN it comes to men," admitted Hallgerdur Höskuldsdóttir to her suitor Gunnar of Hlídarendi when he asked for her hand in marriage on the very day they met.[13]

She was not exaggerating. The strong-willed and vengeful Hallgerdur was married three times, Gunnar being her final husband. Thanks to an increasingly intense feud with Bergthóra, the wife of Gunnar's best friend, several men were killed at the behest of the two women. And that final husband? Hallgerdur was directly responsible for his demise too.

Hallgerdur was known by the nickname Long-Legs, recognition of both her height and her hair, which was soft as silk and grew down to her waist.

This beautiful woman lived in the late tenth century. We know her story today from *Njáls Saga*, the longest and arguably greatest of the many Icelandic sagas. Proud and honorable, she was not shy about expressing her displeasure with her husband's behavior or with any indignities she felt she suffered.

When famine ravaged the land, Hallgerdur instructed her

servant Malcolm to rob a neighboring farm for food. Theft, nota bene, is one of the worst sins one can commit in the sagas. When Gunnar returned home to discover a feast, he realized the dishonor that Hallgerdur's instructions had brought upon the household and slapped her across the face.

Hallgerdur did not react, other than to say she would remember the injustice and pay him back.

Years later, Hallgerdur found her opportunity.

Gunnar was ambushed by enemies and surrounded in his home. He managed to stave them off to a tremendous degree, until the string on his bow broke. Forced to find a solution, he asked his wife for two locks of her legendary hair so that he could repair his weapon and return to battle.

Hallgerdur asked him if anything depended on it.

"My life depends on it," Gunnar replied plainly.

"Then I'll recall the slap you gave me, and I don't care whether you hold out for a long or a short time."

She refused his demand, and Gunnar was felled by his attackers.

For this deed, Hallgerdur has been painted as cruel and heartless. The final words about Hallgerdur in the saga come from Skarphédinn, the son of Njáll, who calls her "either a cast-off hag or a whore."

Yet she was using the tools at her disposal to fight her battles. When Hallgerdur disobeyed her husband Gunnar, who was praised as one of the "finest" men of the sagas, she was defying convention and vilified, but in modern light, we see her as one of Iceland's earliest feminists.[14]

3

THE STRENGTH IN SISTERHOOD

*On with the butter**

THE FREQUENTLY RAGING, FREEZING NORTH Atlantic Ocean that surrounds Iceland is unwelcoming. It is frigid, threatening, and often dangerous. It was therefore a surprise to me that sea swimming—wading into the salty, chilling waves and taking a few strokes—is actually a thing in Iceland.

My first dip was in January, only a few months after I had moved to the country. My "Icelandic for Foreigners" language class was made up of a patchwork of people of different ages and nationalities, including three architects from Mexico. The trio, at least one of whom grew up along the semitropical shores of the Pacific off the Baja Peninsula, began each Sunday by gathering other naïve immigrants at Grótta, a nature reserve at the sandy tip of the Seltjarnarnes Peninsula just outside downtown Reykjavík, passing around a bottle of vodka for a hurried mouthful of liquid courage, stripping down to Speedos as the midwinter sun began to lazily peek above the horizon, and racing into the waves. After a few moments of frolicking—or actual lap swimming for the heartiest souls—they would rush out, towel off, drive two minutes to the nearest geothermal swimming pool to reheat, then fill up on brunch at a greasy spoon in town.

When my friends asked if I wanted to join in the fun, it seemed impossible to decline, purely for the novelty of it. So I dragged Gudni

---

* *Áfram með smjörið!* means to keep going, to get a move on.

out of bed one morning when the temperature hovered around freezing, and we tried it all: the changing on the beach, the vodka shot, the "swimming," the hot pot, and the brunch. Gudni, who was amazed and impressed by this assortment of foreigners in the sea, actually began swimming regularly with them. I, on the other hand, was happy to have ticked that box off my nonexistent list of life goals and made a mental note never to endure that masochistic "pleasure" again.

When you're an immigrant, your friends are an international family in your new home. In the absence of close family members and friends in your adopted country, you celebrate birthdays, holidays, and other milestones together and call one another for support when you suffer from culture shock or simply want to ask practical advice.

For those born and raised in Iceland, extended families often serve these purposes, and actually virtually all Icelanders who are not descended from the immigrants of the last few decades are related six or seven generations back, a fact not as surprising as it might initially seem, given that the current population is about the same as that of Anaheim, California. A compact one- or two-parent family with a couple of children is often supported by relatively young grandparents, aunts and uncles, cousins of varying degrees, and step versions of all the aforementioned. Nuclear families are not usually self-contained units that exist as a bubble. And without the nomenclature of surnames, there's less emphasis on distinguishing the Joneses from the Jónssons.*

---

* Most Icelanders don't have last names per se but instead use their father's first name in the genitive case, with -son or -dóttir tacked on at the end. (It's increasingly popular, but still only in the minority, to use the mother's first name for the same purpose or indeed to have a double-barreled name that encompasses them both.) So Anna Magnúsdóttir's father is called Magnús. If Anna has a child with a Sigfús Matthíasson, that daughter might be called Katla Sigfúsdóttir, giving all three members of the same family different "surnames." The three boys Gudni and I have together all have the patronymic Gudnason (son of Gudni), while our daughter has my last name, Reid. This convention is also the reason Icelandic women don't change their names upon marriage. Being wed wouldn't make you the son of your father-in-law, would it?

Everyone has their own name—mom, dad, kids, or a combination thereof—and with a little help from an open database that maps out Iceland's relationships, it's not hard to see how everyone is family.

Iceland has one of the world's highest proportions of women working outside the home, and an "it takes a village" mentality is a crucial component of this achievement. There is little discussion that one parent may wish to remain at home with children instead of sending them to preschool or child care. To generalize, most people in Iceland would question why someone would choose *not* to have a paying job. For the very few parents who take the stay-at-home route, it can even be difficult to find daytime activities or places to visit with their kids, since the demand isn't there when most of the toddler's peers are in day care. For the most part, "Mommy and Me" classes for the preschool age are an alien concept witnessed only on imported television programs.

Children in Iceland have a level of freedom that parents in many non-Nordic countries can only recall with a fond nostalgia from decades ago. This convention stems somewhat from necessity, because both parents often work outside the home; it helps to ease the juggle of supervising young ones. But it's more likely because society never developed the helicopter paranoia that it was anything but normal to let kids be, well, kids, exploring and learning, each in their own unique way. If distance and weather allow, starting at age six or earlier, most children travel to and from elementary school alone or with an older sibling. Not many years later, many eight- or nine-year-olds are trusted to take public buses by themselves to or from school and between after-school activities. In fact, Icelandic society decidedly encourages elementary school children to get involved in after-school programs by subsidizing activities, from horseback riding and archery to drama clubs and even circus lessons. After all, if kids are trapezing, they're not smoking and drinking. Rates of substance abuse and vandalism among Icelandic teens have plummeted since these recreation grants were rolled out.[15]

Among younger kids, it is not unusual to see a seven-year-old at the supermarket on an errand to buy some bread or picking up a younger sibling from her soccer practice. Ten-year-olds can visit public swimming pools without an adult. Many children in the third grade and up will travel home alone after school ends at around 2:00 p.m. and be by themselves until their parent(s) return from work. I remember being shocked when my oldest son began school at age six and another mother called me one afternoon to enquire whether her son of the same age was playing at our place. He hadn't appeared home since school ended several hours before, she calmly explained, so she was calling around a few homes to investigate where he had ended up. Sure enough, he was located at the third place she tried.

In areas where distances are greater and public transportation less accessible or in the dark of winter or the not-uncommon bad weather, extended family members can cover for working parents. If grandparents are already retired, they are often happy to shuttle between practices or provide pancakes or pâté on bread as an after-school snack. Younger, working grandparents—in Iceland, it's not uncommon to become a grandparent in one's forties—often have the energy to host little ones overnight or for extended visits. Families help each other, and somehow, in an unstructured but unchaotic way and with helpful systems in society, such as that affordable child care, and a very low crime rate, it all just works out for most people most of the time. That's not to say that all families have this extended network of unpaid au pairs, drivers, and errand runners; some grew up in another community or have their family in another country. It's commonplace enough, though, that this group-responsibility mentality affects the collective and usually makes employers, teachers, and other institutions more flexible when these more traditional networks are not feasible support options for one reason or another. If your son has a dance recital during school hours, you don't need to book a half-day vacation; you just disappear from your desk for an hour or so. And if the same son has the day off school, workplaces often have an unsupervised kids' room so you can bring him to work with you.

As we say in Iceland, we all just *get on with the butter*, greasing the rails of social norms so it's easier to shift between worlds, whether that's more women in the workplace or more men doing the carpooling. This builds a trust and reliance that gives more people the flexibility to work outside the home and take on more challenge and responsibility, whether professionally or personally.

As an immigrant who moved to the country to build a life with a native-born partner, I arrived to find a built-in extended family that would provide a reliable nest for our children after they were born. Learning to use this network did not come naturally to me. I had moved hundreds of kilometers from my childhood home at the age of eighteen and never returned—it was easy to assume I was on my own. I soon discovered, though, that reliance on these close contacts and the interdependence of families with young children had evolved a support network that stretched across different dimensions of society. As my children grew, they could take the bus to *amma* (their grandmother) for snacks after school, and there were regular cousins' birthday parties to attend, not to mention playdates with the children of other immigrants whose own extended families were far away.

When I first met Gudni in the UK, I asked him whether he was from Reykjavík, thus deftly showcasing my vast knowledge of Icelandic geography. "No," he firmly corrected me. "I am from Gardabær. It's a town *near* Reykjavík."

The town center of Gardabær is 5.6 miles from Reykjavík city hall. Even if you catch all the red lights along the way, you can drive it in ten minutes. Cyclists can easily commute it. My preteen children have walked the distance.

But even if an Icelander is explaining it to someone from another continent, Gardabær is most definitely its own municipal entity, not— god forbid—a suburb of the capital. Ironically, in a small society, small distances can be vast in terms of identity.

The first place we lived in Iceland was a tiny, furnished one-bedroom apartment we rented very close to the University of Iceland. It was walking distance from the central restaurants and pubs and most places I wanted to go. One evening a few weeks after I arrived in the country, my mother-in-law drove me back to the flat after a dinner at her house. She told me she was so happy that Gudni had finally re-turned to Iceland and that we were settling in the country. She added that she completely understood that because I was new to Iceland, I wanted to live downtown, somewhere I could easily get between places and commute to work.

"But once you get more accustomed," she concluded, "I hope you'll think about moving a little closer to home."

"Home" being Gardabær, where Gudni sometimes jogged on a lazy Saturday morning, not, you know, the *four thousand kilometers* it was to where I had grown up.

I realized I needed to adjust my perception of distance; my mother-in-law was merely expressing a sense of the unique communities in Iceland—that each has its own character—and this gives the country a closeness that I think would be hard to recreate in any other capital city in the world. Each community is strong and supportive as its own unique neighborhood, yet like Russian dolls, each also belongs inside a larger region where it equally has a place. At every level, these communities form part of the web of familial support, but it's often the smallest, closest knit one that a mother may expect her son to return to. Even in the capital region, it's not uncommon for in-laws to live within walking distance of a family.

Regular extended family gatherings are woven into the fabric of Icelandic society. They begin with baptisms. Although Iceland is a very secular place, there is an official religion—Lutheranism—and a majority of babies are baptized by ministers, albeit often in a private home and only rarely as part of a regularly scheduled religious service. Extended family and friends are invited to witness the occasion, and strong coffee and cakes with marzipan topping or whipped cream are served afterward. On our way to the first baptism I was invited to in Iceland, I suggested to Gudni that we stop at the liquor store to pick up a bottle of bubbly for the new parents. "It's a *child's baptism*!" cried Gudni, aghast at the idea of bringing alcohol to an event that was celebrating a child. It was but one of several cultural quagmires I have inadvertently wandered into over the years.

Families also come together for confirmations, similar alcohol-free events that signify a new teenager's coming of age, as well as milestone birthdays (those are any number ending in a zero) and sometimes wedding anniversaries. There is usually no alcohol at parties with children present and copious amounts at those without. Coca-Cola is always on offer, as are savory dishes made of presliced bread, canned asparagus or mushrooms, and mayonnaise. The sweet courses could be the subject of a book all to themselves. I have yet to attend a birthday party that involves fewer than three different cakes.

Many families attend a baptism or birthday or other family event each weekend, flitting between one pavlova and another, sipping an ice-cold Coke directly from the bottle. It's almost always the women of the home who have prepared everything, planned, decorated, shopped, cooked, and tidied up. Family matriarchs all know how to make the best crepes, which direction to fold the ones that contain whipped cream, how to fry the best cardamom doughnuts and decorate the lightest meringue.

Although they are also working in large numbers outside the home, it is still overwhelmingly the women in families who coordinate these social events, plan and host them when their children or significant others are due a celebration, and no doubt feel the guilt or pressure if in their eyes their event does not live up to the social standards set by others. Some things are pretty universal across all countries.

For the women of Iceland, just as with women around the world, even the most supportive familial networks can only provide a limited amount of help, and it is often of the practical variety. Female friendships, both those within organized groups and those less structured, provide invaluable aid, companionship, and the opportunity to develop and contribute in a meaningful way to society. They are also a chance to push limits and foster personal growth, to paraphrase a great many pop psychology bestsellers.

The time when an Icelandic woman was judged on her baking and social hosting skills is easily within living memory; she still is sometimes, especially where birthday parties and other formal gatherings are concerned. These abilities were often honed at regular meetings of local chapters of *kvenfélög*, or women's associations, formalized organizations with annual dues, articles of incorporation, and an elected board. But more important than informal instruction in the social niceties of being a wife and household manager, the women's associations provided a venue for female friendship and interaction, an opportunity for women to take on leadership roles in an era when they were often denied this in the working world, and a commitment to social responsibility through extensive fundraising campaigns and donations to worthy causes and individuals in need.

My mother-in-law was a member of the country's only Catholic women's association for decades, gathering with a handful of other ladies in an empty staff room of the Catholic school on a weekly basis to knit mittens and sew tablecloths for their annual bazaar in support of the church. I too am a sort of honorary member of the Women's Association of Álftanes, the capital-area community where the presidential residence is located; I confess I fall far below par in both event attendance and knitting skills.

Associations today largely continue much of the same work as years ago, as they simultaneously adjust to the demands of a society in which people are increasingly pulled in all directions yet still seek the value of female companionship and the satisfaction of donating time and effort to necessary causes in the community. In Iceland, these groups retain a special influence in the sparsely populated countryside, where there can be arguably less diversity of volunteer opportunities but an equal need for the services that such an association provides. They remain active in many regions, although the average age of members continues to increase, and the popularity of these groups has started to wane among younger women, who get their social fix from their workplaces. Also, so many more women now live in an urban setting and are therefore less geographically isolated.

A more modern and less structured incarnation of female social gatherings often takes the form of "sewing clubs," usually semiformal collectives of childhood friends who continue to meet regularly well into adulthood and old age. Sewing clubs are almost like an informal sorority with five to ten women. In their early editions, showing up to a get-together with something to sew was probably compulsory, but the twenty-first century sewing club (or *saumó*, as they are commonly known) has evolved into just another excuse to meet, eat, drink, gossip, and solve the ills of the world both big and small. Think of it as a book

club with even more food and wine and no literature. The other distinguishing quality of a *saumó* over any loose circle of girlfriends is that the
handful of members in each one determines who is in the club; I moved
to Iceland in my late twenties, and no matter how many local friends I
have made, I missed my *saumó* window by a few years.

Combined with an emphasis on family bonds, these groups still
thrive in modern, busy Iceland because they foster companionship,
confidence, and support of a uniquely feminine variety.

In 1942, the rural county of Hrunamannahreppur in the southern
region of a not yet fully independent Iceland had a population of just
over four hundred. In an area larger than Los Angeles, only two farms
had a telephone, two had electricity, and there was one pickup truck for
the entire area.[16] Roads, which had been built for horses rather than ve-
hicles, were often difficult to traverse and could be impassable in winter.
Several rivers were unbridged. Reykjavík, just over an hour's drive away
in a modern vehicle, was almost another universe, a distant community
only rarely visited.

It was under these conditions that the women's association of
Hrunamannahreppur was established on a March winter's evening
that year, with seventeen women present to attest to the occasion. The
association was one of the later ones to be established in the south of
the country, the oldest being from 1888, which is itself one of the first
known women's associations in the world. The goals of the group were
similar to others: to fundraise for the needy in the community and to
provide a venue for women to meet and interact.

Almost eight decades later, the Women's Association of
Hrunamannahreppur boasts a healthy seventy members and holds
three formal meetings a year (except during the COVID-19 pandemic),

which about a couple dozen women attend. The members take part in innumerable activities, staying abreast of meetings and other news via a Facebook group. The region is still largely rural, though farms now have the latest high-tech tractors and fiber-optic internet connections. The nearest community, the village of Flúdir, attracts day-trippers from the capital for its spicy Ethiopian restaurant and is known throughout the country for its extensive greenhouses that use geothermal energy to grow a disproportionate amount of Iceland's fresh vegetables, all with virtually zero carbon footprint.

Gudbjörg Björgvinsdóttir, the seventy-five-year-old former chair of the women's association, known as Bubba to one and all, invited me for coffee at her rural home near Flúdir. Two other members of the association were there and two from a neighboring group, the Women's Association of Gnúpverja, which was founded in 1929 and now has thirty-five members.

After almost two decades of living in Iceland, I have discovered that an invitation to coffee is much more than an arrangement to meet in a private home and consume hot, caffeinated drinks, already a favorite pastime in my adopted homeland. To "go for coffee" at a private home, especially among the older generation, is to go for a sugar-laden miniature banquet in that midday interlude between lunch and supper.

As a decades-long member of the women's association, Bubba did not disappoint with her coffee offerings. The tablecloth-covered dining table was adorned with fresh flowers and tea lights burning in Finnish crystal holders. The china plates and cups were the exact pattern with red and yellow roses that I used to collect as a child.* The six of us in

---

* Yes, I collected chinaware when I was young, mostly from money I earned by picking up fallen crab apples in my grandparents' backyard in northern Ontario during my summer vacations. Really, it's a shame there was no women's association for nine-year-old girls in my community growing up, because with my interest in porcelain collection and culinary pursuits, I would have been a shoo-in for membership.

attendance shared platters of sugar-sprinkled rolled "pancakes" (more like crepes), jam-and-whipped-cream–filled pancakes (both standard repertoire for any self-respecting women's association member), home-made rolls, four kinds of crackers, three kinds of cheese, jam (cheese solo on a cracker is far too savory for Icelandic palates), homemade date pesto, and another homemade antipasto. The crowning glory was a towering, fluffy pavlova—two layers of lightly crunchy meringue disks with whipped cream in between, all smothered with a thick layer of milk chocolate sauce and sprinkled with chopped fresh strawberries and generous chunks of chopped, caramel-filled chocolate pieces. Strong coffee lurked somewhere in the background. (Woe to the woman who drinks only tea or abhors white sugar in Iceland!)

The four other women Bubba gathered at her home that day had all held various roles of responsibility within the two different women's associations. Now ranging in age from fifty-six to eighty-five, all had joined in their twenties because they craved social interaction and wanted the opportunity to contribute to their communities. After decades of volunteer work with the association, it was inevitable that they would all have fond and funny stories to share about their experiences. They took a charmingly formal approach to telling me what was and remains so worthwhile about women's societies like theirs, speaking in organized turns and often referring to notes that they had arrived with in preparation for our discussion.

I have gradually, but not entirely, adjusted to the warm solemnity with which I was greeted by these women. Perhaps in their minds, they were first and foremost welcoming the First Lady of their country into their home, not a novice book author. They wanted to be as helpful to me as possible with their research and as respectful with me as my role deserves. Indeed, though I sometimes wish it were different, I know that even when I'm "off duty," I am still seen as a representative of the office of the president, and I do my best to conduct myself in a manner that maintains the dignity of that office. But I'm still Eliza, the childhood porcelain cup collector from small-town Canada, and it's important to me that I maintain the line between acting with dignity and acting as myself, without pomp or pretense. I do my best to keep my professional life and my life as spouse of the head of state separate. Perhaps I was a disappointment to Bubba and her friends, arriving as I did in my secondhand family minivan and not driven by the presidential chauffeur. But if they inwardly sighed at not seeing the luxury car with license plate number 1 pull up outside, they kept it to themselves.

By the time the conversational wheels were greased with a day's worth of sugar in one sitting, we were laughing and joking, formality much reduced.

"At first, the main social contact was merely talking on the phone," recalled Rosemarie Brynhildur Thorleifsdóttir, a former chair of the Gnúpverja association. Before joining the group in 1964, she got her social fix by capitalizing on the limited number of telephone lines in the county so that a group of women could talk together at once, a sort of mid-twentieth-century audio-only Zoom.

That social contact was no doubt vital for her and others in that situation, but the association itself then, as now, was busy with all sorts of structured activities. Rosemarie Brynhildur had arrived at our meeting with an itemized list. Their endeavors included preparing coffee, cakes, and sandwiches for postfuneral receptions. They sold Christmas cards and supported the local hospital with the funds raised. They knit hats to give to every newborn baby in the area. They stocked ambulances with teddy bears to soothe nervous younger passengers. They offered a grant that housewives from the area could apply for to get a few days' vacation from the 24/7 duties of running a household. In 2010, now seventy-eight-year-old Rosemarie Brynhildur added rather gleefully, they even blocked traffic on a main bridge to protest planned cuts to the local hospital they had so loyally supported.

"Since 1999, we have raised over fifty million krónur [about U.S. $390,000] for various causes," she proudly concluded.

In addition to the fundraising, the association worked to improve the situation of its own members. Sick housewives could expect help at home from fellow association members.

"It was a complete housewife's school," said Rosemarie Brynhildur. There were courses on topics such as sewing and speaking English, all valuable additions for the women, many of whom had no formal education beyond the compulsory tenth grade. But they also unofficially learned to be bookkeepers and psychologists.

"I call it the school of life," said Bubba with a grin.

"You have to have a certain mindset to join a women's association," dairy farmer Arnfríður Jóhannsdóttir told me as she crowned the wedge of Brie on her cracker with a dab of strawberry jam. "You have to be ready to devote your time and energy, but of course you always get something in return."

The warm, gracious women who shared their memories with me that sunny autumn day might not have defined themselves as feminists—though I never asked. Yet they have lived through decades where their work was underappreciated and their labors often unacknowledged, at least not formally in the way gifts from, say, male-dominated Lions or Kiwanis clubs were.

"Women are always told not to make a fuss in their words and actions," said fifty-eight-year-old Sigrún Símonardóttir, a hairdresser by profession and another former chair of the Gnúpverja association. "It's only gradually changing."

"Half of my work in my life has been voluntary," estimated Rosemarie Brynhildur, who has also served on numerous other local boards and associations, including as the first female head of the local horse association, a male bastion if ever there was one.

"My son works with me, but I own it and run it," explained Arnfríður of the farm she operates with her twenty-four-year-old son. "But people call and ask him to make all the decisions."

"So many women work outside the home now, so they have less time and less need for this sort of organization. But we all got so much experience and so many friends through it. I've learned so much from both the younger and the older members," said Bubba. "It's especially nice to see how young couples today work together in child-rearing and household chores. When I was younger, it went without saying that you wouldn't leave home without having prepared supper or gotten everything ready for afternoon coffee."

Before I recused myself from the conclave of women, they formally presented me with a hardback, glossy-paged book published in 1978 and commemorating the fiftieth anniversary of the formation of the regional women's association for the southern area of the country. In Iceland, many anniversaries warrant the publication of a book, and the half century of this women's association was no exception. Each women's association from the south of Iceland is represented in its pages, detailing how their group was founded, their fundraising priorities, and fun anecdotes or memories from the past decades. Black-and-white photos of the inaugural and current (at the time) boards of directors are included, the women of the earlier photos almost always wearing traditional *peysuföt* hats with long, black tassels attached and the serious faces reserved for the uncustomary occasion of a photograph. The Gnúpverja group, whose modern-day members I met, included a poem by one Ólöf Ó. Briem, who composed her piece in response to a no doubt lighthearted remark by an instructor that she was not progressing enough in her sewing class that was sponsored by the association:

The formidable task has come to its end.
The fruits of this labor, a tremendous feat.
And what I've come to now comprehend:
No women of stronger mind will you meet.

So long have they gathered, each taking her seat
to stitch and to trim and to tie up loose threads.
Day and night they toiled, never a bite to eat,
never dropping their hands or resting their heads.[17]

"Tell her about the man you heard speak," Bubba encouraged Gudrún Sveinsdóttir before I left the house, my belly full of coffee, meringues, and crackers and cheese.

"Well," began the oldest and chattiest member from that day. "We once met a man at an elderly people's home, and he told me, 'People going about their everyday lives don't understand how important the women's association is when one leads a life where nothing noteworthy happens except the rising and setting of the sun.' I thought that was rather nice."

"Rather nice" was the modest way of putting it. Although Icelandic women still struggle to have their efforts heralded on an equal par with men, their work is not invisible to members of the opposite sex. These women's associations form a matrix for community in a rural and formerly unconnected region. They are a vital glue.

With the country's lilliputian population, it's unsurprising that most conversations between strangers in Iceland begin with finding the inevitable personal connection between them. So it was in 2018 with the gathering of women that became the outdoor adventure group known as the Jellyfish. Thórey and Soffía went to school together. Birna's and Brynhildur's daughters are good friends. Halldóra and Thórey are cousins—though had never met in that capacity. Brynhildur and Soffía worked together in Saudi Arabia, of all places. And Thórey and Soffía were two of the founders of the now defunct, but forever popular, walking group intriguingly named "Shut Up, Magnús."

Birna and Thórey were the ones who brought this disparate group of women together with the possibly quixotic aim of swimming across the English Channel, both to raise money for charity and, presumably, to earn the notable bragging rights of having done so. Beyond the co-incidental connections outlined earlier, they were all linked by a shared love of outdoor (though diverse) pursuits and by being women over forty, fully into their golden fuck-it years, in which trying to impress everyone else finally takes a back seat to personal ambition.

Sixteen years after my first foray into sea swimming, I found myself with this group of even more die-hard sea swimmers than my Mexican friends, this time on a sunny, unseasonably warm (19°C, 66°F) August day at the Nauthólsvík geothermal beach in Reykjavík.

Nauthólsvík is the most popular location in the capital for sea swim-ming because it's at a protected cove and has a hot pot and changing rooms right at the unusually sandy beach. Most significantly, the city actually pumps some of the community's plentiful hot water directly into the man-made lagoon in the sea, making its temperature a very manage-able 15°C–19°C (59°F–66°F) in summer. That's warm enough to warrant its own ice cream stand nearby—not that Icelanders ever restrict them-selves to heat waves as occasions to indulge in a cold dairy treat.

An ocean with artificially heated water is of course not authentic enough for the Jellyfish, though. Each Wednesday at lunchtime, they choose instead to partake in several laps in the unheated area of the bay reserved for hard-core swimmers.

"Walk in up to your neck and stay there until you are breathing normally and can count to ten," advised Sigrún Geirsdóttir, who has crossed the Channel four times (including one solo outing) and was awarded the Order of the Falcon, Iceland's highest honor, for her efforts. "It's awful for everyone at first, every time."

Breathing normally? Was that the adult substitute for the vodka shot I had imbibed on my single sea swimming occasion all those years ago? Or was it just that as a nearly middle-aged woman and mother of four, I somehow felt less daring than I did in my twenties?

Yet the Jellyfish are the same age, or older, than I. They are celebrities at Nauthólsvík, where the other regular swimmers cheerfully greeted them.

The water that summer's day measured 12°C (54°F), maybe just a few degrees warmer than that one time I went skinny-dipping in Siberia's Lake Baikal with a honeymooning Swiss couple. Clad in my inexpensive swimsuit purchased from the Icelandic equivalent of Target, I did as instructed and waded in up to my neck. I couldn't help but shriek a little, and I used a term I had last employed in the throes of childbirth. But I counted to ten at a normal pace and was then granted permission to return to shore. After silently congratulating myself for completing a "sea swim" with the Jellyfish, they told me that on a regular day, they take a few kilometers of laps before returning, not the prebeginner version they had indulged in for my benefit.

After accepting polite praise for my nonexistent sea swimming mettle, I spoke with the Jellyfish about the value of their friendship for their own well-being and its importance in inspiring others, especially women, to set high goals and defy expectations. Like the members of the women's associations, the Jellyfish are also performing good works for good causes, but this isn't a formalized organization, despite an aptronymic name. It's more like an athletic sewing club, or *saumó*, with better health benefits—a place for busy career women to prioritize personal development.

"This is really important. It's our therapy time," said Sigrún, the lauded sea swimmer. "We talk about everything, but what is said in the water stays in the water."

Prioritizing time for oneself without guilt was a general theme of the conversation. "It's important for women to have something in the pipeline," said Soffía Sigurgeirsdóttir, who handled logistics and PR for the group but did not swim across the Channel, though I have no doubt she would have the ability. "Men feel as though they can just check out whenever they please, but with something like our project, women have a chance to go off the grid for a while too."

Their off-the-grid, grueling training for the relay thirty-four-kilometer journey across the Channel was a tough combination of regular mountain hikes, swims, and even consultations with a sports psychologist. Rules governing what qualifies as an official swim across the Channel are strict, with dictates covering what type of bathing suit can be worn (a nonthermal one-piece, with no additional equipment allowed except goggles and a cap) to the order in which swimmers take on one hour at a time (if someone cannot cover their prescheduled hour, the whole system falls apart). At one point in their training schedule, the Jellyfish swam from Nauthólsvík across the bay to the official presidential residence and our home, called Bessastadir, to be met by Gudni, who merely had to wade a few meters in to greet them.*

It was rigorous and both mentally and physically demanding. But the Jellyfish took up their space.

"It's important that our kids see that we are taking up that space and

---

* That was literary license based on my faulty memory. When my husband read an early draft of this chapter, he had very few comments, except at this point in the narrative, where he scrawled in large capital letters across the page: I SWAM DOZENS OF METRES OUT.

we are allowing ourselves to take that space in our lives," said Thórey Vilhjálmsdóttir Proppé, a consultant. "Groups of women don't often take on these big physical challenges in the way that men do. There are always people who comment 'what about the kids?' or 'what does your husband think about that?' Men don't get those questions."

"When you hear that kind of thing, then you have to do the opposite," added Birna Bragadóttir, who runs an urban planning institution. "Let nothing stop you."

"We've had so many role models, though," said Soffía, crossing her legs Buddha-style on the grass next to the beach. "Even back as far as Hallgerdur Long-Legs in the sagas, or having Vigdís as president. That makes such a difference. All of us also have strong role models closer to us—our mothers, grandmothers, and great-grandmothers. Many participated in charity work through women's associations and other groups that are still operating all over the country. It's important to be raised up hearing those stories of women making a difference in their communities and having strong voices."

The Jellyfish act as role models for one another and for those around them. "I was nervous at first about all the cold," admitted Halldóra Gyda Matthíasdóttir Proppé. (Icelandic middle names are not merely decoration for birth certificates. They are used often and proudly.) "But we encouraged each other to go for it. We each invented our own motto, and mine was that I'm positive and tough as nails. And I thought about that each time I went in the water."

"My mantra was that I'm calm and composed," added Silla M. Jónsdóttir, a psychologist.

"This was way out of my comfort zone," Halldóra added. "Mentally, physically, it was hard, but we were really strong together."

Thórey wondered if it would be harder for women in other countries to organize and complete a physical challenge such as this one without running into great resistance. Many people, she said, don't like women taking up their space.

"I have taken part in a lot of Ultra-Trail races abroad," said Halldóra. "There are often several Icelandic women in these competitions. And in places such as France, Italy, Spain, if you try to pass a man in a race, they are furious. They'll let a man pass, but they just try to block you if you're a woman. That would never happen here. We all just consider ourselves more equal. You don't have to be first or best, but you have to show some self-confidence, to take a chance."

"Now when I tell the family we're going on a hike, my kids ask me if it's going to be normal difficult or 'Mom' difficult," Thórey commented with a smile.

Affixed to my bright-yellow home office wall with four pieces of blue poster putty is an A4-size printout of a photo of me from my solo backpacking trip to West Africa in 2006. The image was taken at Kakum National Park in Ghana. Visitors to the park can get a bird's-eye view of the area's diverse flora and fauna by walking along a canopy trail composed of seven bridges that hang over 39 meters (130 feet) above the ground, each about the width of a single person.

I hate heights. It's one of numerous irrational quirks (read: fears) I have about situations in which physical harm might come to me. So while travelling alone in several of the world's less touristed countries didn't cause my blood pressure to rise, I have never attempted downhill skiing, riding a scooter at speed, or enduring an adult-sized roller coaster ride. Somehow, though, when you're travelling, you're more willing to test your limits and try something you wouldn't do at home.

Such was the canopy walk for me. While others skipped happily along, smiles of exhilaration stretching across their faces while making the bridge wobble as violently as possible, I tentatively put one foot in front of the other, each hand gripping the mesh rope sides as I willed my breath to slow to an even pace and tried not to look down at the jungle below but rather to the security of the end of the bridge, opportunity to feel like a bird be damned.

The photo in my office captures me midway along one bridge, knuckles nearly white with tension as they cling to the sides, facial expression fixed in concentration and effort to remain calm. At the top of that photo, I have scrawled the words "YOU CAN DO IT!" It's my ongoing visual reminder that when I encounter something challenging, if I could face my personal fear of heights and traverse a series of canopy bridges, I can surely contend with the next test I will face in life, or at least I shouldn't be afraid to try new things.

We all have different definitions of what feels comfortable for us, of the baseline of our status quo. When external factors shift those, it helps to have a mental tool kit of ways to cope: nurturing our mental health on a regular basis, getting fresh air and exercise, and relying on the support of family and friends, whether that's learning new skills and feeling the reward of giving to our community in an organized group like a women's association or gathering to jump, literally or proverbially, in the sea with our friends. This mental tool kit comes in handy throughout our lives as we navigate the twists and turns and grow in our own confidence, experience, and abilities.

Brynhildur Ólafsdóttir, a dauntless member of the Jellyfish, completed her master's degree in international relations in New York City. She talked positively about her experience in the United States and the friends she made and stayed in touch with.

"But after we began to have kids, I started to see some differences between us," she told me after the sea swim. "One of my friends bemoaned the fact that she really wanted children but didn't have a husband, and I kept telling her that didn't matter. 'If you really want them, just do it,' I told her. But she couldn't even contemplate that.

"That's maybe a really Icelandic perspective because the support network here is so strong. The idea of both you and your partner working demanding jobs after you have kids, that was something that some of those friends just didn't understand."

The Jellyfish are in the very privileged position of being able to carve out time to nurture their friendships and to use their means to pursue audacious physical challenges that double as charity fundraisers. I saw that sisterly affection reflected in another way among the women of the long-running women's associations in the south of Iceland—the satisfaction of having helped the community, of learning new skills, of supporting one another through illness and personal crises and natural disasters, mostly uncomplaining, often unrecognized.

These robust social networks, and ones created by the genetic bonds of family, have done much to foster an independence in Icelandic women but also an acknowledgment and acceptance that no one can do it all by themselves and an awareness of the benefits of learning to push one's limits. The extra burden of the mental load from managing households, the guilt about carving out time for oneself, is still there and a real impediment to achieving gender equality. While we do struggle along that path, these friends and extended family do a lot to help along the way—in mental health, physical challenges, and all those cream cakes.

4
STIGMA-FREE SEXUALITY

Give it under the foot

ICELANDIC, THE NATIONAL LANGUAGE OF my adopted homeland, is an ancient tongue almost identical to the one spoken by the Norse Vikings and voyageurs who populated the island along with their Celtic slaves beginning in the ninth century. English speakers can thank Icelanders for words in our vocabulary such as *berserk* and *geyser*, while numerous other colloquialisms still in use in the British Isles, such as *fell* for mountain and *bairn* for child, have roots in the same Norse history. Even the contemporary French word for lobster, *homard*, is a relic left from some southward roaming Norsemen.

Visitors to Iceland often comment on the locals' strong command of English and numerous other languages. Nevertheless, the Icelandic language remains a source of pride and identity. Famously, rather than adopt foreign terms for new technologies and concepts, various committees establish new Icelandic words to enter the lexicon: *tölva* (a mixture of "number" and "prophetess") for computer, *friðþjófur* ("thief of peace") for a pager, and *skriðdreki* ("crawling dragon") for an armored tank.

There is a national day of Icelandic, and many government agencies now focus on bolstering the language and its protection in a global age where English has become somewhat of a lingua franca for planet

---

* *Gefa undir fótinn* can mean to flirt.

Earth. Once a year, the state broadcaster publishes the newest Icelandic words and phrases that have entered common usage over the previous twelve months. Words that have entered the Icelandic lexicon under the illustrious auspices of this annual announcement include *loftslagskvíði* (anxiety about climate change), *líkamsvirðing* (respect for one's own body), and *smitskömm* (shame at being infected with the virus that causes COVID-19). They join a host of other notions that English lacks specific words to describe.

One uniquely Icelandic term, which helps to capture simultaneously both the country's approach to sexuality and its smallness, though not usually in an admiring way, is the word *kviðsystur*, literally "stomach sisters," or two women who have both slept with the same person.

Like its Nordic neighbors, Icelandic society is open-minded about sexuality. Kids are taught about birth control options in elementary school. Only 30 percent of children born in 2019 were born to married mothers (though a majority of those unhitched moms were cohabiting with the other parent at the time of the child's birth). Although the average age for a woman to have her first child has steadily increased over the decades, from under 22 between 1960 and 1980 to 28.6 in 2019, there is virtually no stigma surrounding single or young mothers. Members of the queer community encounter relatively little prejudice and are supported with legislation in their fight for equality, although we need to remain vigilant, especially when it comes to codifying the rights and needs of trans people in law.

There is no single theory as to how this open, liberal attitude to sex evolved. One interview I read suggested it was because back in the eighteenth century, the king of Denmark, who ruled Iceland at the time, encouraged women to give birth to six children each to help rebuild the population that had been devastated by a smallpox epidemic. Perhaps it has to do with a tolerant live and let live attitude, some sort of national philosophy that says, to quote former Canadian prime minister Pierre Trudeau (because I too suffer from small nation complex), "there's no place for the state in the bedrooms of the nation." I also wonder if it has something to do with the general state of life in Iceland. When things are going well, we don't look to lay blame for any ills on the morals of others. And because we are few, many cis people personally know, say, a trans person, giving that entire community a crucial relatability. Or maybe it's just that Icelanders really do embrace the island attitude of marching (and canoodling) to the beat of their own drum.

Whatever its origins, a liberal attitude helps level the playing field for women in all facets of society. A young university student whose child has chicken pox can submit her economics essay a few days after the deadline without penalty. A woman in her thirties who willingly spent the night with a stranger she met at a bar can tell her friends about the adventure without fear of judgment. It would not raise an eyebrow if a forty-two-year-old woman expecting her third child with a third father takes extra time off work to be with her twenty-year-old daughter as the daughter prepares to become a mother herself. The minister of a community church can attend a local party with her wife and their children. Not only do situations like this happen on a regular basis, they are in fact quite unremarkable in everyday discourse.

It's a quarter to three in the morning, fifteen minutes before the traditional last call at Reykjavík's legendary bars and dance clubs. Between mid-May and early August, the sun is high enough in the sky that an observer dropped into Laugavegur, the capital's main drag, could be mistaken for thinking it was almost 3:00 p.m. rather than 3:00 a.m., given the light and the crowds mingling on the street. That is, until the realization dawns that almost everyone is under the age of forty, and a great many of them have the glow and cheer—or anger—of the inebriated.

If you've been building up some liquid courage and had the goal of hooking up for the evening, now is the time known as the "quarter to three"—the last chance to *gefa undir fótinn* ("give it under the foot")—to flirt and find a mate with whom to enjoy a few more hours. If you meet someone you'll go home with, there will be no unspoken longer-term commitment, just an agreement to enjoy the rest of the evening.

There is no expectation that a man should make the first move or spend a long time wooing a member of the so-called gentler sex. Maybe it's the historic unpredictability of life in Iceland. After all, you don't know when the next volcanic eruption or famine may hit the island. If you want to sow your oats, whether man or woman, there is no time to waste.

I was a relatively young adult when I made my home in Iceland, but I did so with a partner to whom I was monogamously committed. I have no firsthand experience of quarter to three culture. But a friend of mine does.

In our first year living in a small apartment in central Reykjavík, when I was in my twenties, Gudni and I hosted one of our friends from overseas. At the end of a day of sightseeing, he met a woman in a bar at the proverbial quarter to three.

The next day, our friend told us he and his new friend had made plans to have dinner that evening. He had only her first name and phone number scribbled on a scrap of paper, but a quick internet search unearthed some other details about the woman in question, namely that she was, legally speaking, barely a woman at all; she was an eighteen-year-old secondary school student who had clearly lied and said she was the legal drinking age of twenty to get into the nightclub where my friend and she met. After a friendly ribbing from us, my friend thought he would go ahead with the date but that he'd call out her omission about her age.

It turns out, he told us afterward, that she arrived at the meal prepared to tell him the truth immediately. When she'd told him the night before that she was an engineering student, she confessed that she meant she *hoped* to be an engineering student—once she finished high school. My friend smiled at this. She was funny, smart, and interesting, but he was several years older and only in town for a few days. Besides, he added, she still lived with her parents and had the same adolescent gripes about their house rules as teenagers the world over. Well, sort of.

"My mom is so strict," the adolescent future engineer lamented to my friend. "When I bring home a guy for the night, she insists that I introduce him to her the next morning."

"Expressing your sexuality and claiming your space as a sexual being are very important to gender equality," asserted sex advisor Ragnheidur Eiríksdóttir. "The empowerment of my daughter and her seventeen-year-old friend here in Iceland is important with regard to our sisters overseas. It's one world."

Like most Icelanders, Ragnheidur wears a lot of proverbial hats. Sporting glasses with thick, vibrant red frames and tattoos on hands, feet, and many places in between, the forty-nine-year-old, charismatic Ragga, as she is more colloquially known, has been a nurse, journalist, sexual health and self-confidence instructor, and, of all things, knitting tour operator. I know her from the last hat, having first interviewed her in 2009 after Iceland's economic collapse on the resurgence of the traditional hobby of knitting during hard times. On this most recent occasion, we met to talk about sex. Ragga was diligently knitting, legs crossed under her on the sofa, pausing occasionally to count stitches yet never letting the yellow woolen sweater she was creating for her grand-daughter derail her train of thought.

"I have been working both with knitting and sexuality, so people have sometimes asked me how I can combine these two seemingly different activities," Ragga told me, her needles clacking away. "But they're quite similar in my mind. In both cases, I am trying to make people braver and encourage creativity. And there is a connection between them both and mental health.

"I think women in Iceland are more assertive," Ragga continued. "We don't have the burden of the patriarchal dating culture where the man is the controlling one who picks you up and pays for the date. Of course, it's always fun to go somewhere and someone pays for you, but in dating and romantic settings, that's not expected at all." She paused to sip her coffee. "Usually you have slept together before going on a date anyway."

This sexual assertiveness has not been lost on foreign visitors. About two decades ago, a maligned campaign by a local airline encouraged London Underground commuters to visit Iceland for "a dirty weekend." The billboards featured mud and mess from an outdoor geothermal spa, but the implication was clear. More recently, bogus claims that Icelandic women will pay foreign men to have the privilege of marrying them have circulated, and local women have no qualms in telling gaggles of patronizing, boorish male tourists who confuse assertiveness with low standards exactly what they think of such arrogance.

A few years ago, an Icelandic app also garnered a few minutes of international glory. The project itself was not new, but the app was. Dubbed the "hookup" app by foreign media, it was a genealogical project that showed how those with an Icelandic ID number (like a social security number) are related to each other.* (Thanks to centuries of good record keeping and a relatively homogenous population, all ethnic Icelanders are related to one another within, say, seven or eight generations.) The story was that if you wanted to have a one-night stand, you could use the app to make sure you weren't about to commit a socially unacceptable level of incest. But do people really do that?

"No, of course not," Ragga told me. "But if you go home with someone and sleep together, then the next day, you might be super stalky and go online to see *how*, not whether, you're related."

Society's nonjudgmental approach to sexuality has also helped to limit, though by no means eliminate, slut shaming.

"Girls and women are not shamed as much as they were for showing that they have sexual urges and that they are sexual beings," Ragga told me. "It's a double-edged sword, though, because with more freedom and more overt expressions of sexuality comes a massively increased need for awareness on respectful limits and consent. Girls growing up in the wake of #MeToo are going to be so much more prepared to set their limits. Thinking back, I didn't have a clue about consent, and enthusiastic consent, when I was their age."

Remember those charming, independent little ones from the last chapter, the ones who are treated as miniature adults mature enough to, say, run an errand at the grocery store or walk a younger sibling home from school? By the time they reach adolescence, they are also behaving more like adults.

---

* In its more innocent incarnation, the online version was used to show how you were related to famous people or others you met. Finding the whole concept intriguing, I once plugged Gudni's details into the program to see how he was related to the two other colleagues who worked in my department at the time. It turns out he was third cousins with both of them.

The age of sexual consent in Iceland is fifteen. A teen who has been dating the same person for more than a year may quite possibly refer to their date's parents as their mother-in-law or father-in-law. She or he would almost certainly be spending many, if not most, nights of the week in the arms of their beloved, snug in their adolescent double bed at home, with parent(s) down the hall.

Is there a concern that a teen might fall pregnant? Yes and no. "Teenage pregnancy isn't the same total and utter drama here that it would be in the United States," said Ragga. First of all, it happens less and less frequently, with easy access to affordable birth control and abortion not the hot political issue it can be in some countries. Girls do not require parental consent to terminate a pregnancy.

"In any case, we're close. Our families are close, babies are always welcome, and we all just help to take care of them." She shrugged, pausing to add a new color of yarn to the yellow jumper.

A few years later, as young adults starting independent lives in Iceland's cities, where rent prices are challenging at best and prohibitive at worst, many couples take the plunge to move in together after only a few weeks of "dating." If things are serious enough that you might consider keeping a toothbrush at your partner's place, why not save a couple hundred thousand krónur a month and just have one toothbrush at one location? If the relationship doesn't work out, there is usually a parent's spare room to crash in. Facing stigma about a failed or misguided relationship is about as likely as being told off for addressing your professor or doctor by their first name. It's just what one does.

Ragga has led popular workshops on sexual health and sexual self-confidence for women on and off for the past two decades. "If the exercise involved nudity, I allowed them to do it at home," she joked. Ragga told me she had seen a difference in tone over the years. At the beginning of the century, people used to ask nervously how they would locate the class, whether there would be a sign on the door proclaiming SEX HELP HERE so "everyone would know" they were about to learn about open relationships, consent, and pelvic floor exercises. But in more recent times, participants proudly posted photos of themselves on social media showcasing new dildos they had bought on a class trip. Yet along with an increase in self-awareness, Ragga also saw self-doubt.

"That probably has to do with social media and the demands it places on you," she mused. "When we were growing up, it was just when we came across *Vogue* that we began to doubt our bodies, but my daughter is getting bombarded with TikTok and Instagram messages about what bodies should look like.

"But I also see a lot of empowerment," she continued, expertly backtracking a few stitches as she spoke. "With these young girls, I also see that they are very conscious about how you should speak about your body, about their rights as people. And they call us parents out when we are being too 'old school' for them."

This is perhaps an example of the evolution of Icelandic society prompting changes to legislation. Although the national curriculum now includes more guidance on positive self-image, communication, gender, and sexual orientation, the topic of sex education from a personal health point of view is covered more under the auspices of the healthcare system via a school nurse. It remains up to individual teachers, schools, or even municipalities to determine whether they wish to expand these very basic guidelines. The ways in which they add to these basics, if at all, are as diverse as the schools and districts themselves.[18] Meanwhile, an NGO, Stígamót (the Education and Counseling Centre for Survivors of Sexual Abuse and Violence), has taken it upon itself to produce short and entertaining videos to distribute to schools (they have been banned from sponsored distribution on social media platforms such as Facebook and Instagram because of what is deemed to be "offensive" content), in which a diverse range of Icelandic teenagers educate others on topics such as masturbation tips, porn versus reality, consent, and positive body image.

Does all the casual sex and partner swapping lead to moral decay or decreased outcomes on some quantifiable lifestyle indicators? Not at all. But there are challenges, including Europe's highest rate of chlamydia infection and nearly chart-topping levels of other STDs (all per capita, as if you had to wonder). Look up "Reykjavík handshake" on urbandictionary.com if you want more proof.

"Maybe it's that we live in such a tiny little country that sometimes we feel invincible," suggested Ragga.

Reports of sexual assault are also comparatively high in Iceland (and, indeed, throughout the Nordic countries, a phenomenon known as the Nordic paradox). It is unclear whether this is from more incidents of sexual assault in real terms or a result of a combination of good trust in the police, relatively easy access to reporting mechanisms, and broader legal definitions of sexual assault. Women in Iceland tend to be more well versed about what constitutes sexual violence than their sisters in countries where such topics are taboo. They are less afraid to seek justice here than in more patriarchal societies. Iceland's drinking culture is also a factor; when bars and nightclubs were forced to close early during the COVID-19 pandemic, there was a noticeable drop in reports of rape to the police in the capital area (but an increase in reports of domestic violence). Generally speaking, although many women, including me, have felt safer in Iceland walking alone after dark than elsewhere, unwanted advances, verbal and physical harassment, and occasionally assault occur here too. And it should go without saying that there is no acceptable level of harassment.

These progressive attitudes nurture increased activism, so laws help conform to social mores and support gender equality at the same time.

For example, in 2009, Iceland's parliament passed a law that makes sex work itself legal but purchasing the services of a sex worker or profiting from someone else's sex work illegal. This places the criminality on the johns and pimps and not the sex workers themselves. Across the board, legislation now refers to "parents" and not "mothers and fathers." In 2019, the country's law regulating abortion was updated for the first time in forty years, eliminating the need for approval by a committee before the procedure could be carried out between the sixteenth and twenty-second weeks of pregnancy. In February 2021, a new law passed that criminalizes so-called revenge porn and other forms of breaches of sexual privacy.[19]

"Somebody said that women's bodies are political battlefields, and we don't have to go far to see that," said Ragga. "Look at what's happening in Poland, in the United States. Women haven't been in charge of their bodies in a global sense, and the body and sexuality are so intertwined, so the way that a woman is allowed to express her sexuality is such a good measure of how much self-determination she has over her body."

There are also more creative ways to advocate for social change. Iceland has held an annual "slut walk" since 2011, only a few months after the first such event was held in Toronto, Canada. The walk is designed to eliminate victim blaming and turn the focus of sexual assault on the perpetrators instead of the victims. In 2015, Reykjavík Mayor Dagur B. Eggertsson appeared in a poster for that year's walk with the caption "I am a slut."

In 2015, after a female patron at a local pool was chastised for bathing topless, the hashtag #FreeTheNipple trended, under which women posted photos of the offending body part online. In egalitarian Iceland, one such post was by then member of parliament (and later minister of the environment) Björt Ólafsdóttir, who published a photo of her own bare breast on Twitter with the caption (in Icelandic), "This is for feeding babies. Shove that up your patriarchy."

Advocacy led by happily unabashed politicians (among others), young women who refute slut shaming, and all those who celebrate control over their own bodies has helped to reinforce the ongoing fight for equality among a specific marginalized group within Iceland: the country's queer community. The Icelandic word that envelops the LGBTQIA+ community is *hinsegin* (literally "the other way around"), an inclusive definition that encompasses all who identify as queer.

"I think the feminist movement goes hand in hand with the lesbian movement. After all, there is even more reason to push for gender equality if you're going to be with another woman!" Eva María Thórarinsdóttir Lange told me from the comfort of her elegantly de-signed central Reykjavík apartment, panoramic views of the capital surrounding us on all sides of the sixth-floor penthouse.

Charming and confident, forty-year-old Eva María ran the capital's pride festivities for seven years and is a nationally recognized voice on queer issues. I know her best, though, in her capacity as cofounder and owner of Pink Iceland, a travel agency she runs with her wife, Birna Hrönn Björnsdóttir, and their friend Hannes Pálsson that caters to the LGBTQIA+ market and is popular for weddings, events, and other bespoke travel experiences in Iceland.

From a legislative and societal perspective, Iceland has a well-deserved reputation as a leader in queer rights. In 1996, it was the fourth country in the world to recognize same-sex unions. Same-sex couples have been able to adopt since 2006 (although Colombia is the only nation Iceland's single adoption agency has an agreement with that allows for same-sex couples to adopt, and domestic, nonkinship adoption is extremely rare because there are almost always extended family members willing to step in if needed). The government legalized same-sex marriage in 2010, by no means one of the first countries in the world, but perhaps one of the few whose legislation was passed with no votes against the motion.

In 2009, Iceland earned international praise for LGBTQIA+ rights when Jóhanna Sigurdardóttir became the world's first openly gay head of government and the country's first female prime minister. I remember this moment as well, but mostly because the domestic news hook for Jóhanna's selection as prime minister was that before entering politics, she worked as a flight attendant. The fact that she was openly lesbian and had been with her partner, the writer Jónína Leósdóttir, for well over a decade was common knowledge within Icelandic society. As an immigrant who was less au fait with her backstory, I was pleasantly surprised that her sexuality was not considered a salient point to highlight.

Jóhanna served as prime minister until 2013, but in that time and beyond, numerous heterosexual leaders have also expressed their support for the queer community. Former mayor of Reykjavík Jón Gnarr, a heterosexual father of five, famously rode in full drag on one of the lead floats of the annual, and very family-friendly, pride parade in Reykjavík. The current mayor has continued the marching tradition, if not the drag. My husband is patron of the National Queer Association, Samtökin '78, and as far as we know was the world's first sitting head of state to address a national pride parade. (Many correctly pointed out that Canadian prime minister Justin Trudeau had already taken part in several such parades, but, pardon the quibble, he is a head of government rather than a head of state.)

When he became patron of the Queer Association, Gudni was gifted a narrow, cotton rainbow bracelet, the type that's popular for young people to weave. He wears it every day, replacing it with a new one if the old one frays or loosens. It was on his wrist for official photos when he shook hands with Russian president Vladimir Putin at the 2017 International Arctic Forum, and during then U.S. vice president Mike Pence's whirlwind visit to Reykjavík in 2019.

It wasn't always this way, of course. The queer community has fought hard for its rights and recognition. It was not so many decades ago that activist Hördur Torfason fled to Denmark after facing physical threats for his sexuality, or when openly gay couples were occasionally attacked for showing affection in public. In Iceland, as elsewhere in the world, it has taken time for society to acknowledge and tackle its own prejudices.

Back at her apartment, Eva María spoke of how Iceland compared to other countries in her own experience. She lived in Naples, Italy, with her Icelandic mother and Italian stepfather between the ages of eight and fifteen.

"Being lesbian there wasn't really an option," she told me. "I literally didn't have a word for it. So for me, Iceland was my paradise, the place I wanted to go. For the family in Italy, I'm not gay, even now."

Coming out in Iceland, which she did as a teenager, was not a big deal for Eva María, though. "I was so relieved that I had come out to myself. When that happens and you're finally comfortable in your own skin, then you can take anything."

But a lack of diverse role models in the queer community was a problem. "When I started coming out, people were like 'you don't look like a lesbian,'" she told me, smiling to herself at the memory. "I'd go into a lesbian bar in a skirt with nail polish and lipstick, and people thought I was a straight girl who had stumbled in there. We need all the role models—the super flamboyant gay guy, the butch lesbian, the femme lesbian."

These stereotypes are certainly all on display in Iceland, where the queer community is generally not segregated into its own neighborhoods. Same-sex couples express affection in public, school forms ask for details of parent one and parent two, not mother and father, and gay people feel comfortable hitting on potential partners at any bar, not just one "designated" for their own gender.

"People come here because society is so accepting, not just because the legislation exists," explained Eva María of her clients.

Eva María also works toward what she dubs "tiny steps" of improvement in attitudes and vocabulary. "I was at a meeting where someone remarked that another person 'took it like a man,' so a while later, I managed to comment that someone else 'was such a lady about it all,'" she recounted. "Everyone realized what I was doing, and I think he won't make that sort of comment again."

I too have adjusted my language after Eva María pointed out to me, following a speech I delivered on gender equality, that I needn't discuss how our country's parental leave policy gave some months to the mother and other months to the father. "It's easier to say they go to one parent and to the other parent," she corrected me politely. I have learned my lesson and always think of her when I speak of our policies for both parents, regardless of gender.

There are several Pink Iceland customers who stand out in Eva María's mind: The couple from West Hollywood, "probably the gayest part of any city" according to the Pink Iceland owner, who said holding hands in a tiny North Iceland village meant they were "just normal human beings" who didn't have to live up to some stereotype of a gay couple. The first wedding she planned for Pink Iceland, at the UNESCO World Heritage Site Thingvellir, between an American army doctor who was about to be posted to the Middle East and his German boyfriend, who wanted to wed "in case anything happened" to him on post. The nuptials during which the sister of one of the grooms read out a touching letter from their estranged mother, wishing him well. The two fiftysomething upper-class Indian women, in love for more than a quarter of a century, who said, despite helicopter tours, glacier hikes, and horseback rides on black sand beaches, that the highlight of their trip was the freedom they felt strolling hand in hand along Reykjavík's main shopping street, the first time they had ever held hands in public.

"One of the strongest human needs is the sense of belonging. If you don't feel you belong anywhere, you'll never be happy," Eva María said of the effect these experiences had on her and the clients themselves.

Even as legislation is finally catching up to society and being gay is not the stigma-inducing crisis it was, there are still challenges to overcome, according to Eva María.

"For the first time, we have older openly queer people. Would a gay man who is ninety years old move into a seniors' home here and be proudly gay? I'm not sure about that. Young people don't really need to come out of the closet now. Maybe they are even just gender fluid. But the older generations had to fight for their very existence and maybe continue to face prejudice within themselves.

"If I had the choice at fifteen to be straight, I would always go for gay, because it has made my life much better and has given me more opportunities. I've never thought I couldn't do something because I'm a woman or I'm a lesbian. It has never crossed my mind. Is part of that due to living in Iceland? Of course."

If Iceland's lesbians are feeling socially and legislatively connected with Icelandic society, trans women and nonbinary individuals are still fighting for their rights to be further enshrined in law.

Ugla Stefanía Kristjönudóttir Jónsdóttir came out to their parents, a farmer and a housewife, via a typed five-page letter, frequently asked questions section and all, that explained how they felt their gender assigned at birth did not match how they felt as an individual, which is nonbinary, or not exclusively male or female.

"'Take your time digesting this, read it, and then go out and milk the cows,' I told them. 'And then when you're ready, we can talk about it,'" Ugla Stefanía recalled when we met at the downtown Reykjavík headquarters of the Queer Association of Iceland.

They did so, sat down around the forty-year-old farmhouse's sturdy kitchen table, and after assuring Ugla of their support, the first question Ugla's father asked was "Which changing room will you use at the swimming pool?"

"It's such an Icelandic thing to have swimming as your first concern!" Ugla told me, smiling. "I said we will just take everything one step at a time."

Ugla Stefanía was born and raised in a farm near the village of Blönduós in northwest Iceland. The town itself is generally known to visitors as the home of a popular swimming pool and interesting textile museum. A verdant region with treeless hills and clear streams, it has a positive reputation for its good farmland and a less favorable one among some for arguably the country's most assiduous police officers, who love to pull over drivers speeding between the capital and Akureyri, the largest town of the north. Ugla's school had fewer than one hundred students from grades one to ten. The next house was a five-minute drive away. There was no mobile phone reception. Ugla's father, who was born at the farm in 1959, did not live with electricity until he was almost a teenager. Their parents, Kristjana Stefanía Jóhannesdóttir and Jón Gíslason, have been running that farm together since they were only seventeen and nineteen years old.

"People think being raised in the countryside is quite conservative, but I'm really grateful and happy that I was raised there, because I was able to connect with nature in a much deeper way than my friends raised in the city," Ugla recalled. "When I was growing up, I was obviously very different from typical boys, and my parents were always good with me. They never made me feel bad about being different."

Ugla Stefanía identifies as a trans feminine nonbinary person who uses they/them pronouns. In Icelandic, a new word, *hán*, representing a gender-neutral third-person singular, has been used increasingly often in recent years, although unlike *tölva* for computer and *sími* for telephone, this word originated within the queer community itself and is still not included in the official Database of Icelandic Morphology.

"I find more solidarity and understanding with women," Ugla told me, who is "perfectly fine" with being interviewed in the context of women's support for gender equality in Iceland.

"My entire world and experience are around being seen as a woman, and my experiences are the same as women in almost every instance," Ugla told me. "So I feel a real connection to that, even though I feel that my gender identity is broader." Ugla is also a vocal trans activist in the UK and Europe more widely and was named one of the BBC's 100 Women in 2019.[20]

As I spoke to Ugla, I made a mental note about how frequently they used the words *fortunate*, *lucky*, and *grateful*. Ugla, who is better known in the UK, where they live, by the moniker Owl Fisher (*ugla* is the Icelandic word for "owl"), is most decidedly an individual who sees opportunities instead of challenges, blessings instead of curses. No access to internet until the early years of this century? "It makes me appreciate the technology now." A challenging number of identities trying to be part of the conversation of LGBTQIA+? "Our language creates solidarity around this with the word *hinsegin*; we are so lucky to have that."

The facts about trans individuals remain stark, however: trans people have a significantly higher risk of depression, anxiety, and suicide. Many don't feel comfortable using public restroom facilities. Trans youth in many countries are bullied, refused access to basic services, and stigmatized.[21] Statistics on the mental health of trans individuals in Iceland are hard to find, but it's safe to assume that while percentages may be more favorable in this country, there is still plenty of room for improvement.

Slowly but surely, these improvements are being made and enshrined in law. Trans youth in Iceland can start taking hormone blockers when they hit puberty, effectively pressing the pause button on its effects. From the age of fifteen, an Icelander can legally change their name and gender marker. After the age of sixteen and in consultation with physicians who evaluate the person's physical characteristics and emotional state, trans individuals can begin taking cross-sex hormones. In 2020, the rights of intersex minors were also protected by banning medically unnecessary surgeries without their consent.

Ugla is "in awe" of trans kids in Iceland today. "They just do what they need to do and are so nonchalant about it. Being trans is just one facet of who they are."

Since 2012, transition procedures have been covered under the national healthcare scheme, and there is a "trans team" at the National Hospital to help coordinate the myriad procedures and services many trans people elect to have—from laser treatment for the removal of unwanted hair to psychological counselling to the genital surgery itself. No one requires any sort of official permission to transition.

"If people can't afford to medically transition, they literally can't afford to be themselves," Ugla pointed out.

Individuals in Iceland can select a gender-neutral option when applying for a passport or update to this option with their national identity number. People who are registered as gender-neutral can choose a gender-neutral family name ending in -bur ("descendent"), instead of the more traditional -son or -dóttir.

The social discourse on trans issues is also becoming more mainstream. A city bus in 2020 was painted with the trans flag colors during the nation's pride month. The same year, a television show about trans kids in Iceland garnered positive reviews. Even the Lutheran Church, the state church of Iceland, advertised its Sunday school by featuring a drawing of a bearded, full-breasted, Caucasian Jesus, admittedly stirring strong debate and controversy, but without broad national outrage.[22]

"I think the majority of folks really want trans people to feel good about themselves and to participate in society," asserted Ugla. "I experience Iceland as a society that wants to be open and respect people regardless of who they are."

Ugla has lived in the south of England for the past five years, and the differences in trans rights are stark, they told me. "Most people in Iceland will meet a trans person, whereas in the UK, the chances of you meeting a trans person become much smaller. The problem with prejudice and fear is that it's the unknown.

"When I do an interview in the UK, it just becomes a fight. You have to be prepared for war, and it can be really exhausting," they continued. "I've never had an interview in Iceland where people have been rude to me, even though I've been asked challenging questions."

Ugla Stefanía persists in helping shift perspectives and keep trans issues on the table. "Finding common ground and shared values is where the real activism happens. That's when people can relate to you as a person."

Equality in this field, as with others, will foster it in other areas too. And just like the word *hinsegin* that gathers in so many disparate orientations, for the activist from a farm near Blönduós, it suggests lessons that can be applied elsewhere.

"'Feminist' still often focuses on a particular type of woman. We don't see disabled women, immigrant women, women of color, and we need to have them part of the conversation. They need to be in the room, because otherwise we'll do something that won't include them, and you'll have the same dynamic as always."

My conversation with Ugla Stefanía took place on a sunny summer's day, the year that locals took over the country for themselves as travel slowed to a masked trickle in the global coronavirus pandemic. Ugla and I donned rainbow masks provided by the Queer Association to move from place to place. There was a bittersweet feeling around having plenty of space to ourselves in some of the capital's most interesting locations, knowing the paucity of visitors meant economic agony for many.

In the center of town, in the midst of those colorful corrugated iron homes that feature in so many postcards, runs one of the main, partially pedestrianized arteries of Reykjavík. Moving up a steep hill from a busy shopping street and straight along almost one kilometer to the towering city landmark that is Hallgrímskirkja, a Lutheran church, the first block of Skólavördustígur Street is painted with a rainbow. It was originally set there to recognize a pride month but is now a permanent—and regularly repainted—reminder of the city's and society's commitment to diversity and equality.

We all need these reminders. Equality doesn't happen of its own accord, and while we celebrate all steps forward, we must never forget how easy it is to slip back. A diversity rainbow, a colorful ribbon threading its way through the city center, is a tangible nod, both to what we've achieved and to the journey yet to be. It's also a signal that we all belong, no matter where we fall on the spectrum.

Eva María's penthouse apartment looks out over the Skólavördustígur rainbow, one of her favorite features of the flat. In souvenir shops lining the sides of the street, locals can stock up on wool and visitors can buy sweaters and mitts, in the same style as those that the sex advisor and knitting devotee Ragga finds so soothing to create. Late into the night, anyone who may have chosen to take advantage of quarter to three culture may stroll hand in hand along this pedestrianized portion of the road.

Despite the unprecedented times in which we met, true to character, Ugla Stefanía was upbeat about everything and about the opportunity to visit their homeland.

"Whenever I come here, I have a moment to breathe," they told me. Regardless of all the hours spent catching up with friends and family, buying culinary goodies not available in the UK, offering advice to shy trans kids, or conducting interviews with the national press, there is space to relax, to soak in the pool, to be oneself without justification, to breathe.

Ugla Stefanía's optimistic tenacity inspires me—to elevate others' voices when I can, to remember the unseen and unspoken challenges so many are facing, to consider that minor amendments to my wording can have a more major impact on others. I don't always succeed. I unconsciously fall back on stereotypes I absorbed long ago, judgments about people's choices in their romantic lives: the open-minded attitude to sex is probably what surprised me most when I moved here. But none of this is about me. It's about allowing people to live the lives they want, as the people they know they are. It's about speaking up and increasing social pressure to help change attitudes in our communities and into laws that enshrine and secure everyone's rights.

Nothing is perfect, but in this country, we try to free the nipple, march in our slut walks, and give it under the foot whenever and with whomever we want. While there is still some prejudice and ignorance, we're fortunate that promiscuity and indecency are not the stigmas of present-day Iceland.

THE NO-HOLDS-BARRED
SPRAKKI OF THE MIDDLE AGES

ICELAND IN THE FIFTEENTH CENTURY: The island of about seventy thousand souls lay under the Danish realm. Earthquakes, volcanic eruptions, and general storms could wreak enormous havoc without warning. The arrival of the Plague roughly halved the population to somewhere around thirty-five thousand at the very beginning of the century.

In this era of general poverty, an elite group of well-connected individuals lived off the pocket of the Danish king and exploited increasing trade with far-flung nations.

Ólöf "the Rich" Loftsdóttir was one half of a Middle Ages Icelandic power couple and the closest Iceland has come to having a "noble woman." The daughter of a governor, she grew up in privilege and luxury. Ólöf and her husband, Björn Thorleifsson, were the wealthiest pair on the island. Together they owned great swathes of land in the western part of the country. Ólöf also bought and sold property in her own name and led sailing missions. Indeed, it seemed to some of her contemporaries that she acted as both wife and husband.

The couple also earned favor with King Christian I, who

paid a hefty ransom for the couple's safe return after they were kidnapped by pirates on the Orkney Islands off the coast of Scotland.

Years after their return to the homeland, in 1467, a gang of English merchants upset with new Danish-imposed tariffs on their growing trade with Iceland attacked and beheaded Björn and seven other men. They dismembered the governor's body, salted the parts, and sent them in a sack to Ólöf.

Upon receiving the gruesome package, the steely Ólöf is reputed to have said, "Do not grieve for Björn, but gather men to avenge him."

Avenge him she did. Ólöf amassed men to round up dozens of English merchants and held them captive. Assisted by her eldest son, Thorleifur, Ólöf took three English fishing vessels and all their crew. She forced many into slavery at her farmstead, sent others back to England, and had others killed.

Legend also has it that Ólöf travelled once again to meet the Danish king and share the story of her husband's murder with him. The king was so impressed with Ólöf's assertiveness and grand demeanor that her complaint may even had led to a five-year war between Denmark and England.

Following the death of her husband, the determined Ólöf continued to manage the large farm after his passing, including building a church there that stood for three centuries.

As Ólöf's final years approached, she asked God for something significant to occur. When she died in the waning days of 1479, a fierce storm blew in the region. Churches, homes, and boats were destroyed. In England, fifty ships were sunk, and in Norway, houses were blown from their foundations.

Henceforth, the storm was dubbed Ólöf's Tempest.[23]

5

CLAIMING THE CORPORATE PURSE STRINGS

*Never peed in a salty sea**

LIKE SO MANY GOOD IDEAS, this one began over a bottle of wine. In the dark autumn of 2012, my friend Erica Jacobs Green and I were enjoying a full-bodied rioja while she told me about the inspiring American writers' conference she had recently returned from.

"Icelanders love writing so much," she mused. "I wonder why there are no similar conferences here?"

"That's a great point," I responded, two drinks in. The light bulb in my brain flickered on. "Why don't *we* create something like that?"

That is how our business, the Iceland Writers Retreat, was conceived. Erica and I quickly buckled ourselves into the emotional roller coaster that is launching an event from scratch, pitching to sponsors, creating marketing plans and budgets, inviting a dream list of authors to lead writing workshops, learning the ropes of social media advertising, and devising book-themed tours to showcase beautiful Iceland to our clients, who would travel to the country from around twenty different nations. The idea appealed to both of us: Erica and I love to organize, plan, and execute events. She had worked for almost two decades as an editor, and I had years under my belt writing magazine articles, mostly in the travel genre. I was editing Icelandair's in-flight magazine, and generating much of the content. The IWR seemed like the perfect mix

---

* *Að míga í saltan sjó* refers to someone inexperienced (because they have never had to try the balancing act of peeing overboard when on a fishing expedition).

of doing something we both loved (planning) about topics we both loved (writing and Iceland).

Eighteen months, dozens of meetings, many worries, and probably a case of rioja later, we held our first IWR, and we are still going strong. We have managed to weather snowstorms in April, one of our most famous authors cancelling the night before she was to arrive to teach fully booked workshops, running a smooth show as rumors swirled surrounding my husband's possible presidential run, and the bombardment of challenges the COVID-19 pandemic sprang on international conferences such as ours.

The Iceland Writers Retreat is my professional baby, and its gestation taught me a lot about the process of being an entrepreneur in Iceland. Before its management took over most of my working time, I was employed at both a start-up and a magazine. I had gained insights into dozens of other organizations through my freelance work in copywriting and marketing. But I had never "peed in a salty sea": I was inexperienced and unaccustomed to having the buck (well, the króna actually) stop with me. The transition from employee to freelancer to entrepreneur was never dull. That said, the reward—seeing people from around the world gathered to enjoy what many claim to be one of their most fulfilling experiences—is more than worth it.

Unlike my brief working years in the UK, when as a twenty-something executive, I was often taken for the secretary at meetings, I have not experienced overt sexism during my workdays in Iceland. Of course, like every other individual of my gender, I have been interrupted and ignored. Some Icelandic men are as skilled as their counterparts around the globe at mansplaining, at raising their voices to bully female colleagues instead of speaking to them with respect. To say that sexual harassment in the workplace does not exist in Iceland would be disingenuous.

And yet. More than three-quarters of Icelandic women over fifteen who are economically active work outside the home, their presence felt in virtually all sectors (labor force participation for women in the United States is 56 percent, 61 percent in Canada).[24] Admittedly, many fields such as nursing and teaching are dominated by women, and the salaries in those areas are unsurprisingly lower. Many other fields, such as fisheries and, crucially, investment, remain primarily male domains. Nevertheless, all-male enclaves are few and far between.

Iceland is not immune to problems and conditions that exist elsewhere, but it does tend to be cognizant of the role of gender in professional inequalities. As is the case in other countries, lower-wage jobs are often filled by women. In 2020, a national strike by the lowest-paid workers, such as municipal workers, including preschool staff, was branded by union organizers as a battle against sexism. After striking for more than month, a new contract was agreed to that gave those workers a raise, a shorter work week, and a greater emphasis on education and training when calculating wages. The union whose workers were striking called it an important step in updating the contracts of the minimally compensated workers and jobs filled mainly by women.

As is often the case, the view of the country is rosier when seen from an outsider's perspective. Iceland topped the *Economist*'s glass-ceiling index in 2020, praised for the number of women in the country who have a university degree (more than half) and for the proportion who make up the boards of public companies (thanks to quota legislation).

But from inside this nation, we focus on the outstanding challenges. In 2019, women's average annual employment income was 30 percent lower than men's, and when women make less money over the duration of their careers, they earn far less in pensions for retirement. At the time of writing, female CEOs are notoriously absent from any of the companies traded on the Iceland Stock Exchange. Only 13 percent of CEOs in the country's top eight hundred companies are women.[25]

In Iceland's corporate world, there is increasingly urgent hand-wringing on the lack of gender parity in the boardroom and the corner office. Legislation that mandates a gender balance on boards as well as laws on equal pay for equal work have helped to hasten the process. Men generally seem to be in agreement with the concept and recognize overall that increased gender and ethnic diversity increases the bottom line.*[26] Vocal role models ensure the issue remains in the minds of decision makers. But the money—the companies on the stock exchange, investors such as powerful pension funds—remains firmly in the hands of men. Meanwhile, a growing number of immigrant women face unique challenges in the entrepreneurial and private sectors. However, the oft-cited barrier to greater corporate parity—the challenge of balancing work and family—is surprisingly absent from the dialogue of the women I spoke to and in my own experience as an entrepreneur. Here is where Iceland's social structures facilitate more professional involvement, even though we have much to improve, especially when it comes to parity in holding the purse strings.

In 2010, the world's eyes fell on Iceland and its unpronounceable volcano, Eyjafjallajökull, when the ash plume from that eruption caused the worst disruption to European air traffic since the Second World War.

In a way, the eruption ended up being a blessing in disguise. All of a sudden, the world realized that Iceland wasn't really that far away. After

---

* In fact, a 2020 McKinsey & Company report revealed that companies in the top quartile for gender diversity on executive teams were 25 percent more likely to have above average profitability than companies in the bottom quartile.

all, it was close enough to spew ash over continental Europe. And as far as the pictures indicated, it had some very photogenic natural wonders. Thanks to that unplanned event, the country's preexisting notoriety from surviving one of the largest bankruptcies in history (all publicity is good publicity!), and a concerted ad campaign by government-funded tourism boards, visitors flocked to the island. The number of tourists ballooned from 360,000 in 2004 to 2.3 million in 2018. In 2013, tourism overtook fisheries as the sector with the greatest contribution to the country's gross domestic product.

With the exponential increase of tourists and their dollars, euros, yen, and rubles came a blossoming of the services offered. Or, put another way, Icelandic entrepreneurs found innovative approaches to help vacationers part with those funds while here.

Let's say all this volcano publicity and an increase in potential audience sparks a thought. You have the nutty idea to melt lava in front of an audience and pour it onto ancient glacier ice to demonstrate the awesome power of nature. At face value, it sounds daunting and quite possibly dangerous. In reality, it's even more difficult than that. You need to source real lava that has no more than 5 percent alkali metal oxides to ensure an even flow. You need to procure a furnace and ventilation system that can securely store heat up to 1250°C (2500°F). You need 1800 kWh of energy over the four or five hours it takes to melt 100 kilograms of igneous rock so it can be transformed into lava and poured into the showroom. And you need to make sure it's melted to a Goldilocks viscosity: neither too thick nor too molten to ruin the show for viewers.

This is exactly what Ragnhildur Ágústsdóttir and her husband, Júlíus Ingi Jónsson, did. In September 2018, in the village of Vík, under the shadow of the massive Katla volcano, they opened the Icelandic Lava Show, an immersive experience in which up to fifty guests at a time sit spellbound in a small auditorium while Júlíus recounts the story of his ancestors from the area. Then he calmly reminds the audience that should Katla decide that moment is the one in which its long overdue eruption would come, in a worst-case scenario, the town and all its people would potentially have as little as fifteen minutes to seek higher ground before a torrent of melted glacial water floods the community.

Next, Júlíus asks everyone to don the safety goggles they are given upon entry and suggests that they may wish to remove any thermal outerwear. "It'll get kind of warm in here"—an understatement he's perfected for these shows. Then he unleashes the lava. Few would fail to be awed by the close-up glimpse of molten rock steadily streaming onto the glacial ice. The room almost instantly heats a good ten or fifteen degrees as the ruby-red rock spits and hisses upon contact with the ice. All eyes remain fixed on the show as Júlíus explains the science behind the forms the rapidly cooling lava takes. Lucky audience members get to take home a piece of the new rock.

Ragnhildur and Júlíus's professional baby was a hit. By January 1, 2020, they had already prebooked 68 percent of all the visitors they had had the previous year.

Ragnhildur is used to being a woman in a man's world. Not only is she an entrepreneur, but she also works in the IT industry, becoming a CEO for the first time at the age of twenty-five. She and Júlíus are such idea incubators that before they had kids, they would regularly turn off their devices and other distractions and just brainstorm concepts for start-ups or solutions to all kinds of problems. Charismatic, articulate, and enthusiastic, Ragnhildur has a lot on her plate, but her confident buoyancy is infectious. Talking with her, you soon begin to think that you could probably take on that much too, maybe even generate a new entrepreneurial initiative of your own. But then you realize and accept that there are few people as skilled at multitasking as she is.

"Even in Iceland, there is a difference between being a male and a female entrepreneur," Ragnhildur acknowledged in a video conversation with me from her suburban home, piles of folded laundry sitting on a table behind her. "But you are not going to have it better in many places than here.

"I believe that a lot of us women are more risk-averse in general and less likely to take chances when it comes to our careers. I think that some of our other responsibilities, such as parenting, housekeeping, and all the little things like birthday presents and doctor's appointments, still weigh more on us women even if men are generally taking a more active role," she continued, right before her young son toddled into view to get some help with his headphones. "Very few of us have that luxury of a partner who just takes on that responsibility. If a man is the entrepreneur, it's sort of expected that the woman picks up the slack. But if you're a female entrepreneur, is it expected of your male partner?"

While society may reward the gumption of men who risk everything to bring their ideas to fruition, Ragnhildur told me that she felt women were judged more for their outside-the-box ideas. Women and men alike bear a responsibility to work toward diminishing that double standard.

"What are the messages we are sending out there? Are we trying to highlight equality?" she mused without missing a beat as what I can only conclude was a stuffed dinosaur turned projectile soared behind her.

In this challenge, as in so many others, role models are of vital importance. Ragnhildur didn't pause for a moment before she rattled off the names of numerous of her role models, both within the corporate world and without.

"When I was eight, I said I was going to be president," she told me. "That was because we had a female president. I had never known any different."

In addition to the too few women who are trailblazing in the boardroom, Ragnhildur pointed out that we should emphasize their importance in all facets of society.

"We need to highlight not just the biggest role models but also the everyday woman who is doing an amazing job on this front or that front. And we need to bring male role models who support equality movements into this too. We need to influence both men and women in this. And we need to raise our boys to become such men. It's not just enough to have *a* woman on the board of directors or team of executives. The gender glasses need to be worn all the time. If there is only one woman somewhere, she is the exception that proves the rule."

Role models alone cannot manage all the heavy lifting needed to create more gender-equal companies. The company Marel is one of Iceland's biggest corporate success stories. Founded in 1983 by several male former engineering students from the University of Iceland, Marel is now one of the world's leading providers of solutions for the meat, fish, and poultry processing industries. Using the country's historic foundations as a fishing nation that thrives on innovation and sustainability, Marel's products include the patented FleXicut, a machine that optimizes fillet utilization, and the Innova software solution for real-time monitoring of the entire production process.

If all this sounds like a marketing brochure aimed at customers who work in food processing facilities, there's some truth to that. I worked on a freelance basis in Marel's global marketing department for a few years before becoming First Lady, proofreading texts in English on the FleXicut or the latest service contracts for Innova and polishing slogans for upcoming billboards that would be displayed at international seafood shows. I worked there with a team of lively and dedicated people; the company aura was positive and energetic.

If there was ever a traditionally male-dominated industry, the design and production of tools for these processing sectors has got to be in contention for top place. At Marel's first location and headquarters in Iceland, just under one-quarter of the staff are women. In the global context of this industry, that statistic falls to 15 percent.

"We just acquired a company in Germany that was about six hundred employees and relatively few women," Gudbjörg Heida Gudmundsdóttir, the executive vice president for Marel Fish, told me when we had a chat about women in this male-dominated Iceland success story. "So every time we buy a company, the dial gets fucked up again."

She laughed, an ebullient, contagious expression of joie de vivre. "It's crazy. We're striving for equality here in Iceland, but the global scene is not the same."

Even that 75/25 gender ratio of employees in Iceland is not terribly impressive at face value. Yet the management team in that location is a slightly better 65/35, the company's board of directors comprises four men and three women, and the global management team is five men and four women. For the ten-year period from 2017 to 2026, Marel is aiming for 12 percent average annual revenue growth, so something in their alchemy must be working.

Those corner office–level gender ratios, which are more in line with a society that prides itself on aiming to achieve parity, are the result of legislation that has been created to nudge diversity in the right direction. In 2013, Iceland's parliament passed legislation that required the boards of companies with more than fifty employees, such as Marel, to have a gender ratio of at least 60/40. In 2017, Iceland again made global headlines when it became the first country in the world to make it illegal for companies to pay men more than women (equal pay for equal work).* Marel acquired the certification that they were an equal pay employer in 2019.[27]

"I am sure we would not have had the equality on the boards if it were not law," asserted Gudbjörg, the first woman to be responsible for one of the brand's global P&L (profit and loss) accounts. An engineer by training, she was the company's head of the Iceland office until March 2020, when she took on her new responsibilities. In this capacity, she heads a team of just over two hundred people and is responsible for an annual turnover of about 150 million euros, in a role that, prepandemic, would have seen this single parent of two on the road for at least one hundred days a year.

Ragnhildur of the Icelandic Lava Show agreed with Gudbjörg's assessment of the importance of legislation. "I was extremely against the idea of quotas at first. I was really young and was confident things were changing," she recalled. "I was arrogant, thinking that the older female generations just hadn't shown what they could do. But as time has gone by, I've completely changed my mind. I know that to accelerate change, we need this."

Despite the law, though, in 2019, the average percentage of women on boards of the companies to which the law applies was only 34.7 percent, albeit a significant increase from the 12.7 percent total in 2007. Perhaps the growth has not been more significant because there are no repercussions for failing to fulfil that particular requirement.†

---

* Of course, many nations, including Iceland, already had equal pay stipulations in law, but this was the first time that companies with more than twenty-five employees had to *prove* they were doing it and faced fines if they did not comply. The law was passed in 2017 but took effect January 1, 2018.

† It is not possible to legally register company boards that do not meet the gender balance requirements. However, boards that existed before the legislation took effect do not face consequences such as fines, even if they do not meet the current standards.

"If there were a fine for not meeting the minimum 40 percent gender equality rule on boards, I'm sure the results would be much better," Ragnhildur argued. "That's what we've seen with the extensive GDPR (global data protection regulations) on how companies store personal data. The potential fines for not complying to those rules are immense [up to 4 percent of total revenue], and as a result, this has become a business priority.

"In the ten years or so since the law was introduced, we are still far from achieving equality," she continued. "This makes me really mad. Things are still moving too slowly." She said this also applies to the newer law on equal pay for equal work.

Ragnhildur's peer Gudbjörg had been working at Marel for several years before she was tapped to run the Iceland office, and she didn't feel she was treated any differently in that role because of her gender. On the other hand, after her appointment to the global executive team, an opportunity she described as "a dream come true," she said some of her new sales team were skeptical about being led by a woman.

"They had probably never had a woman boss before," Gudbjörg acknowledged. "But once you get the connection, you start to have success, and everyone wants success. Once you have that, then gender is forgotten."

Gudbjörg believes the corporate culture in Iceland is more conducive to gender equality.

"I can see it in the Netherlands, for instance. They are still debating whether they should have quota laws. It's very uncommon for women to go back to work full-time after they have kids. In Iceland, we're a tiny country, and I love how passionate we are about equality. I think we're way ahead of other countries."

Nevertheless, when Gudbjörg moved into the top job in Iceland, she decided it was time to introduce some different values into the corporate culture. "When you get the power, you have to dare to change things," she said. "I sent all seven hundred employees here on gender awareness training, anti-bullying training. I hired more female engineers."

Legislation to hasten equality and impose consequences on non-compliers is an important component of achieving parity in the corporate world, but so is an individual's self-confidence, Gudbjörg told me. She was quoted in a television interview saying that her biggest challenge is herself. "It's really about a belief that you will be able to achieve something," she revealed.

"A guy once asked me what my dream was. I got angry and told him I didn't get to do that. I'm a single mother. I need to make sure I have everything I need for my family. I don't get to dream," she recalled. "He said to me, 'Actually, you do. You're living in this rich society with all this equality. If you don't get to dream, then I don't know who does.'"

The time and support to dream are certainly luxuries afforded many women in Iceland. But making dreams a reality in the corporate world can't be accomplished in a bubble. For decades, if not longer, men have exploited their access to male-only enclaves. These membership clubs, sports venues, and—often in Iceland—fishing and hunting lodges become the venues where familiar bonds are formed. So when Jón is looking for a new member of his executive team or his board or when Magnús has some extra krónur to invest, human nature shows they will be inclined to first seek those with whom they have already established trust and personal connections.

To level the playing field, women too need the opportunity to build professional networks. "You don't get a promotion because you're hardworking. You get one because you are well connected,"

Gudbjörg told me. Groups such as the traditional women's associations I discuss in Chapter 3 have provided much-needed friendships and, very often, skill building, but for the private sector in recent decades, associations for professional women have gained increasing influence in Iceland.

I too have made new friends and enjoyed gatherings in these groups, which focus on building the connections between professional women who are often leaders in their fields. The Association of Women Business Leaders (FKA) and EXEDRA (from the Latin word for a room configured to facilitate dialogue) are societies that hold lectures and social functions but also, more importantly, provide a strong network of women supporting women, regardless of age, profession, or political stance. If a member finds herself unfairly targeted on social media, other members have her back. They confront trolls in comments sections, share positive news stories, or simply send an encouraging text message. We meet at lunches that feature a well-known speaker to discuss hot topics of the day, or, in the case of the women business leaders, push for women's increased involvement in the corporate world and increased representation in media. For those more athletically inclined than I, women can socialize at golf tournaments, mountain hikes, and yoga sessions.

For the academically minded, FKA also commissions studies and research into gender balance in corporations and offers an annual award to companies, municipalities, and public organizations that have at least a 60/40 gender balance in their senior management. The first year they ran the program, eighteen companies were recognized as having achieved this milestone. By 2020, forty-five groups were on the list, with a further seventy-one pledging to achieve it before 2027.

The awards have an influence on shaping policy within companies that are seeking to boost their reputations as socially responsible organizations, not to mention their bottom lines by attracting the best talent of all genders.

Gudbjörg has made the most of membership in these groups. She had been in senior management or running Marel's Iceland office for almost five years but was more ambitious. She had not yet had success with gaining the attention of the board of directors.

"So I thought I would work my way into the executive team by using the outside world," she said. "In early 2020, I was named woman of the year by FKA." The award garnered extensive local news coverage and, "two weeks later, I'm an EVP."

One of the most well-publicized segments of FKA is a database of its members who are willing to serve on company boards or be available for media interviews. The idea is that organizers can no longer cling to the excuse that they didn't know of any qualified women to fill a position or an interview.

Ragnhildur is not convinced of the database's effectiveness, though. "I've been on the FKA list for people willing to be on boards for many, many years, and I don't know anyone who has been asked to be on a board because they are part of that list," she told me. "Too often, it's the same few women occupying way too many boards. It's a real shame not to use the opportunity to bring in new, talented women who have a lot to offer."

Yet the stronger networks and increased collaboration fostered by these groups have created benefits. Their meetings have resulted in members founding companies together, buying other companies together, and using encouragement from peers and friends to apply for high-ranking positions in their fields.

If networks are important for professional women who were born and raised in Iceland, they are even more so for others who can't boast a built-in hive of contacts from extended family and childhood friends.

Fida Abu Libdeh has always been diligent at nurturing her professional networks. The forty-year-old has been a member of FKA for five years and sat on the board of the group's innovation committee. She is also on the board of the Association of Start-Up Enterprises and a member of the Women in Geothermal Energy Association, which helps foster female solidarity in a very masculine environment.

"We are stronger together and working to stand together," said Fida of her fellow female entrepreneurs.

Fida relocated to Iceland from Palestine as a teenager but moved to Jerusalem in her early twenties to reconnect with her roots.[28] It was a difficult time, as she had failed to complete her secondary school education due to a missed diagnosis of dyslexia and the challenge of having to complete her studies in a new language. Her journey from mature student to founder of a geothermal energy company that is selling to five countries is thus all the more impressive. Her success is a testament to her own persistence but also to a start-up ecosystem whose relative homogeneity was both a blessing and a curse.

Visitors to Iceland often remark on the fact that it's one of the few places in the world where you have to let the water cool down when you turn on the tap. It is a place where a steamy shower whose temperature stays consistently hot also has a potent, eggy aroma. Those are both manifestations of the country's extensive geothermal resources, tapped from naturally hot water that flows beneath the Earth's surface.

This source of energy heats almost all the nation's homes and many of its outdoor swimming pools, greenhouses, and fish farms. Combined with extensive usage of hydroelectric power, this means almost all the country's heating and electricity are provided by renewable energy sources.[29]

Fida's company, GeoSilica, uses the minerals that are extracted as by-products from the water that is pumped by geothermal power plants in the country. It is the process of extracting these undesirable (from the power plant's perspective) minerals that is the primary feature of her technology. Yet it was the applications of the minerals themselves, specifically silica, that first attracted the attention of investors. The silica mineral that GeoSilica's process extracts is incorporated into a supplement that can help prevent osteoporosis and strengthen skin and hair, among numerous other benefits. The company has plans to expand by extracting other minerals that have health benefits, including calcium and magnesium.

It was a long road for Fida to found a successful start-up. When she returned to Iceland for good, Fida completed her high school qualifications at a new school that had opened on the site of a former American military base. After that, she could move straight into a bachelor's degree in energy and environmental engineering technology.

"I chose it because the school was close to my home and the kids' preschool. As an immigrant, you do what is practical when grandma and grandpa aren't nearby to pick the kids up from school," Fida admitted.

"When I finished my studies, I knew there was no chance I was just going to find a job," Fida told me in Icelandic. (I always feel a special pride when two immigrants have mastered their second—or more—language enough that it becomes the one of choice for them to communicate.) "Immigrant, newly graduated, with young kids. No. I applied for about fifty jobs and got one interview. I knew I would have to find something on my own."

The result was GeoSilica, which has done well from the outset. Meanwhile, Fida's Palestinian roots have been both a challenge and an advantage for her.

"I was introducing the company at an event in Reykjavík, and one woman just kept asking me, 'Yes, but who owns this company?'" Fida recalled, recounting a tale that many immigrants find familiar. "On the third try, she even switched over to English, thinking that I didn't understand her. She couldn't conceive of the idea that I was behind it all." Fida hastened to add, however, that the majority of women she has met have been very supportive of her endeavors.

On the positive side, Fida's immigrant story has been appealing within the media and organizations keen on promoting their diversity. "It's really good to be an entrepreneur in Iceland and even better to be one of foreign origin," she told me. "You need to fight to have yourself heard, but then it helps you stand out."

Still, Fida admitted that "I get more phone calls about societal issues than something about my area of expertise, which is energy and environmental technology. In the eyes of people abroad in this industry, I'm an Icelander. Here in Iceland, I'm seen as a foreigner."

Whether immigrant or locally born, whether in a nation that appears at the top of the glass-ceiling index or at a depressingly average juncture, Fida, Gudbjörg, and Ragnhildur all agreed that whoever controls the pocketbook controls the decisions. Twenty-first century Ólöf the Rich equivalents—overwhelmingly wealthy women who stand up to the big boys—are few and far between. A recent Icelandic study showed that only 11 percent of the people who run the largest funds in Iceland are women. Only 1.4 percent of funding from private investment funds goes to companies founded entirely by women. Eighty-eight percent goes to those founded solely by men (though this also shows us the need to encourage more women to start companies). As long as men continue to manage most finances, they may, inadvertently or not, pay mere lip service to gender parity.

"If a guy had the same idea as me, he is much more likely to get the investment," Fida believes. "Women don't have the same opportunity to know where to look for funding. To level the playing field, we really need to offer more funds just to women."

As Fida told me, that applies in the European Union too.* "I applied for a grant there, and only two percent of the funds went to women. If you look at [some of the most successful companies in Iceland] Össur, Marel, CCP, they were all started by men. I will never be big like that if I don't get investment now. It's almost like it's just a hobby for me, even though I have developed a unique technology."

"Men own 95 percent of the money, and the money rules," agreed Gudbjörg. "So if men aren't also willing to better women, then it won't work. Iceland is so social, and it's all about networks. All the guys with all the money just call each other in the evenings, so women never stood a chance. Equality won't come until women get the money.

"You don't take risks with money and hire someone because you feel you should," she continued. "You hire the person you think will bring your company the most success, and that's why men are usually hired into these positions—because those are the types you are familiar with in those roles. I have been asked 'Can you make decisions?' I think no man has been asked that."

Few men have also had to deal with harassment in the workplace. Ragnhildur was one of the first women to come forward in the wake of the #MeToo revolution with her story. She published a detailed account of an experience when she was pregnant with her second child. Speaking a short while later on a nightly current affairs television program, she recounted the incident during which two male board members of the

---

* Although a European country, Iceland is not a member of the twenty-seven-nation European Union. Along with other non-EU nations Norway and Liechtenstein, however, it is a member of the European Economic Area, a body that gives the country access to the same "four freedoms"—freedom of goods, people, services, and capital—as the EU nations.

company she ran locked her in a room to pressure her into signing a resignation letter that also removed some of her rights to severance payments. Ragnhildur pressed charges of forcible confinement against the men, although they were later dropped.

Ragnhildur was praised for her candor in coming forward and is happy she did it, despite the lack of repercussions for the perpetrators. "It made me feel as though I had the upper hand, rather than being the silent victim. I had overwhelming support from both women and men after I spoke out. Women were generally complimentary about my bravery in opening up, while men just said something like, 'Good for you. Never let the bully win.'"

Did the bullies in fact win because they weren't punished? They didn't lose, at least, and guys like that will likely get away with a lot before they face any comeuppance. But for now, for her, Ragnhildur knew that, at the very least, she had done the right thing, and she felt empowered by the responses of those around her.

On the morning of the very first meeting Erica and I had with a potential sponsor for the Iceland Writers Retreat, I found out I was pregnant with my fourth child in five years. I recall being fairly distracted during the meeting itself, mentally calculating weeks and dates and thinking that, if all went well, I would have a seven-month-old baby during our first event. That should work out fine, I reckoned. If I could avoid morning sickness and other pregnancy ailments, the growing baby should not impede any of our planning meetings. I could use the five months of parental leave I would take to try and build some word of mouth for the upcoming conference. And by the time we would greet writers from around the world, the little one would be in the capable hands of her father on his parental leave.

It all went according to that plan—we even secured that first sponsor! Our little girl, Edda, was the youngest participant on our day tour, strapped to Gudni in a BabyBjörn carrier as he taught our participants about the history of Iceland (we had a very limited budget and needed a guide, and Gudni came cheap).

Could I have managed starting a new business and running an international conference as well as my other freelance work, which included editing the glossy magazine with Iceland's largest print run, if it weren't for the subsidized child care for our other children and the paternity leave for my husband? Absolutely not. Perhaps this is why I take so much pleasure in talking about the benefits of entrepreneurship in Iceland when I deliver speeches abroad as First Lady. I know from personal experience the joys and challenges of creating something new and what Icelandic society offers to help that process along.

This is so ingrained now in our working culture that the challenge of balancing family and work life was not a prominent factor for Ragnhildur, Gudbjörg, and Fida—all of them mothers—when it came to evening the playing field in the corporate world. Two of Ragnhildur's three preteen children have special needs and require additional care. Single mother Gudbjörg became a parent for the second time thanks to an anonymous sperm donor; she was not willing to wait around to find the perfect man to help her make her dreams come true. Fida's three children did not have grandparents on the next block to help with school runs and soccer practices. Yet none of these women identified any complications in their personal lives as major hindrances to success in their professional lives.

Despite bringing a newborn along with me to meetings around the founding of the Iceland Writers Retreat—an unproven endeavor for which we were often seeking funding and needed to make a good first impression at meetings—I felt that having a baby, two children in preschool, and a first grader would not prevent me from having a successful professional career. There was no nanny or au pair at our wee yellow house, but there was an equally involved and caring partner, excellent, inexpensive child care, and a safe environment that encouraged independence in lieu of helicopter parenting. I wasn't "doing it alone" because there was no expectation that I should. (I am sure no one even asked my husband, who was teaching and writing a book at the same time, whether he could handle it all.)

I consider this freedom a remarkable statement of societal support, both formal and informal, that helps us all in the long run. It's also important to acknowledge, though, the privilege this assumes. Despite the strong social safety net, it's fair to say that women who work in more labor-intensive service industries or other low-wage jobs with fixed working hours and who cannot work remotely find it much harder to juggle everything.

We must see more women in decision-making roles within companies and in charge of allocating loans and funds to new enterprises. These are effective tools for getting skilled women the experience they need to become senior executives. But we must also continue to make it easier for working women in all sectors to balance work and play, to live out their dreams. Most importantly, though, we must stop assuming that a benchmark for success for women is the length to which each can efficiently balance personal and public, carer and worker. There is no magic, one-size-fits-all formula for how to achieve this, and to assume so does a disservice to all women, adding pressure and wasted energy that we all know can be well used elsewhere.

"In our culture, we are independent and passionate and high spirited," Gudbjörg said at the end of our conference call. "We've built a social structure that is good for everyone, even if we're not there yet."

In the meantime, the male-dominated corporate world could do with further injections of male allies to the equality cause. These are men who actively work to discredit any corporate cultures that value bullying, condescension, or even downright misogyny that is garbed in the language of competitive spirit or a "plainspoken" approach. These are men who realize that gender equality is not a zero-sum game where they stand to lose if they support women too overtly. Quite the opposite, in fact: companies with more gender balance do better on their bottom line. Aside from the simple ethics of it, gender equality will make things better for men too. While such a disproportionate amount of the financial control still resides with them, as we elevate and encourage *sprakkar* to fulfil their professional ambitions, it does no harm to strive to bring more men in agreement with this approach by using the simple argument that Gudbjörg has so often made: more women means more success. Everyone benefits from that.

6

BEING SEEN AND HEARD IN THE MEDIA

*There lies the buried dog**

IN JANUARY 2018, GUDNI AND I visited Stockholm for a three-day state visit to Sweden at the invitation of King Carl XVI Gustaf and Queen Silvia. State visits are highly choreographed events, rigid with protocol, that are designed to strengthen ties between two countries. A visiting head of state, almost always accompanied by his or her spouse, will travel with an official delegation of representatives that usually includes politicians, businesspeople, and unofficial cultural ambassadors. The program is scheduled down to the minute, from the time it takes for the president to inspect a ceremonial guard to the three minutes allocated to the head of a research institute to summarize her organization's latest work. At the usually white-tie-and-tails gala dinner, with several hundred in attendance, we have often literally been trumpeted into the room. It is during moments such as these that the surreal feeling of progression from my rural Canada roots to acting as one of the guests of honor in a palace bubbles to the surface.

By the time the Sweden trip rolled around, Gudni and I were becoming more adept at the protocol and procedure of a state visit. We had already been on similar tours to Denmark and Norway and had attended an international gathering of Nordic heads of state in Finland. I was no longer worried that I did not have gloves to match my handbag

---

* *Þar liggur hundurinn grafinn* refers to identifying the crux of the matter, getting to the point.

(advice I had been given before our first state visit) or that I even dared to use the same handbag the entire time rather than coordinate it with each of the eight or so outfits I had for the three-day trip. When news arrived just a couple of days before departure that all women in the delegation to Sweden would be required to wear hats for the official welcoming ceremony, I didn't let the fact that I owned nothing more than a toque and that Iceland was devoid of milliners let my blood pressure rise. (In fact, after a last-minute bulk order of hats from abroad, I even got positive reviews on none other than royalhats.net for my final choice!) By now, I was pretty used to delivering remarks at events in royal presence, waving for cameras, and asking challenging yet noncontroversial questions during stops at universities, museums, and institutes. The king and queen, with a lifetime of experience in the public eye, were expert at making us feel at ease and at giving us gentle nudges in the right direction should we forget who was meant to get out of the car first or walk ahead of another. They were charming hosts in every way.

One facet of the visit was the inescapable presence of paparazzi. In Iceland, while our official events are almost always covered by local media, the closest we usually get to nosy cameramen is a savvy ten-year-old with an iPhone and a social media account. In Sweden—and other countries—each stop was trailed by a gaggle of journalists, flashbulbs popping and questions flying. It was invigorating to experience it for a few days, but I am grateful not to live with it sans respite.

Midway through the afternoon of the second day, on about our fifth stop, I stepped out of the car to notice that one of my earrings had fallen off. They were of Icelandic design, but there were no carats or precious metals harmed in their creation. I asked the queen if she had seen it on the car seat next to us, mentioned it in passing to the security officials surrounding us in case they came upon it, and thought nothing more of it, popping the other earring in my handbag.

Later that day, in the (exactly) fifty-three minutes we had to change into our gala clothing for the evening, I was googling myself (we've all done it, admit it) only to discover that a major Swedish newspaper had a big story on the First Lady of Iceland's vanished earring. "Chaos at the King's lunch: Jewelry mysteriously missing" trumpeted the headline in the *Expressen* tabloid. It had close-up photos of me at stops earlier in the day, when I was wearing the earring, and one where it was missing, and it revealed that palace staff had been dispatched to see whether the lost object could be located. Such was the scrutiny of a state visit, and "chaos" was certainly an overly sensationalist choice of words by *Expressen*. (I never did find the earring either.)

It's true that media coverage was and is significantly more low-key in Iceland. But since becoming First Lady, I had learned to morph from Eliza changing wet bedsheets and wiping stray child snot off the sofa in the morning to Eliza putting on a crisp suit or to-the-floor gown later and having the image appear in the paper, on television, and online. And as a woman who had arrived in the spotlight less with my own identifying characteristics than as someone's spouse, I began to learn both how I could use that to my advantage to carve the image of how I wanted to be seen and how society was already imposing some expectations of their ideal of a First Lady through media coverage.

Really, though, why should I care how the media portrays me? It's not mere vanity. (That said, please see comment above on googling myself.) It's important how all women are represented in the media. For "there lies the buried dog" or the crux of the matter: the media is largely our window on the world, and that includes gender equality. When media interviews are predominantly with men, when the editors and the photographers and the broadcasters and the writers are mostly of one gender or don't represent in other ways the diversity of the society for whom they claim to speak, we lose insight and narrow our subconscious assertions about gender and diversity. In the comments section and in social media that assure everyone with a smartphone that the world's population is desperate to hear what they have to say about everything, statistics show that women are judged more harshly and subjected to more threats of violence and attacks than men, discouraging them from further engagement and thereby effectively silencing them. This is as much of a challenge in Iceland as it is elsewhere.

And yet, international media outlets have often portrayed Iceland in astonishingly oversimplified terms, sacrificing the nuances of a nation that few know intimately for the allure of a good (if wildly inaccurate) story. According to too many parachute journalists, Iceland is a gender paradise, a country where we can rest on our laurels as we bask in the benefits of a near-perfect nation where we all have a quaint belief in elves, jailed all our bankers after the economic collapse, crowd-sourced a constitution that protects the Earth as well as humanity, and where women and men live in complete harmony. (Please excuse the hyperbole.)

International inaccuracies aside, we cannot understand Iceland's successes and ongoing challenges in the field of gender equality without examining the role of the media in the fight. So one December, I invited a quartet of women who work in various media for a traditional Christmas buffet to discuss this field. Ranging in age from early twenties to midforties, the women have experience in various media forms, both in generating content and being subjects of public discussion themselves. They were eager to deliberate how far we've come in covering women in the media in Iceland but also how the comments section has become increasingly appealing for newly connected older men who fervently believe the rest of us are keen to absorb their wisdom, how our representation of marginalized groups such as people with disabilities also does a disservice to women overall, and whether we can ever live up to the hype about Iceland as a nation populated with intimidating Valkyries. If I could get tips on how to steer attention away from the proverbial mystery of the missing earring, all the better.

A disproportionately large number of people are big fish in Iceland. After all, it's a small pond. Sometimes it can feel like everyone is known for something, their fifteen minutes of fame extending to several hours or occurring regularly. At cocktail parties, you can never be sure whether that person you vaguely recognize is your husband's second cousin or the former minister of interior affairs. Or both. As such, those who work in the media and those covered by it are close to each of us. It is all more personal, for better and for worse.

Iceland's media climate has evolved greatly in recent decades. As any Gen X Icelander will tell you, in the early 1980s, they felt hard done by with only one television station (color broadcasts only becoming commonplace at that time) and two local radio stations. There was no television broadcast on Thursdays or during the entire month of July, when, in any case, you should be outside enjoying the daylight. Print media was usually politically affiliated, and the daily newspaper to which you subscribed would be a reliable indicator of which party you'd vote for in the next election.

We are less insular these days. We have plenty of digital television channels to choose from, in Icelandic and other languages, and Icelanders are some of the most connected people on the planet, with one 2018 study showing 99 percent of residents between the ages of sixteen and seventy-four use the internet.

We have also become more progressive in what topics we cover and who covers them. Women still receive less prominence in Icelandic media and online—on average in mainstream media, just one-third of interviewees are women. There is, however, an active and vocal movement to draw attention to unconscious bias that is shifting the line of what is acceptable in public discourse and the way in which women are portrayed in the media.

The chatter started as soon as we had topped some squares of rye bread with slices of cured salmon.

"I could talk forever about the importance of the media in the fight for gender equality," began Thóra Arnórsdóttir. A familiar face on Icelandic small screens, forty-five-year-old Thóra has been a television and radio journalist for over two decades at RÚV, the state public broadcaster. She has run a popular nightly current affairs program, produced an award-winning documentary on the economic collapse of 2008 and a later series on female pioneers from the country, and is now one of the brains behind *Kveikur*, one of the hardest hitting homegrown investigative journalism shows.

Funded as it is by taxpayers, RÚV has an obligation to ensure diversity in its on-air reporters and newsreaders as well as the people interviewed. Society's awareness of the importance of gender parity and public pressure have ensured that RÚV's success at balancing gender coverage is quantifiably monitored on a regular basis.

"There are always some things we can't control, such as whether cabinet ministers are men or women," Thóra said, uncrossing her legs and leaning back on the sofa, composed and impeccable as always. "But now we're getting more women serving in roles like minister of health and chief medical officer. Then *Landinn* [a lifestyle show featuring stories from the Icelandic countryside] decided they would cover an equal number of men and women as subjects. That's easier than news because you have more choice, of course. They used to get more recommendations about men to interview because they were more visible, but when you dig deeper, you see women are doing all kinds of things."

Sitting next to Thóra was Steinunn Ása Thorvaldsdóttir, another television celebrity. Steinunn is also a singer, one-time political candidate, and general woman-about-town, but she is best known as one of six hosts of RÚV's *In Our Eyes*, a groundbreaking and award-winning interview-based show that was conceived by the National Association of Intellectual Disabilities and run almost entirely by people with disabilities. Steinunn has Williams syndrome, which is characterized by developmental delays, distinctive facial features, an aptitude for learning languages (she relishes speaking English and Italian as often as possible), and a joyously optimistic, friendly nature. Steinunn's age is hard to pinpoint (it's thirty-seven), and she had dressed up for the occasion of the dinner, sporting one of her favorite silky Icelandic-designed dresses and locally created rings on almost every finger.

Taking a sip of her drink, Steinunn brought up a topic that is dear to her heart and for which she fights tirelessly. "I am always thinking of the way disabled people, including disabled women, are covered in Icelandic media," she told me. "Media forget us when things are going well and then cover us when they are not." For her part as a member of the media, she said she enjoys interviewing all sorts of folks, from a local priest to public figures (which is how we met), and the team ensures gender balance among the people they cover on their show. One of Steinunn's points struck a personal chord with me: the fact that women with disabilities often get lumped into a single group when naturally they are as diverse as, say, we immigrant women.

Dabbing some red currant jelly on her cube of reindeer pâté, Thóra detailed how every program at RÚV, both on television and radio, monitors its gender balance.

"After every show, you report how many men and women you interviewed, and we regularly review those stats," she explained.

Newspaper editor Tobba Marinósdóttir agreed. "You have to make sure you have diverse content but not obviously cater material to one gender or another," she said. Tobba is a glamorous woman in her late thirties who was sporting my favorite shade of power red lipstick and let long, enviable curls hang over her shoulders. Tobba has earned a reputation as a woman with her finger on the pulse of the nation's social calendar and a writer of romantic comedy novels. After becoming editor of the once-a-week print edition of *DV* newspaper eight months before we spoke, she featured twenty-four women and sixteen men on its cover.*

Interview subjects are one thing, but making sure people are prepared for an on-air hit or the tough questions is another. Thóra pointed out that women are frequently more nervous about television interviews than men, perhaps in tacit acknowledgment that they are often questioned more vigorously about their qualifications to speak on a certain topic.

I found this relatable. I am not usually nervous appearing on live television or in other interviews, but given that in Iceland I am not speaking in my native language, I am more cognizant of any mistakes in my delivery or my more limited vocabulary detracting from my message.

Yet I also know that the more I am recognized via the media, the more I can use it to help shape the image I want to portray of myself. When my instinctive responses to glowing coverage of my fashion choices (an irony given that I don't know my Versace from my Vuitton) were a mixture of dismay and curious surprise, I decided I could use it to my advantage. I wore a silky black blazer I bought for $20 at a local charity shop to a major awards show. The story that the First Lady shops secondhand helped promote the concept of reducing our purchases and

---

* In March 2021, Tobba announced that she was leaving her position as editor of *DV*.

supporting a good cause. I have subsequently worn secondhand clothes at other high-profile events such as when receiving heads of state and on the day my husband was reelected for a second term as president.

I also repress what is sometimes my first instinct—to politely decline—if I'm asked to speak at an event where I feel I am not an expert. We need to hear women's voices more, not less, I remind myself with almost mantra-like regularity, and if the organizers trust the importance of any contribution I can make, then I ought to do so too.

"I notice this when I talk to preteens in school," added Sólborg Gudbrandsdóttir, the last of our dining quintet. In just a few years, the twenty-three-year-old law student and singer has garnered a huge following on Instagram for her posts condemning sexism online and answering candid questions from anonymous adolescents on everything from puberty to dating rituals.[30] This success has led to steady work speaking to teens at local schools.

"I often have to shush the boys when I'm talking, but I never have to with the girls," she continued. "They have already learned by this age what space they take up in society. And the girls know, if they screw up, they won't get as many chances."

"That's right," added Tobba, recalling in a broader sense than merely the media how women cooked all the meals at home and then made sure everyone had something on their plates before filling up their own. "You can't take up space." She threw up her hands in exasperation. "You can't even take a meatball! I mean, come on."

There are more modern examples of this phenomenon—of pushing women to take up room. In an effort to credit women for the space they are owed, local activist Hildur Lilliendahl opened a popular Facebook album called "Do women exist? Do they have names?" She and her friends populate the album with clips from Icelandic news headlines and photo captions that neglect to name women or that identify them exclusively in relation to men: a photo of three people with only the two men identified; "sister of [a former male prime minister] now a member of parliament"; "Króli [a popular male singer] debuts girlfriend at film festival." Another image is of Gudni and me shaking hands with a stream of anonymous visitors during an open house at the presidential residence. The caption reads "The president greets guests."

In an era of fake news and ridiculous deep-state conspiracies, does the omission of a single name in a photo caption matter? Is being identified solely in relationship to another person really such a big deal?

Absolutely yes, these things matter. It is indeed a privilege to worry about these issues, as opposed to even more grievous ones. And because it costs us less to speak up, we are all the more morally obliged to do so. Women, in the spotlight and out of it, have enough to contend with aside from the slow culling of our identities by a thousand cuts.

And beyond the endless need to remind others of our existence, what about when we aren't charting out the genders of interview subjects or hiring female writers? When we leave it up to the big, wide world in social media, how do we tackle the misogynistic silencing culture that can sometimes emerge, leading women to abandon their online presence and effectively removing their voices from the debate? My dinner colleagues didn't have all the answers, but they were keen to provide a few suggestions.

About eighteen months after our state visit to Sweden, Gudni and I hosted the president and First Lady of India for a similar occasion. There was not the same level of paparazzi as in Stockholm, but plenty of photos circulated nonetheless. A few days later, I received a very polite message: "I saw the photos of you greeting the Indian presidential couple, wearing a green dress. Pardon the forwardness, but green is definitely not your color. The blue dress was lovely, though." It was signed respectfully by a woman who identified herself as a master tailor.

Although I appreciate the kind intention and positive sentiment behind the letter (to save me from myself and my dreadful sartorial choices, presumably), I have since made an effort to wear more green clothing.

This message is not something to lose sleep over. I mostly cannot complain about the way in which the Icelandic public talk about me online, though there are a few minor exceptions: the woman who scoffed that I looked like "a convict" when I wore a bright-orange pantsuit during a state visit to Poland; the complaints that I am starved for attention anytime I speak up about an issue (the identical criticism too often hurled at any woman who does the same); the "helpful" summary of the most vitriolic accusations someone once compiled into a single blog post (it was designed to criticize them, not me); and, more sinisterly, the small social media outcry when I visited the local mosque (the first member of a presidential couple to do so) and removed my shoes as a sign of respect. I should also add that these negative comments are always dwarfed by opposite and more positive feedback and occasionally direct pushback against the trolls themselves for their statements.

This was a concern when Gudni ran for president. I thought that it would be tough to read cruel and false statements about him online, statements it would not be possible to directly reply to or to engage with to correct erroneous assertions. I was relieved that our children were too young to be on social media and that my stepdaughter, Rut, was old enough to know it was all part of the dance.

In the end, I surprised myself with how little I was fazed by anything that was said online. It takes me longer to read in Icelandic, so I could make a conscious decision about what I wanted to absorb. And when I encountered an unknown adjective that was clearly something derogatory given the context, I felt no need to waste time translating. Even when I did understand every word, some statements were such patent falsehoods that I could only smile at how ridiculous they were. Thankfully, their sheer preposterousness prevents these assertions from gaining any traction among the mainstream public.

It's not the same for everyone. As we advanced to the main courses of our Christmas buffet, Sólborg opened up about her experiences as a young, outspoken female activist online. About 10 percent of the population of Iceland follow her on Instagram, many times more than other, older public figures. (She posts exclusively in Icelandic, which means it's a virtual certainty that those followers are locals.)

"I've had threatening DMs, rape threats, messages like 'I know where you sleep.' If I were a guy, I wouldn't get these threats. Is this something women are just supposed to accept when they are in the public eye?" she queried our group.

"I let them hear it," she continued defiantly. "I answer them and I stand up for myself. They aren't used to that. But I'm not a politician or a journalist. I'm an activist, and I can tell them to go fuck themselves.

"Then I post my response publicly," she continued. "There are other young girls and boys who are also getting messages like that, and they don't have the chance to see that it's possible just to tell them where to stick it. People used to ask me why I didn't just block them. If they threaten me, then I do that, and I report it. But I don't begin there. If you want to talk to me, I have a right to defend myself. And these teenagers aren't used to that." She paused, chewing her nut roast before continuing.

"Actually, some people then say to me, 'Aren't you being a bit mean to him? He's just a kid,'" she mused, incredulous. "Then they say I'm just as bad. But calling out online abuse is not the same as committing it. All my work on this in recent years has shown me that it's important to take up our space and that it's okay to stand up for myself and tell people to shove it."

Misogyny and threats like this are all too common throughout the world, but because Icelandic is only spoken here and the population is relatively small, it is easier to weed out many bots and identify otherwise anonymous accounts. For attacks coming from real profiles, it doesn't take much effort to track down the offender. When someone sent Sólborg a threatening message under an anonymous account, it took just a posted screenshot and a few hours for someone to unmask the offender. He was a fifteen-year-old student, and he apologized only after Sólborg told the boy she had filed a formal report with the police, an important step Sólborg said was necessary to show that words have consequences.

TV host Thóra agreed with that approach. "We need clearer laws about what you can say or not say. We need to update them in order to increase the likelihood that they will actually be enforceable." She dipped her potato into some béchamel. "I mean, you don't have to send people to jail, just…"

"…take 20,000 krónur off their salary the next month!" suggested Tobba jokingly.

If only it were as easy as that. Iceland's legislation on free speech stems from the European Convention on Human Rights—as does the legislation in most other European countries—and laws limiting speech will be interpreted in light of the right of freedom of speech. In practical terms, this extends to comments posted on social media, especially concerning public figures, making it very difficult to prosecute cases of what essentially amounts to digital misogyny unless outright threats have been made. Furthermore, website hosts and internet service providers bear less responsibility than individuals, meaning that if a person sets up a website with offensive content that he or she needs to remove, it would generally be up to the offender to do so rather than the company hosting the site. So despite any desire to make the comments section and the online world in general a friendlier place for women, the paths to improvement here likely lie more with the actions of individuals— including educating young people about online communication—than from legal protections.

There is also potentially more threatening activity online. A November 2020 report by the Centre for Digital Youth Care on online misogyny and antifeminism in the Nordic countries overall indicated that although researchers could not identify a "delimited subculture or movement," there were "active" Nordic users on the forums examined and clear instances of misogyny that needed to be tackled.[31] In other words, the Nordic region may not yet have reached the point where there is an urgent, acute risk of mass misogynistic hate crimes or a systemic, organized movement, but there is enough concern not to be complacent. Added reason for worry in Iceland is that Icelandic law is fairly vague about what constitutes hate speech or hate crimes.

Legal measures (or lack thereof) aside, moderators are less tolerant of this belittling of women's voices. "At DV, we block and then ban people from commenting," said Tobba, whose newspaper has been notorious for somewhat sensationalist stories, a reputation she is working to erase. "That's because no one was monitoring it." She also admitted that they sometimes now close the section for an interview if the subject is concerned about online backlash.

Such backlash can be swift and unanticipated. In the summer of 2020, a children's theater troupe performed in the tiny northeastern village of Kópasker. One of the group's actors posted on social media that she didn't recommend visiting the town (they had been particularly unlucky with the weather); she later apologized, but the comments section responded with an almost nuclear strike. For her frankness, she received rape threats as well as threats to slit her throat and beat her to the point of being unrecognizable. Iceland is no better than other locations in this regard, although it is arguably easier to track down offenders, just as Sólborg did. The woman involved in the Kópasker situation, Thórdís Björk Thorfinnsdóttir, reported all threats she received to the police, but to date, no charges have been brought against any individuals.

Steinunn listened with interest to the discussion, then added her own spin on the dialogue. "We don't get criticism in the same way," she said of people with disabilities. "We are often seen just as grown children and so beyond criticism in some ways. It means we are not taken seriously."

"Two words that always come up in the discussion are 'attention seeker.' Women are always labelled as attention seekers merely for taking up space," added Tobba, slathering a piece of crispy *laufabraud* flatbread with butter. "Sometimes when someone writes something really ugly about me, I just 'like' the post to remind him that I have the internet too and I see him."

"I am really scared of the comments section," confessed Steinunn. "I avoid it like a raging fire."

To make the online world less blazing to women (well, to anyone), we need to take certain steps. That Centre for Digital Youth Care report made three primary recommendations to tackle online misogyny. One was to require identity authentication in order to reduce online fraud. Another involves working with the forums to train volunteers and moderators so that instead of harmful, polarizing, echo chambers, these communities could actually try to provide the support that many men who go online are actually seeking.

Finally, the report suggests "building literacy and developing a more equal perspective on the possibilities and capabilities of each gender" in an effort to expand gender norms and stereotypical gender roles. Here too is where positive male role models can be very important.*

"I am aware that I'm living with extreme privilege," admitted Sólborg. "I have much more of a platform than a lot of women. The violence I have been threatened with is a totally different level than, say, getting shot or something that could happen in another country. But I can't be satisfied by thinking 'Yep, I should just be happy I'm allowed to vote.'"

In the Icelandic presidential election of 2012, six candidates stood for the position of head of state of the country. The incumbent, Ólafur Ragnar Grímsson, was running for a record fifth term in office; Iceland's constitution has no term limits. He won, handily as it turned out. Grímsson's main competitor throughout the campaign was none other than one of my companions for the Christmas buffet, then thirty-seven-year-old television host Thóra Arnórsdóttir.

Unsurprisingly, Icelandic presidential elections garner little international attention. But during the two-month campaign, Thóra was featured by outlets such as the BBC and the *Guardian*.

The brouhaha had little to do with her pledges or her approach to the office. Rather, halfway through the campaign, Thóra took a fortnight's break to give birth to her third child. Prebirth, she delivered her speeches, shook hands, and attended various gatherings in admirably high heels. Two weeks later, the heels remained, and her common-law partner cared for the newborn girl from backstage as she continued the fight. Thóra finished in second place.

---

* Positive male role models are by no means unique in Iceland or even in the Nordic countries. An excellent Icelandic example, though, is Thorsteinn V. Einarsson, who runs a very popular Instagram page called Karlmennskan ("masculinity") that campaigns to open up discussion about oft neglected aspects of masculinity, such as emotional accountability and the strength of kindness.

"Of course, when the foreign media show an interest in something like this, you want to do your part," recalled Thóra of the international attention her campaign garnered. "But it also reflects the situation in other countries and reminds us that it would have been unthinkable in many places for someone like me to run. So we're in a different place here. I was aware of the limits we were pushing, but they were further than in a lot of other countries."

Thóra admitted she did get several questions on the campaign trail, mostly from women, about how her potential election would affect their children (there were six of them, including the newborn and three from her partner's earlier relationship). She was firm on the fact that the decision to run was hers and her family's and considered what they knew they could manage.

"We are always told it's not the right time. You're too young, then you're supposed to be having kids, then your kids are too young, then you're in menopause, and then you're too old and collecting your pension, and all of a sudden, you realize there was no time for you to do anything because someone else thought it 'wasn't the right time.' How does someone else have the right to do that?"

If the world's media love the inspiring novelty of a woman who doesn't let a pregnancy stop her from standing for the highest office in the land, in many other ways, outlets are still employing twentieth-century judgment when it comes to reporting about young women.

Take, for example, a story from the early autumn of 2020. After a national men's soccer match between Iceland and England, two young players from the latter team invited two similarly aged Icelandic women they had been chatting with online back to their hotel room, breaking strict COVID-19 quarantine regulations that had been imposed on the visiting squad. The women said they didn't know about the regulations or the fame of their newfound friends. They posted a few photos on a closed Snapchat group without realizing that the images would inevitably be shared publicly because of the fame of the men, one of whom was married with a young child.

The story rapidly became top news in both Iceland and in the British tabloids, which are not known for their gender-neutral coverage. The England players made public apologies, were fined for breaking quarantine, and were not allowed to take part in their next national match against Denmark.

As for the two women, UK media framed them as promiscuous gold diggers intent on milking fifteen minutes of fame. In Iceland, prominent people, from a member of parliament to a pop singer, publicly defended the women against such accusations. These defenders rightly claimed that it was not the young women who had broken regulations and pointed out that a great many of us perhaps behaved in ways we are not particularly proud of in our youth, blessedly before the dawn of the social media era. Other commentators simply mused at all the attention and pointed out that perhaps there were more newsworthy topics to cover.

Comment sections for UK news articles lambasted the "Icelandic beauties" on their looks, their motives, and their backgrounds. In Iceland, comments were often a mix of sympathy for the young women and indignation at the extent to which the story was covered.

"We were nothing like the Brits in our coverage," Tobba recalled about the incident, which took place when she was newly at the helm of *DV*. "They [the UK media] identify them by their first names, call them idiots, etc."

It hasn't gone unnoticed by media outlets outside Iceland that we often strike a different tone in how we endeavor to reflect gender equality, overtly and otherwise, in our media.

"I sometimes get questions from overseas that 'it's going so well in Iceland, so how can we do it in the U.S.?'" Thóra told me. "But we can't send over a blueprint, drawings of a century of developments. We can point out many things that we do, but there is still just as much work left. It's like getting an oil tanker to change direction. God didn't dictate from heaven that we needed to change our attitude. Bit by bit, we made changes to do so, and we're proud of that."

Thóra reminded us that this is an equality battle, not a women's rights one. She was preaching to the choir as she pointed out that men must be involved too. "If our feminist role models are only women, how can young boys see themselves in that?" asked Sólborg. But the relentless pressure and small successes come with a price—a "burnout from the fight," as Steinunn put it.

"The women of my generation are dropping like flies," agreed Thóra. "For more than twenty years, they are working and working, have kids, keep a tidy home, are thin and cute, go to yoga, found a company. Then all of a sudden, they're sitting in the car outside their home one day, and they can't breathe."

It shouldn't be like that. Turning that oil tanker around takes more than a blueprint, more than relentless calling out of microaggressions in photo captions and reporting more blatant threats that appear in social media. It involves rewarding women for taking up their space, for using their voices, not dismissing them as attention seekers and questioning their experience and wisdom. We all need to treat subject fields in which there tend to be more women—from fashion to education—as equally important. Those of us who are able to must speak up to those who try to silence or diminish women's voices. Women need the same chance as men to make mistakes in the public eye, to not get it right the first time, and to allow them room to grow. Finally, turning that tanker around incorporates the voices and perspectives of all women—with or without disabilities, locally born and immigrant, of various gender identities and religions and ages and ethnicities.

Through the media in all its forms, women must claim their space. Not just the space they have been allocated but the space they deserve. It can be intimidating and stress inducing. It's most definitely tiring.

Ever the optimist, Steinunn had the best approach to moving forward: "Every morning, I get up and look at myself in the mirror, and I say, 'Today is going to be the best day,'" she said, sitting upright, straightening her rings, running her fingers through her cropped hair, and practicing for us as if she were in her bathroom at home. "'It'll still be okay even if something doesn't go quite as I expected it would.'"

That's an important sentiment to keep in mind as we ponder how to really tackle the ongoing and pervasive problems of the portrayal of women in the media, especially online. In Iceland, we have the advantage of a small community and a language spoken by few people, which helps to name (and hopefully shame) offenses. As a society, we are also pushing back against old-fashioned representations of women on television, in radio, and in print. This is an ongoing issue, a marathon struggle, so we need to keep Steinunn's positive attitude. But we also need to find the strength, within ourselves and those around us, to stand up to online attacks, report hate speech, turn the shame on the perpetrators, not the victims, and generally persist in allowing women's voices to take up their own space. There is security in numbers. Speak up. Speak up for others, speak up for yourself, and more will follow.

THE UNDAUNTED SPRAKKI
WHO FOUGHT FOR NATURE

GULLFOSS, THE "GOLDEN" WATERFALL, IS one of the most famous pearls of Icelandic nature and part of a trio of natural wonders on the famous "Golden Circle" tour that is one of the country's biggest tourist attractions. Hundreds of thousands of visitors witness the majesty of the tumbling, three-tiered fall every year (COVID-19 pandemic excepted).

As one of the most visited places in the country, Gullfoss stands as a symbol of Iceland's natural beauty. The person whom many credit with saving the falls from being destroyed was one of Icelandic history's resolute, headstrong women.

At the turn of the twentieth century, Sigrídur Tómasdóttir lived at the farm Brattholt, whose lands included Gullfoss. A largely self-taught woman, Sigrídur used to guide the rare visitors across rough tracks to view the falls.

During this period, when a not-yet-independent Iceland still struggled with poverty, Sigrídur stands out for her environmentalist outlook that was decades ahead of its time. During Sigrídur's years as a young adult, volcanic landscapes, glaciers, and waterfalls were not seen as wonders or attractions but rather impediments to good farmland or locations with the potential to be exploited for economic gain.

Such was the situation with Gullfoss. When an English investor approached Sigrídur's father, Tómas, with a generous offer to buy the falls to harness them to generate electricity, he is said to have rejected the offer because he did not want "to sell my friend." A few years later, however, he agreed to lease them.

"Harnessing" the falls meant in practice destroying them by creating a dam farther upstream for generating hydro-electric power. Sigrídur would have none of it. She hired lawyer Sveinn Björnsson (who would later become Iceland's first president upon its independence from Denmark in 1944) to advocate for her cause. She travelled several times to Reykjavík to argue in person for the preservation of the falls; legend has her taking the trip of more than one hundred kilometers barefoot across volcanic landscapes. When she felt that these meetings were not having the desired effect, she threatened to throw herself over the falls if the plans to destroy it were confirmed.

Sigrídur's protests took place during an era when women's rights activists were fighting for legal protections for women in society. Sigrídur was not active in that battle, but she was nevertheless tirelessly passionate for her cause. Fighting to have her voice heard in a male-dominated world, she faced the stigma and prejudice with which modern women remain all too familiar. She was accused of being too sentimental, too emotional about something as insignificant as a waterfall—adjectives that would also be widely deployed by politicians who wanted to deny women the right to vote.

As society has increased the value placed on environmental sustainability, Sigrídur's passion has become admired and respected. During her lifetime, Gullfoss and the surrounding land were eventually sold to the government. About two decades after her death at the age of eighty-six, the area was officially protected from development. A memorial to her stands at the top of the waterfall, and she has rightfully earned the title of the country's first environmentalist.[32]

7

FINDING HARMONY IN THE WILD

I come from the mountains[*]

I COME FROM THE MOUNTAINS. Not literally, of course. Far from it. Canada's Ottawa Valley is flat, rich farmland for long stretches, with the Gatineau Hills (ancient mountains worn down by glacial activity long before the time of the dinosaurs) off in the distance. But metaphorically speaking, I come from the mountains. This Icelandic idiom is a self-deprecating way of expressing the fact that you're out of touch with something. If your postmillennial granddaughter is talking about TikToks and Reddits and you assume she's namedropping new varieties of Girl Scout cookies, then you come from the mountains.

When folks in Iceland discuss their relationship with the countryside, I come from the mountains, especially compared to many locally born people. I rode an Icelandic horse (slowly!) for the first time in 2020. I felt queasy on board a retired coast guard vessel that was anchored in harbor on a calm day. And although I grew up on a hobby farm with plenty of sheep around, I had never seen the birth of one until I became First Lady and Gudni and I regularly toured the countryside during lambing season.

An increasing number of Icelanders come from the mountains in this respect too. After all, in the last fifty years, the population has morphed from one that was primarily based outside the capital area to

---

[*] *Ég kem alveg af fjöllum* means to be out of touch with something.

one that has a much more urban focus. Back in the old days, for those who were not raised directly in a fishing or farming household, children of city slickers were often sent to grandparents or other relatives outside Reykjavík for long stays during the summer months. They were expected to help out on the farm with everything from shoveling manure to babysitting younger children. In fishing communities, they took day trips on small vessels to catch cod or helped land and process it for sale. When not contributing unpaid labor, these children could roam free in safe communities at a time of year when darkness never fell.

Although this tradition is much less common today, it is impossible to separate Icelanders' general national character from their natural landscape. The oxygen-rich sub-Arctic air, the sound of the waves crashing against a rocky shore, puffins nesting against craggy cliffs, lunar barren highlands, treeless hills and green valleys, snow-capped peaks and moss-covered lava fields: they are all etched into our bones. (My bones have had fewer years here, but I can feel the scratches beginning.)

Mother Nature has been at turns both benign and vicious toward the hardy Icelandic people. Only the adaptable, determined, and practical would survive for centuries with the threat of earthquakes, volcanic eruption, famine, and erosion, not to mention despair-inducing winter darkness. Yet treeless mountains uninhabited by predators ensure endless grazing for livestock, and the seas surrounding the island are rich in fish and other seafood. On land, there is virtually unlimited fresh water for drinking, hot water for heating, and no endemic poisonous creepy crawlies to wreak havoc on food supplies or immune systems.

Since the era of Sigrídur of Brattholt and her quest to save Gullfoss, Icelanders have developed an appreciation for the beauty and wonder of nature for its own sake. Harnessing nature for economic benefits, such as in the case of developing power stations, which often require dams to be built, is always the subject of fierce debate. On one side, there are those who see the benefits of increased employment and other financial incentives, and on the other, those who highlight the irreparable damage to nature. Nature on its own has also led to a huge increase in wealth for the country, thanks to the tourists who flock to the island for its highly Instagrammable environment.

Iceland has even become somewhat of a showcase for the climate crisis. You can hike up to a memorial plaque for a "lost" glacier, called Ok, and witness up close the dramatic effects of other rapidly shrinking glaciers, which research indicates could disappear entirely from our island within two hundred years. For decades, the country has had a strict system of fishing quotas to manage its valuable stocks, thus avoiding the disastrous collapses that have occurred, for instance, within the cod stocks off Canada's Grand Banks. The land surrounding the village of Höfn in the southeast is actually rising about one centimeter annually as the weight of nearby Vatnajökull glacier—Europe's largest—decreases as it melts, reducing pressure on the land. Even foolhardy tourists who venture off piste in tiny two-door rental cars and encounter inclement weather—gale force winds, or snow in late May—can be said to be experiencing the ongoing effects of climate change. And research shows us that the acute, global climate crisis disproportionately affects women around the globe.[33]

Somewhat paradoxically, this intimate dependency on the whims of nature led to both a fairly clear division of gender roles in the various tasks required to run households, farms, and businesses and a certain indifference to gender that called for all hands on deck in times of crisis, which could mean a woman fishing at sea or a man knitting his own woolen sweaters. The reality that many men in coastal communities were often at sea for days at a time (some never to return) meant women ran their households, handling all expenses. They would then also arrive at the harbor to chip in and help land and salt all the catch when the men returned. This division of labor is an oft-cited explanation for the strength of women in the country today. After all, there is a long history of tough, independent women taking control and being adaptable, reliant, and resilient.

Areas such as farming and fishing often remain segregated today; farms are usually officially owned and managed by men, and men also tend to be the ones away at sea, while women work mostly in fish processing facilities (especially in administration and not, of course, in the management of these companies). But there are women who buck the trend and keep their own livestock and captain their own vessels. Whereas in past decades and centuries, some women may have inadvertently ended up in charge due to a dearth of men, today's female farmers and fisherfolk have chosen to be where they are.

They often have to prove themselves in the field before being fully accepted in the cliques that form around the industries. These women would not consider themselves trailblazers, and indeed while they may be rare, they are neither unique nor the first. They are merely following their dreams, irrespective of gender. They are not waiting for legislation to push for equality. They effect the change themselves and believe that if you put your mind to something, then you can do it, laws or not, role models or not.

Aside from professional pursuits in agriculture and fishing, there's another rural area where women are increasingly having their say. Thousands of well-trained volunteers, including a growing number of women, perform heroic tasks in the countryside—and in the towns— as part of highly respected search and rescue squads that are based around the country. Despite the physical demands of the job, these squads are perhaps one of the country's most gender-blind organizations. Although women are still in the minority, their numbers are growing. The barriers to entry—the physical and mental requirements that need to be met to become members of these elite groups—are high for everyone, so there is no additional need for women specifically to show their mettle. Here, perhaps, we see the best embodiment of success achieved without regard to gender.

Heida Gudný Ásgeirsdóttir lives at the literal end of the road in the southern region of Iceland, about midway between Reykjavík in the west and the town of Egilsstadir in the east. It's a region so sparsely populated that each individual farm (they are all named) is marked on the large map posted at the last junction before turning on to her unpaved street. Heida's almost 40.4 square miles farm (about the size of the UK Channel Island Guernsey), called Ljótarstadir, is also her childhood home. It has a relatively high elevation, meaning it snows here early in the season, and has plenty of grassy slopes on which her flock of some four hundred sheep spends the short summer weeks freely grazing.

"We need nature, but nature doesn't need us," Heida told me when I visited her at the farm. "Farmers especially need nature. In a good summer, the outcome is better, and in a cold winter, it's worse. We're so connected to it here. When there are bad storms, you feel like you're tiny."

Ljótarstadir is also a mere fifteen miles from Katla, Iceland's most threatening volcano, and its lava and ash have laid the farmstead to ruin on more than one occasion in its nine-hundred-year history.

Heida is characteristically sanguine about this permanent threat. "If we spent the day thinking there might be an eruption tomorrow, then we'd do nothing today," she shrugged.

Tall and stereotypically Nordic in appearance with a light complexion, strong cheekbones, and long blond bangs she probably chooses to trim herself, Heida exuded intelligence, compassion, honesty, and a principled willingness to do good. She was the subject of a well-received book in Icelandic that was published in 2016 and did a lot to personify the life of the modern-day farmer for city dwellers in the capital.[34]

Heida struck me as a somewhat reluctant celebrity, however, an introvert who is not always at ease leaving her comfort zone of solo work with animals and machines, yet one who believes we all sometimes have an obligation to do so. In Heida's case, it was her passionate support of the environment and her efforts to prevent land in her region of the country from being sold to developers that brought her out. She was against harnessing delicate nature for new power plants that would provide energy for a foreign-owned aluminum smelter.

"They send some charming men over for coffee, and they dangle money in front of people who have never seen that kind of money before," Heida told me over strong black coffee in the kitchen of Ljótarstadir. "And they say if you just let us build this small dam far off in the distance, we'll let you have that money. Then they promise better cell phone reception, better roads." She rolled her eyes. "I'll never sell my land to them."

Some of the farmers in her region have agreed to sell rights to use the water on their land, though, should development plans be approved by the government. But Heida is not your typical farmer. Her gender is the first testament to that. (Although there are a great many women who work primarily on farms, since a majority are run by couples, few of them are the official landowners and managers of what are effectively small businesses.) Yet one doesn't need to share more than one cup of coffee and a couple of salt-licorice candies to know that there is nothing else Heida would be.

Heida grew up on this land, the youngest of five sisters, one of whom died when Heida was only three. Her oldest three siblings are her mother's with her first husband, a man who was killed in an avalanche in 1967. In a small society, with a farm to run, Heida's mother formed a bond with and ultimately married a man who was around a lot during those challenging years: her late husband's brother. She had two children, including Heida, with him.

"I always wanted to be a farmer and to work with my hands," Heida told me during a short, well-earned break from the labor-intensive work all farming requires as she relaxed in a well-worn La-Z-Boy chair ingeniously placed in the most accessible corner of her kitchen, facing the table where I sat. (Everyone should have a reclining chair in their kitchen, I realized as I watched her. The guest can sip coffee sitting at the table, and the hardworking farmer can relax with her feet up.) "We took on all the jobs because farming is a man's world and still is, but in our case, there weren't any," she told me. "We are basically four sisters who are hard-core feminists and know we can do anything."

Heida remains unabashed in these convictions. Her father was born in 1929 and "wouldn't have used the word *feminist* but was proud of us, of course," she told me. "Despite that, he still thought I needed a husband to remain here, someone to take over the farm. There is this narrow-minded thinking that everyone needs to keep inside the box and stay along the same path, get married, have children. There's nothing wrong with that per se, but there is so much pressure to be like that."

It required a bit of work to convince the outside world of this too. Heida took on two days of a modelling photo shoot in New York once, which led to a BBC profile about Iceland's model turned farmer, when in fact the photos were a mere blip in what she had always intended to do, which was to take over the family business. "I kept trying to tell the journalists that I'm just lucky in the gene lottery, but that's not something I wanted to do as a career."

When she returned from studying at the agricultural university and after stints as a teacher at the local school and as a police officer, she had to prove herself as a farmer and as a sheep shearer, one of her other jobs (you usually can't earn a living simply farming in this day and age). She is also a party chairperson for the district council and, at the time of this writing, is an alternate member of parliament for the Left-Green Movement.

"Very few women in Iceland do sheep shearing, especially for others," Heida explained of her second profession. "When I started, people said I was doing it because I was desperate for attention—not because I thought it was fun and I could do it well. It's such a chauvinistic environment."

Next to her La-Z-Boy, Heida has posted one large map of Iceland and one of the world, with little thumbtacks marking the places she has visited for sheep shearing, hiking, or other travelling; each activity has its own color. They reach as far as New Zealand, where there is a small red tack in Invercargill on the South Island, representing a 2017 sheep shearing tournament at which she was the only female competitor.

But day to day, at Ljótarstadir, "I'm alone most of the time working," she admitted quite happily. "The arrival of mobile phones and the internet changed everything and made the world a lot smaller." She helped herself to a couple more licorice sweets. "But I'm bloody unsocial, so I really just feel good being by myself."

The professional interaction Heida most often encounters is through her sheep shearing, when she travels to other farms and trims the thick wool off the sheep. It is by doing this that she has acquired a lot of observational knowledge about the role of women in the farming sector in Iceland.

"Women in the world of farming tend to be hidden," Heida told me earnestly. "Usually they are working just as much in the stable, doing the bookkeeping, budgeting, helping with lambing, although the whole farm is legally run under the husband's name. When I visit a farm, the man is often made out to be the one in charge even though you know they are both equally responsible. I've visited farms where a couple are both hard at work outside, and then she puts together a fancy lunch and he just goes in, sits down to eat, and leaves her standing up pouring coffee and everything else. It just seems that the men have the last word."

Heida is convinced that only a shift of mentality will fix this, and she told me she has seen some improvements, for example in the "chauvinistic way" in which men talk about women. "That's no longer considered acceptable." Having said that, she pointed out that "the financial arrangement that puts the farm in the husband's name also keeps women down."

Perhaps some women, but not Heida. And not because she's running the farm on her own.

"I have proven myself [as a farmer]," she concluded before heading back out to repair something in the barn. "But it was a long process."

Having to prove oneself is not exclusive to Icelandic women in agriculture. The other traditional economic backbone of the economy, the fishing industry, remains relatively segregated. The low-paid, labor-intensive roles in the fish factories processing the catch in monotonous eight-hour shifts are dominated by women, nowadays the large majority of foreign origin. On the vessels themselves, from smaller three-meter boats to huge trawlers with twenty-person crews, men make up over 90 percent of the labor force. Women hold only 1 percent of the captain's licenses. This work can be very lucrative but even today remains a potentially dangerous profession. Since 2004, twenty-six Icelanders have perished at sea.[35]

There have been notable exceptions to this rule, of course. Thurídur Einarsdóttir was a legendary captain at the turn of the nineteenth century who got special dispensation to wear men's clothing while at sea and was very successful with her catches. Women were always ready to jump in when work needed doing, but in more modern times, there have been campaigns by the Associated Icelandic Ports, Reykjavík's Technical College, and the Ministry of Fisheries and Agriculture to increase the number of women getting their captain's licenses and studying to become marine engineers.[36]

Yet if there's one area where genetics has dictated that life must be much harder for women than men, it's when nature calls and you're dressed in a waterproof fishing suit alone on a small boat in the north Atlantic.

"That's actually really interesting," admitted Halldóra Kristín Unnarsdóttir, captain of the eight-meter *Andri*. "There is no toilet on board. So you're in these huge overalls, and you have to pull it down, and you have to be careful you don't fall in, especially if the boat lurches. But that's all part of the experience. It's not luxury."

Halldóra Kristín, or Dóra as she is called by her friends, first went to sea when she was twelve years old, not an unusual age for any Icelander raised in a fishing community, as she was. Her father and grandfather were both fishermen, sailing up to fifty-meter vessels year-round from the harbor in the 140-person village of Rif out onto the wide Breidafjördur Bay, where they would spend a long day catching cod, haddock, and pollack. Dóra's mother was a supervisor at the community's fish processing facility.

Virtually everyone in Rif is connected to the sea in some way. The village is near the western end of the Snæfellsnes Peninsula, which is famous for its eponymous glacier, site of the beginning of the Jules Verne novel *Journey to the Center of the Earth*. Ornithologists also flock there to spot the Arctic terns nesting nearby. Despite these tourist attractions and the services that have sprung up around them, it's the riches of the sea that keep the community in existence.

"It was wonderful to grow up there," Dóra told me. "You go out and you meet someone and chat, and you know everyone. It's like being in a movie."

Dóra wanted to work at sea for as long as she can remember, regardless of the fact that everyone she saw do it was male. "I wasn't treated any differently by my family for doing what I wanted to do," she told me when we met at her winter job as a youth worker supervisor in Reykjavík. "The plan was always that I was going to take over from my father. I think it's natural to be a woman at sea."

After completing her secondary school diploma and a stint at a film school in Norway, Dóra returned to the School of Navigation in Reykjavík to earn her license to captain fishing vessels up to fifteen meters long, a qualification known colloquially as the "Testicle Test." Aside from the fact that it is almost exclusively men who complete this test, the term is also a play on the Icelandic word for "small boat." Dóra was the only woman graduating in her class of 2012. Her father and grandfather were always supportive of the move. So were the retired fishermen, who respected her for completing the schooling and thought it was "terrific."

But there was definitely an informal process of initiation. Dóra recounted her experiences in a cheerful and refreshingly blunt, understated way. That tone, both confident and self-deprecating, is quite possibly why she also wins over the crowds as a stand-up comedian at local festivals and confirmations (Icelanders really do simultaneously wear a variety of professional hats).

"I had to be allowed into the clique," Dóra recounted of the first time she sailed the *Andri* alone after getting her captain's license. "There was a lot of machismo around. The other captains would snigger and say, 'Does your dad know you're looking after the boat?' The first time I went out, I didn't have a plan for where I was going to sail. All the other boats were heading off at the same time, and when I asked where they were going, they just told me that it's every man for himself. But I could see them staying in the same cluster near each other. So I went off on my own and ended up hauling in a huge amount of fish!" she told me, a satisfied look on her face recalling the memory. "I returned to the harbor much earlier than the others, and they were all dying to know where I had found all the fish. This happened for a few days in a row."

Dóra said she "just got lucky," but from that day forward, they all discussed plans together and got advice from one another. And she earned the nickname the Fish Whisperer.

Dóra spends her summers fishing in and around Breidafjördur Bay, in the jovial company of the other vessels. It's "never boring," whether she is using those solo hours on the *Andri* singing aloud to herself or composing new gags for her stand-up routine. Leaving at about six in the morning and usually returning later in the day or the bright evening, she sails out for a few hours, drops the line to collect fish, hauls the catch in, ices it, stores it, and repeats, up to the 650 kilograms she is permitted to catch per day with *Andri*. A sonar helps highlight where schools of fish might be lingering far below the surface, and there are other indications for those who know where to look: more birds circling means more herring swimming near the surface, which means larger fish farther below. Same goes if you spot a pod of whales.

"There is so much freedom in being at sea. I find it cathartic. There's something about nature and working outside, even though it's incredibly cold," Dóra told me. "You get some quality time with yourself and your thoughts. So even if you don't find fish, you just breathe deeply and think 'ah, this is the life.' If you learn to steer your ship well, you can apply that elsewhere in life. Being at sea has helped me be a better person."

Despite all the safety equipment and latest technology, there are some adrenaline-inducing moments. "Maybe you're on the other side of the peninsula where there's great weather and then you turn around to go home and the wind picks up. You're sailing against the current, and in such a small vessel, there are waves crashing over you and the ship is riding up and down, and you're just thinking, 'Well, I've really got myself in it now.' I have been scared, and I have cried and swore to myself that this is the last time I'd go out," she recalled.

After establishing her sea cred as the Fish Whisperer, Dóra is pretty much considered just another sea captain now. "I remember when I started, and people wanted to interview me for TV because they thought it was so fascinating. I was called a feminist, but I really don't think it's all that special just because I'm a woman who works at sea. Who cares what genitals you have to do this job?"

Dóra is also optimistic. "Overall, there is a lot less sexism now. Men are more aware of the situation, and women are just more visible in these roles too. If there were no women around at sea, they would probably still be at it with that talk." And role models make all the difference, she thinks. "I try to encourage teenage girls if they show even a little bit of interest in it.

"For me, being a captain isn't something I need to brag about or showcase. It's just a part of who I am. And sometimes you have to fight hard to achieve what you want to. But you can't do it unless you believe in yourself. That's what makes the most difference."

Thorgerdur Brák is one of many strong but unappreciated women in the Icelandic sagas. She served as nursemaid to Egill Skallagrímsson of the eponymous *Egils Saga*, the epic story of an unruly boy who would grow up to become one of Iceland's most beloved poets. He would never have had this success, however, if Thorgerdur Brák had not saved his life as a young boy when Egill's father, Skallagrímur, tried to kill him in a fit of rage. When the man was unsuccessful, he turned his wrath on the nursemaid, who, to escape him, jumped in the sea near Borgarnes in West Iceland. Skallagrímur threw a stone on her in the water, and she perished.

The spot where these dramatic events took place is now marked with a monument bearing Thorgerdur Brák's name. In the same region, the local volunteer-run search and rescue crew is also named Brák in honor of this fierce and courageous martyr.

There are ninety-three search and rescue organizations throughout Iceland, all run by volunteers. These teams epitomize many of Thorgerdur Brák's admirable traits: they are composed of well-trained, brave, hardy individuals who are ready at a moment's notice to push cars out of snowdrifts, search for flying trampolines after a windstorm, rappel from a helicopter to rescue stranded crew members from fishing boats, climb up mountains to help injured hikers, and locate other missing individuals. According to regular Gallup surveys, Iceland's search and rescue crews have the trust of about 90 percent of the population, the highest level of trust of any officials or institutions in the country. (The office of the president comes in second, not that I'm keeping score!)

Only about one-third of search and rescue members are women, and an even smaller proportion of the organizations—eight of the ninety-three—have female leaders. Brák is one of them, having selected its first female director, Elín Matthildur Kristinsdóttir, in the spring of 2020.

I went for a walk with Elín and my daughter, Edda, one bracing November day in the countryside Thorgerdur Brák herself would have known well. Edda stopped regularly to jump on frozen puddles, and thirteen-year-old Labrador Kleó trotted loyally by our side. Forty-eight-year-old Elín grew up in the city but spent summers with her grandparents in the countryside and has lived her adult life in smaller communities, first Stykkishólmur on the Snæfellsnes Peninsula and later Borgarnes, the old stomping ground of Egill Skallagrímsson. Her current home is a half-hour drive from the town itself, on the property of a family-run dairy farm, an irony not lost on this nature-loving vegan, who is nevertheless content with all her surroundings, bovine and otherwise.

A teacher by training, Elín introduced a new program of relaxation and mindfulness at the local primary school, which has earned praise from students and the wider community. In her personal life, despite raising her four daughters as a single parent, she always found time to remain active in community service, singing in a local choir and working at the nearest charity shop run by the Red Cross.

"When you're alone, you are responsible for everything, and there are many challenges, but you do what you have to do," Elín told me as we strolled tractor paths by a narrow stream. "Then you reach this point where you realize you *can* do something, or you ask for help to learn, even if it's something like searching for a YouTube video on how to fix the washing machine."

It was when her daughters were older and more self-sufficient (and after she had no doubt watched many how-to YouTube videos) that Elín felt she could apply that resourcefulness elsewhere. She would tackle the next challenge in her personal development, moving outside her physical comfort zone, by joining the search and rescue squad at Brák.

"There is a really tough two-year process to join the search and rescue team," Elín told me as the bracing wind took my breath away for a moment. It's perhaps this strenuous training that is the reason why

Elín felt her experience as a woman qualifying for the squad was no different than that of a man. If you can learn to use your ice ax to brace a fall off a glacier, lower yourself into frigid water, or scale a mountain-side, then whether you have a Y chromosome or not really doesn't make a difference.

The qualifications are intense. Courses include not only all the physical requirements above but also practical skills such as first aid, general mountain climbing, and GPS navigation. After completing the training, volunteers are added to their region's search and rescue call list. When a call comes into the center via 112 (Europe's equivalent of 911), a text message is sent to everyone in that area's search and rescue crew. Calls are assigned either level one: drop everything you're doing now and race to the site because every second counts; level two: try to get there quickly; or level three: if you're around and want to help out, that's great.

Iceland's workplaces deserve plaudits for their support of the na-tion's search and rescue volunteers. They are almost universally un-derstanding about the last minute and time-consuming nature of the work and are flexible about time off and other supports needed to allow employees to volunteer in this lifesaving capacity.

Clearly an energetic, perennial optimist, Elín got into search and rescue for the same reason many people active in community work do so: to give back, to invest in the area closest to them, to further develop her own capabilities and confidence. She has been quoted in numerous local interviews about how she was always really afraid of heights, but once she learned how to tie the right knots and to inch her way down slowly, it was no problem to rappel down a cliff.

"It was actually a lot of fun," she admitted to me, "to realize that you could learn how the safety mechanisms all work and trust that. Obviously, your adrenaline is sky-high, but it was such an enriching experience. I used to wonder why people put themselves in such danger, but once you've learned to trust yourself and how things work, then it's no longer dangerous."

Of the many subspecialties available to search and rescue volunteers, Elín chose to specialize in search methodologies. She knows the different approaches to finding a lost person with dementia versus a tourist who has underestimated the weather.

Even with all the training, it was a baptism by fire. On her first call out, Elín was part of a group of 250 people (on a level two call) to search for two experienced ptarmigan hunters who got lost one autumn in pea soup fog on the Snæfellsnes Peninsula.

"The weather was insane," Elín recalled. "We would encounter streams that were normally so small they weren't even marked on the map, but it had been raining so much they were swollen in size, and we had to wade through them all. It didn't matter how well dressed we were. We were all soaking wet."

Happily, the duo were found alive after they had been outside all night. But then they and their rescuers had to return to civilization, and night had fallen once again.

"The streams were now huge, and it would have been impossible to wade back through them," Elín told me. "So they had to call out a special river rescue team. They set up a safety line and drove a huge six-wheel ATV into the middle of what was now basically a river. They made a human chain for us and helped us cross this deep and rapidly flowing water."

Iceland's search and rescue team is not the world's only such volunteer-led group, but it is unique as a countrywide organization that encompasses all aspects of search and rescue. Their calls range from daring escapes at stormy seas and highland searches in unspeakable weather to helping push cars stuck in snow or finding missing kids who have fallen asleep in a cupboard in their own home (it happens more than you'd think).

Elín may be one of only a handful of women in her leading role with Brák. But she doesn't do it to be a trailblazer. For her, the search and rescue recruitment process is the very definition of gender blindness. I asked her if she had ever met men who thought women weren't up to some of the tasks required of them.

"Probably that's somewhere," she considered. "But I've certainly never encountered that attitude in Brák, even though there aren't that many women in the organization. Search and rescue builds security and confidence that you can use elsewhere in life, and that's helpful for both women and men."

Actually, the fact that there are women at all on the search and rescue teams is a relatively new phenomenon. They were few and far between until about the 1990s, when their numbers began to inch up.

That increase is happening organically, believes Elín. "I don't think you need a special initiative to attract more, other than part of any general initiative to attract more volunteers overall." She paused to consider. "Although maybe sometimes women need more encouragement to trust themselves to do it."

After our chilly stroll, we returned to Elín's home, where her partner, Thór Thorsteinsson (incidentally, head of the national search and rescue team), had prepared hot chocolate and homemade scones for us. Elín mused on the concept of being a role model. "I don't think I have to prove myself because I'm a woman. I'm just one of a group that is both men and women. In the search and rescue, gender doesn't make a difference. We have these projects and tasks and responsibilities, and we each do what we need to do."

Elín admitted too that it is nice to have felt she has made a difference with something, especially for her daughters, now older and all living away from home. "I'm glad if they feel like by seeing something I have done, they know that all options are open to them too."

But after rescuing ptarmigan hunters and being on the on-call list for over four years, plus now running this more than seventy-year-old search and rescue team, I wondered if she was still afraid of heights.

"Yes, but less so," she replied cheerfully. "If I know I'm tied in, then I'm fine. I just need to find that security, which is so important."

Near the end of my first year living in Iceland, my rather energetic co-workers asked me if I wanted to join some of them on a hike after work. It was a regular Monday in April, at the tail end of what I thought was an almost intolerably long and dark winter but would later realize was par for the course at the sixty-fourth parallel. By this time of year, though, the sun doesn't set until well after 9:00 p.m. After a full day's work, we drove just over half an hour outside town, parked at the edge of some sun-dappled hills, and laced up our hiking boots.

It took only about forty-five minutes to follow a rough dirt trail winding fairly gently up through the hills to reach our objective: a rather ordinary-looking stream that snaked its way between rocks and over dips in the earth. Its only unusual characteristic to my eyes was the steam that rose from it. This clear creek was about 40°C (104°F).

We ducked behind some shrubs, changed into bathing suits, and soaked for a while in the water, then toweled off and hiked back down the mountain, all before it got dark.

I remember thinking that if I could work a full day and still have time afterward to drive beyond the city limits, take a refreshing hike, and soak in a natural hot spring, then maybe all those dark mornings were worth it. I also realized that no matter how modern our society is, in Iceland, nature is literally right next door.

"People come and go, but the Earth stays the same, the mountains stand the same. The rest is transitory," Heida told me on my visit to her farm.

The days may have passed when a majority of Icelanders earned their livelihood from farming or fishing—though the latter remains a vital economic industry. But both these sectors, and the countryside in general, are strong and integral parts of the Icelandic psyche.

Icelandic women have always made their marks in these fields. Heida and Dóra had to prove themselves to move into the areas of farming and fishing that have traditionally been male domains. After raising four daughters on her own, Elín proved her physical and mental endurance through rigorous search and rescue training.

What all three women have in common is that they have followed their passions, despite what was expected of them. They didn't see a lack of role models in their chosen fields as a barrier to following that path. They saw a route to fulfilling their dreams, irrespective of their gender. Following those dreams, even if they're not the norm, even if they don't fit some sort of outdated feminine ideal, doesn't mean these women come from the mountains, that they are naïve about what they want to achieve. It means that they forged their own destinies. It means they believe in themselves and trust their abilities. It means they know that asking for help, that being open to learning from others, shows strength and not weakness. It was at times challenging for them to reach the targets they set for themselves, but they have found satisfaction and acceptance, both in themselves and among their peers. In accomplishing this, they encourage others to live out their own ambitions and to maintain our vital links to the fields, the sea, the mountains, the valleys, and whatever other earthly surroundings envelop us, both on this island and elsewhere on our beautiful planet.

8

ART AS AN INSTRUMENT OF EQUALITY

Blind is the bookless man[*]

AT 3:42 A.M. ON MONDAY, February 10, 2020, many Icelandic televisions were tuned to RÚV, the state broadcaster. Many more tablets, phones, and laptops were logged on to the official livestream. Some bright-eyed morning people had set their alarms extra early. Others had downed a double espresso or two at about 10:00 p.m. the evening before and stayed awake for the long haul, the adrenaline of the moment blending with the caffeine to help with a final push.

Those who made the effort to witness the moment were rewarded. Seven thousand kilometers away in Los Angeles, California, composer Hildur Gudnadóttir became the first Icelander to win an Academy Award and only the third woman ever to earn an Oscar for composing a film score, in this case for her work on the movie *Joker*.

"To the girls, to the women, to the mothers, to the daughters, who hear the music bubbling within," the gently spoken thirty-seven-year-old told the crowd, her eyes sparkling. "Please speak up. We need to hear your voices."

It's possible this victory made Iceland the country with the most Academy Awards per capita.[†] Judging by the outpouring of emotion

---

[*] *Blindur er bóklaus maður* refers to both reverence for literacy and the importance of knowledge.

[†] For those of you keeping score, add another point to the Iceland Best in the World Per Capita tally.

(Icelandic style: no tears and no screaming but an exclamation mark—even two!!—after a status update or perhaps a smile to a stranger on the elevator the next morning), it was an achievement understandably on par with qualifying for a major sporting tournament or the two occasions the country finished in second place in the Eurovision Song Contest.

Everyone was quick to find their personal connection to the hero of the day. "WOULDN'T YOU KNOW IT, SHE'S MY COUSIN?" exalted poet and writer Gerdur Kristný in all caps on Facebook as she posted a screengrab from the nation's online genetic database showing that they shared a common ancestor seven generations back. Many others showcased their own familial ties to the new homegrown celebrity.

Hildur's success had become Iceland's success, an international validation, from a prestigious source, the Academy of Motion Picture Arts and Sciences, that what we create here matters.

Thanks to the small population, we feel successes—and failures—more keenly in Iceland. Our sporting heroes are not just faces we see on television or collectable cards. We run into them at the mall and movie theaters. They visit schools, hospitals, and sports clubs to inspire young people through a proximity that makes even the most unrealistic of ambitions seem possible.

Athletes are not the only stars through whose accomplishments, large and small, we live vicariously. Our artists, dancers, musicians, actors, composers, writers, poets, filmmakers: we follow their achievements, bemoan their failures, express opinions on their latest outings, and yes, even post on Facebook about how we are related to them. (Except for the singer Björk. Everyone did that calculation the first week the genealogy database was launched.)

Indeed, nothing awakens our passions as a society or unites us as a nation as do our unofficial cultural ambassadors and athletes. (One of my husband's favorite anecdotes stems from a history lecture he was invited to attend on the question of the possible end of nationalism. It had to be postponed when organizers found out it conflicted with a televised game vital for the national men's handball team.)

But is all sport created equal? Does cultural output reflect the diversity of our society? When we put on our gender equality glasses, do we picture Sara Björk's best goal as often as Eidur Smári's? Can we lip-sync to pop star Hildur as well as to rappers JóiPé and Króli?

The short answer is no, but that might also be the pessimist's reply. For although absolute parity is not yet a reality in the fields of culture and sport in Iceland, we can point to many areas where our awareness of the inequalities has led to improvements in the status quo and a larger, general awakening to the ubiquity of gender inequality throughout the society. Members of the women's national sports teams in soccer and handball now earn the same bonuses as their male counterparts.[37] Books by women sell just as well as those by men.

But progress in these fields ebbs and flows. Change here is not driven by legislation that pushes the speed of developments. Nor are there organized advocacy efforts to the same degree that, say, the National Queer Association lobbies to have trans people's rights enshrined in law. But the sheer visibility, the public passion for these sectors of society make them some of the most important areas for levelling the playing field in more than a symbolic way. For the many people who work professionally in cultural pursuits and in athletics, equality *is* personal. For the rest of us, it's the canvas from which we can judge whether we're making real progress or merely swirling the paint around.

Aside from individual sensations like impish singer Björk, on the occasions when people devote thought to Iceland's contributions to global culture, most think of its literary heritage. The sagas have inspired creative minds from Wagner to Tolkien.

They have inspired many modern-day Icelanders too. Several sources claim one in ten Icelanders will publish a book in their lifetimes (though it would be more accurate to caveat this statistic to publishing *something*, even a letter to the editor). Books are the most popular Christmas presents, and a large majority of the year's batch is accordingly published from mid-October to mid-December, beginning when the eagerly anticipated *Book News* catalog of the year's offerings is delivered to households around the country. Thankfully, this remains the case; the Icelandic idiom *blind is the bookless man* warns us all of the fates of those who lack something to read over the holidays. In the weeks leading up to Christmas, during what's known as the Christmas book flood, authors and poets fill their days with readings and other events in bookstores, workplaces, and even outdoor swimming pools. Many former homes of writers are now museums situated around the country, from the ancestral land of the thirteenth century's Snorri Sturluson, who is credited with composing several influential medieval manuscripts, to the '60s-chic sunken living room and outdoor swimming pool (a rarity in Iceland) of Nobel Prize winner Halldór Laxness.

Sadly, there is predictably a dearth of museums devoted to female authors (advances in gender equality do not stretch back far enough to celebrate the homes of the proportionately fewer women scribes).[38] That said, nowadays there is certainly no absence of the female writers themselves. Their fixed place in the pantheon of Icelandic greats means that festivals will no longer inadvertently (or not) feature a "manel" or interview only men for a literary podcast.

The tales of two current writers exemplify the state of gender and culture in Iceland today. They were each born in Reykjavík at opposite ends of the 1970s. One describes herself as a writer for decades; the other has had a single semi-autobiographical novel published, with a second in its nascent stages. One works full-time in this field, travelling abroad several times each year to take part in literary festivals. The other is by day a librarian at the University of Iceland. One was recently commissioned to write a poem for the sixtieth anniversary of a coast guard vessel; the other was recruited to write a book-length work following the viral popularity of her wryly astute tweets. Both are recognizable names, unabashed feminists, cuttingly funny, wizards with the language, and cognizant of their privileged upbringings and the effect that has had on their ultimate success.

Gerdur Kristný and Kamilla Einarsdóttir, despite differing styles, were a complementary pairing to discuss Iceland's ambition of gender equality in the context of the literary world. We met one chilly winter's day in Gröndalshús, another home dedicated to the life and works of a writer who lived there, one Benedikt Gröndal. The cozy, low-ceilinged house is now a writer's apartment and meeting space in the center of Reykjavík, which incidentally is the world's first non-native-English-speaking UNESCO City of Literature. The three of us shared some vegan wraps and a bottle of lukewarm Cosmopolitan Diva, a nonalcoholic sparkling wine that felt tongue-in-cheek fitting for a gathering of middle-aged lady writer types.

"There's never a dull moment here," summarized Gerdur (the same one who is a proud seventh cousin to Oscar-winner Hildur Gudnadóttir) of the literary scene in Iceland as she bit delicately into some falafel. "People want books. And we follow what people are writing and publishing. We're excited for new writers, and they don't need to be young, just telling some new stories. We also look forward to stories from our established, favorite writers."

Gerdur falls into the latter category. She has been describing herself as a poet and writer since secondary school and has been working in the field since not much later than that, regularly captivating crowds with her beguiling contralto voice and deliberate delivery and garnering praise for the inventive use of the Icelandic language in her writing. Gerdur works full-time at her craft, and every Christmas, she releases something new, whether a book of poetry, children's fiction, or a novel. Her works have been nominated for several awards. *Bloodhoof*, a feminist retelling of "The Lay of Skírnir," one of the epic poems in the *Poetic Edda*, won the Icelandic Literature Prize, one stanza of which reads as follows:

> *"I would stay*
> *I chose to remain*
> *in the place where I knew*
> *every cranny*
> *and creek*
>
> *and the rivers ran*
> *through my every vein"*[39]

"There is a lot of inspiration in being a feminist," Gerdur said. "It's not like you go to the library now and see all kinds of books with feminist themes. It makes you realize how much there is left to say."

Kamilla Einarsdóttir, a bleached blond, tattooed librarian with a hearty laugh and an acerbic wit, agreed. "At the library, I see all these books by Icelandic men who are covering women by writing about their mothers. Then you just think, ach, I don't know, maybe someone could actually tell a *realistic* story about motherhood?"

Kamilla did just that in 2018. Contacted by a local publisher who followed her on social media, she wrote *The Kópavogur Chronicles*, a darkly comic semi-autobiographical profile of a reluctant young mother who is explaining the causes of her troubled love life and self-confessed failure to thrive to her daughter; the largest cause is that she has to endure living in the title's middle-class capital area suburb. The book was critically acclaimed and adapted for the stage. A short, striking section was also named "Most Curious Sex Scene" of the year, leading, Kamilla says, to numerous dubious Facebook friend requests from "old guys" and solidifying her professional reputation as a straight-talking maven of modern life for the Snapchat generation. Kamilla identified one of her favorite passages: "It was a good time to hook up with people in Kópavogur. Like the sad-eyed stock boy at the Iceland grocery store on Engihjalli Road, who was known to wipe away his tears on the inner thighs of women."[40]

"At one place I went to read, the average age of the listeners was probably about ninety-six," Kamilla recalled. "I was a bit nervous because the book is quite explicit, but everyone thought it was exciting and fun. These people have been reading all their lives of course, and I realized they have probably also done all the stuff I describe. They weren't scandalized at all by it."

"There is so much excitement around new writers," Gerdur added.

What makes it possible for writers such as Gerdur to make a living from her literary work are the so-called artists' salaries the government subsidizes. These highly competitive grants were originally created to ensure that people were able to produce works in Icelandic and therefore help preserve the language. They have now expanded into other sectors, such as visual arts and music. The monthly stipends the system produces allow several hundred individuals in the country to focus on their craft.[41] And while in times of economic belt-tightening, the general public may grumble about the generosity of the grants, mainstream political parties across the spectrum would never consider eliminating them.

"[A few years] after the economic crash in 2008, the then minister of culture, who was a conservative politician, defended the practice in the media," recalled Gerdur, who was one of a trio of writers that year to receive a three-year writer's salary. "He questioned what kind of society we wanted to live in if we cannot support our artists. It was tremendous."

"I think it's just normal we have this," added Kamilla. "It's like subsidies for a farmer or vegetable growers."

These grants are also a key reason that poets can work as such in Iceland. "It is very inspiring to be a poet in Iceland since people here are always interested in new poetry," said Gerdur, who describes herself as a poet and writer in her entry in Iceland's online phone listings.* She sipped her flute of Diva. "We sell five hundred to twelve hundred copies [of a book of poetry] or more." Per capita, that's equivalent to selling more than one million copies in the United States.

High-selling female poets join other women who also feature on the bestseller lists each year in all categories, from memoir to children's literature to crime.

"There is still so much to be written. And we have strong role models, women who have paved the way for the rest of us," Gerdur said. "It's great to be a woman and to write from that point of view. I don't think I would have written *Bloodhoof* if I were a man. And *The Kópavogur Chronicles*? By a man?" She glanced at Kamilla and shook her head decisively. "No."

For various reasons, women feel free to write from their point of

---

* Iceland's online telephone listing is an interesting study on its own. The country has so many Björg Magnúsdóttirs and Jón Jónssons that in order to distinguish one from the other, listees have the option of including their profession next to their name. So you call Sigrún Björnsdóttir the plumber and not Sigrún Björnsdóttir the pilot. Entries are not vetted, though, so it seems Iceland has at least one hamster whisperer, one Cher expert, and dozens of lion tamers. In the now defunct printed phone books, they were all listed alphabetically by first name, because we are so informal in Iceland that surnames (patronymics, really) aren't significant. Whether addressing your teacher, doctor, or even the president, you just need the first name.

view, and there is less need to compete for media attention or even book deals. And when it comes to that common challenge for writers, thinking up new ideas, Kamilla smiled and said jokingly, "Makes you feel better when you walk around the library and see that there are so many really boring books that have been published, and then you are reassured that yours is never going to be the worst one."

After washing down the wraps with the last vestiges of our drink, the two writers hit on one well-trod area where the old gender stereotypes have cropped up. "I was reading my bio at a literary festival, and it began with 'she has three children,'" recalled Kamilla. "[Icelandic author] Dóri DNA was there too, and he also has three kids and was promoting his first book, but his blurb didn't start that way. I said they didn't have to change mine, but they'd have to begin his bio the same way." She shrugged her shoulders with a *plus ça change* tone. "If a woman has children, it is supposed to be central to her identity, but it can be the seventeenth sentence in a man's bio. It's as though if you're not completely devoted to being a mother, you're a bad person."

"Ah, well, at least we can end on a sour note!" interjected Gerdur with a smile, satisfied that we hadn't painted too idealistic a portrait of women in the literary world of Iceland.

But speaking of idealism, I wondered if there is concern that we are pulling away from this storytelling tradition, this popular image of thousands of Icelanders snuggled up warm with a good book to keep them company on a cold winter's evening. Or of children who can recite the sagas' most famous passages and covet gifts of Laxness over LEGO.

We agreed those days are no longer. But "we are not a PlayStation nation yet. We are a book nation," Gerdur insisted. "I hope so at least."

⟶⟩

Many overseas guests are surprised by the unassuming nature of the office of the president of Iceland, which is located in a formerly private home in a central and quiet residential neighborhood of Reykjavík. Visitors wait for any appointment in a small reception area with two chairs and a large L-shaped desk. The president's private office and meeting area showcase Icelandic design in art and furniture. Outside in that waiting area, however, the largest display is a 43.3 in × 23.6 in photo that hangs on the wall greeting guests as they enter. It was taken on September 16, 2016, and is of Iceland's national women's soccer team celebrating their 4–0 win against Slovenia, a victory that secured their place to compete for the third time in the European Football [Soccer] Championships the following summer.

In the center of the smiling, blue-uniformed squad is my husband, clad in a suitably presidential woolen trench coat, national team scarf tied loosely around his neck, hands clasped together, mouth agape, and eyebrows raised in jubilant astonishment (more likely at his own fortune of getting to meet some sporting heroes in person than the team's advancement itself). The messages this sends to people with an errand at the head of state's office? We celebrate success together. This president is a relatively informal person. And we are just as proud of our female athletes as our male ones.

If many of us think of art as books or music or theater or painting, for Margrét Lára Vidarsdóttir, it is soccer. The beauty of a free kick soaring over a wall of defenders, the finesse required to weave a ball as you move it up the field, an elegantly executed tackle to avert a game-changing goal, the magical union of individual strengths into a cohesive unit, ecstatic fans rising from their seats in the unified and oft intimidating "Viking chant" Iceland supporters have made famous at international tournaments.

"I can't draw or write or create in that sense, but this is my outlet," the highest all-time scorer for the national team told me when we met in the watering hole of the now-retired striker's old local club.

The falcon logo of team Valur is well known in Iceland's sports world. Since their founding in 1911, they have accrued more than one hundred titles in soccer, basketball, and team handball.* Not least of their achievements are numerous awards for their women's teams. This success has led Valur to acquire a local reputation as an egalitarian sports club. In the cozy clubhouse where Margrét Lára and I spoke from soft brown Chesterfield chairs, the walls were lined with trophies, old jerseys, and photos of victorious squads, featuring men and women alike.

Growing up in the sports mad Westman Islands, an archipelago just off the south coast of the country, Margrét Lára always knew she had a knack for athletics. From the age of eight or nine, her skills outshone those of her peers, and she racked up the trophies for most goals (before it became de rigueur to stop keeping score in kids' matches). But Margrét Lara wanted to study sports at university when she was older, not become a professional soccer player, unlike a large proportion of similarly aged boys who, no doubt, stayed up late dreaming about the possibility. The reason? "I didn't know that existed," she told me in her characteristic husky voice. "There were no games on television. I didn't even know what the national women's team was."

In the couple of decades since then, much has changed for women's sports in Iceland. This field remains one with significant inequality: male professionals are better known and earn a lot more money. But progress in gender equality overall in the country has narrowed the gap

---

* Handball is a team sport popular primarily in Continental Europe and virtually unknown in North America and the UK. It's similar to basketball, but instead of a hoop to score, there are small soccer-style nets guarded by a goalie. Iceland's national men's team won the Olympic silver medal in handball at Beijing in 2008, by far the smallest country in population to win an Olympic medal in a team sport.

appreciably. In addition to much publicized equal bonuses for national team members, female sporting heroes have sponsorship contracts and are popular social media influencers (especially the CrossFit champions).

Margrét Lára is now one of the most recognizable players in Iceland, even though she retired from the national team in 2019, having capped off a professional career that included stints in both Sweden and Germany and representing her country in 124 international matches, where she scored 79 goals. Her supernatural skill of being in the right place at the right time to receive a well-placed pass and zing the ball past the goal line made her one of the most watched players on the team. She now works as a psychologist and commentator for various sporting matches, a role for which she has earned a reputation as insightful, opinionated, and engaging.

Despite the lack of role models, she was always following her passion. In high school, she skipped her school's annual party (about as significant as missing the prom) to attend a late-night soccer practice.

"The next day, my teacher asked very earnestly whether everything was all right with me, if I had some concerns about attending, although for me it was the most natural thing to have been at practice instead," she told me. "If I were a boy, I wouldn't have been asked this. They would have seen that as an investment in my future."

At sixteen, all those extra practices paid off, and Margrét Lára was scouted by the then national team coach. She signed a contract with a big insurance provider to travel the country and talk to school kids about the importance of sports. Her image appeared on billboards, and kids were given soccer balls branded with MLV9—her initials and jersey number. Margrét Lára had become one of the country's first female athletes to earn money from sponsorship. She was a familiar face.

That sponsorship and exposure were important for promoting the women's game. "That made women's soccer more popular, and then becoming a soccer player by profession becomes more appealing," asserted Margrét Lára.

In Iceland, those faces on billboards are real, tangible people, usually only one or two degrees away from a personal connection. "We are so lucky with our proximity to things," Margrét Lára told me. "You go to the grocery store or the shopping mall, and you see your role models in the flesh. It's like you can reach out and touch your dreams. That really helps us to believe in what we can accomplish."

This increasing semi-fame occurred at around the same time Margrét Lára left the Westman Islands and moved to the capital to play for Valur, a top division team. When she first started, she immediately picked up on the equal treatment of the men's and women's teams within that same club. Valur's men's team and its women's team had normal practice times on the regular pitch. The women's equipment and clothing were of the same quality as the men's. She told me that even today, those basic details are not as equal with many of the other soccer clubs in the country. "When you get the same quality equipment and practice times as the men, you find that you can make more of a difference and have been shown more respect, and you show that respect in return."

After a few years honing her skills, Margrét Lára turned her attention to Europe, where she could play professionally with world-class players and coaches in larger stadiums that attracted more fans. Surprisingly, though, she said many of the facilities were better back in Iceland. "In Iceland, we had Jacuzzis in the changing rooms," she recalled. "We had a gym to lift weights on-site." She conceded that the human resources—fellow players, coaching, physiotherapists—were of a higher quality abroad, but even at the best team in Germany, where she played, they would still climb onto their bus for a ten-hour drive to the next match, while their male counterparts in the Bundesliga hopped on their private jet.

This stark contrast is indicative of how money propels the game. Men's teams generally have better resources because they generate more revenue and thus garner bigger sponsors and media, making them more popular. It's a cycle that keeps men's teams better funded and women's teams working harder for attention. But it also points to something else. Simply put, as Margrét Lára said, that level of "inequality is deemed unacceptable in Icelandic society." This includes sports, even though that sector remains one of the last global bastions of acceptable sexism, often without even the lip service equality is paid in other male-dominated arenas. But in Iceland, society as a collective has come to expect more. Margrét Lára told me, "if the television station broadcasting soccer matches says it won't also show women's games, some people would threaten to cancel their subscriptions."

This collective understanding of the inherent value of equality is what enabled the team to get the same level of bonuses. "Of course we had to fight for it. They didn't offer it to us," acknowledged Margrét Lára. "But we didn't need to threaten to go to the media and run a big campaign."

This achievement was noteworthy among her peers overseas. "They think it's really important," she said. If her teammates in Germany, for example, had asked for the same treatment, "I think they would just laugh at them, unfortunately."

The high-profile successes of the national team have inspired others to follow in their footsteps. Since 2004, the number of women playing organized soccer with a local team (from preschool age up) has more than doubled. On the management side, Klara Bjartmartz is the first woman in Iceland, and one of only very few in the world, to serve as the general secretary of a national football association.

Now, Margrét Lára is famous and can be the kind of role model she didn't see growing up. "It's a privilege to be a role model," she smiled. "If a six-year-old wants to talk to me in a store, I think that's wonderful."

She and her former soccer mates are also in close contact with their male counterparts, many of whom earn six- or even seven-figure salaries for top-tier clubs like Arsenal and Augsburg.

"The guys really stand with us," she told me. "When we were fighting for equal bonuses on the national team, they told us theirs when we asked. It's not their fault they have it better than us."

There are still voices who loudly claim that watching women play sports is just not as interesting as watching men. But that's like comparing apples and oranges, Margrét Lára believed. "You have to wear different glasses when you are watching men's and women's soccer. It's the same sport, but it's also different because we are naturally different."

Indeed, perhaps this form of art is like comparing a Picasso to a Monet; they are both works of creative genius but are hard to contrast with each other. In the end, she said, the most important factor to continuing to work on equality in sports is "respect."

Soccer is the golden child of sport in Iceland. It receives the most money, and its players are the most well-known. But its success in gender has permeated other fields. The hashtag #dottir, referring to the most common suffix of an Icelandic woman's patronymic, trends during national team matches (ignoring the irony that this identifies the players by their fathers more than themselves). The flag carrier, Icelandair, proudly sponsors various national sports teams and gives equal attention to women and men.

There are large and ongoing disparities, to be sure. At this time, women like Margrét Lára still cannot hope to earn seven-figure salaries if they go pro. Tickets for women's games will still cost less than those for men's matches, and ad revenue will be significantly lower.* In not only soccer but other athletics too, women will have to fight just to have the coaching, equipment, and facilities that men often have by default. Nevertheless, in Iceland, sports is one field where people are cognizant of the inequalities and are working to rectify them slowly but surely. That's good news, said Margrét Lára, looking over the smiling faces of past female sporting heroes of Valur.

"It's not about my voice or the other girls' voices," she said. "It's about society's voice."

While the soccer inspirations for #dottir continue to carve a path in international athletics, other daughters are making waves in Iceland's music scene.

The Daughters of Reykjavík, a nine-person self-described rap collective, have performed their hit "Reppa heiminn" to a crowd of several hundred oat latté drinking feminists (including me) during a #MeToo-themed gender equality conference organized by the office of the prime minister. The bandmates have jumped and jived for discerning five-year-olds at several capital region preschools, assiduously removing words like "fuck" and "beer" from their repertoire but keeping terms like "gender nonconformity" and "counterculture" in any lyrics. And they caused a stir during a live appearance on a Friday night chat show, involving explicit lyrics, much gyrating, and a strap-on. Such variety is par for the course for many musicians in Iceland, most of whom also have other professional commitments. (In the Daughters' case, that includes a graphic designer, a dance teacher, a classical pianist, and several actors.)

---

* The exception to this is for basketball matches, where tickets to men's and women's matches cost the same, and ad revenue is also similar between the genders.

The Daughters of Reykjavík want to be known first and foremost as rappers, creatives who have taken the country's ancient traditions of *rímur* (rhymes performed in an almost musical way and incorporating complicated word play) and applied them to the twenty-first century, with international flavor added. They were featured in the *New York Times* in the summer of 2020, an achievement not accorded to many of their musical compatriots. Their concerts are more shows than musical performances, each singer taking her turn to dominate the stage with displays that have included ripping off their tops and crotch grabbing—all par for the course with male rap groups but not acts in which women onstage are traditionally expected to partake.

Whether it's because of the lyrics or the costumes or the whole performance, "we are known primarily as a feminist act," grumbled one of the band's founders, Thurídur Blær Jóhannsdóttir, when I met a trio from the group over drinks one evening during the COVID-19 pandemic, when there would be no opportunity to witness a concert. "I completely disagree with that characterization. If you're a rapper and a woman, you're automatically a feminist performance act that is trying to push some feminist agenda. We are just doing it because we love to do it. I am proud to be a feminist, but I don't like it when other people take that label and use it to drag down other things I'm doing. If a guy starts to rap, you think, yeah, he loves rap. We have the same motivations, but because we're women, people thought there was something more behind it."

These assumptions are perhaps indicative of the sense of equality (or lack thereof) within Iceland's music industry. "They are great at talking the talk but not walking the walk," explained Blær, as she is known. "So many male singers talk about how great women singers are, but they have never worked with a woman."

There is a lot of lip service paid to the importance of equality, the

Daughters argue, but it's hard to see it in practice. "It's not that these men consciously try to keep women down," continued Thórdís Björk Thorfinnsdóttir, known as Dísa, a local Instagram star, actress, and singer, and acknowledged by the group as the fashion icon among them. (She is also the theater troupe member from chapter 6 who was castigated online for maligning the small northern town of Kópasker.) "It's just not really on their radar."

Daughters of Reykjavík is, in truth, an accidental collective, formed in 2013 after a poetry/rap slam night Blær and her friend Kolfinna Nikulásdóttir organized that was packed to the rafters with participants.

"We didn't have some grand plan to form a group," Blær explained. "It was more that people kept calling and booking this group Reykjavíkurdætur [the Icelandic name that they began with]. It was more chaotic at the beginning, but we have matured since then." At one time, the group ballooned to twenty members, with individuals coming in and out based on other commitments and occasionally the arrival of a baby. Now they are fixed at nine.

On one hand, Daughters of Reykjavík don't represent the mainstream female musician in Iceland, many of whom (notably Björk) have made successful careers even on the international stage, often capitalizing on a stereotype of the Icelandic songstress as a quirky, ethereal beauty. Yet they also encapsulate a contrasting and almost postfeminist concept of rap as storytelling, of performance as provocation.

Their in-your-face style and loud concerts shook up the fledgling and male-dominated rap scene in Iceland. For example, according to the Daughters, misogynistic behavior and objectification of women in lyrics and music videos from other rappers stopped. And although they got a lot of encouraging feedback from the public in their first years, as they garnered a reputation for increasingly outrageous performances (even though they did not explicitly engineer them as such), segments of the population who prefer mainstream music began to be more critical.

"I think we are the most hated band ever in Iceland," said Blær ruefully but matter-of-factly. "Well, us and Nylon." A pop group modelled on the Spice Girls, Nylon reached their peak fame in the early 2000s.

"The most criticism we get is from men who think we take up too much space, although they don't say it in so many words," added Steiney Skúladóttir, the group's unofficial prankster and also member of a popular local improv troupe.

As dissenters became more vocal within some areas of Iceland, the Daughters took their act to Europe, officially adopted the English version of their name, and have been filling clubs from Barcelona to Greenland.

"We go abroad, and people are seeing us for the first time, and in so many places, you realize things haven't gotten as far as we have in Iceland. People have never seen anything like our act before," Blær said. Although they mostly perform in Icelandic, that's not the reason their act is so different for audiences. "People don't need to understand what we're saying. They understand what we are."

Blær, Dísa, and Steiney believe that Iceland's music industry is more chauvinistic than the country's other cultural branches. And those who speak up about it face more blowback. "In theater, I didn't notice this at all," said Blær, who also works as an actor at the Reykjavik City Theater and starred in the acclaimed Icelandic television miniseries *The Minister*. The music industry has less career security, and whistleblowers are more nervous about losing future gigs if they aren't seen as team players.

Neither do the Daughters feel strong solidarity with male rappers (though there are of course exceptions). "We'd meet the other guys, they were so nice, then you'd hear what they had been saying about us when we weren't there," Steiney told me, adding "and [she spits out the name of one of the country's most popular rappers] has tried to sleep with many of us."

Much like corporate Iceland, money in the industry remains heavily in the hands of men, who organize most of the local festivals. "He [the organizer] just wants to sell tickets and thinks male performers sell tickets," Blær said. "So then there is only room for one woman when there should be room for ten."

"That ends up pitting women against each other," added Dísa.

The room made murmurs of recognition and disappointment at this sad observation, and the conversation quickly turned curative. "We have to get rid of that idea that if there are nine spots for men, there is one for a woman. There are ten spaces," began Steiney.

"I can't wait to see a poster for a concert and it's just women and no one says a thing about it," added Blær.

The trio of Daughters I spoke with were in favor of gender targets at music festivals. This is not a new concept; the Keychange movement in Europe, an initiative launched in 2018 and supported by the Creative Europe Programme of the European Union, has a goal of bringing underrepresented genders into the music industry and has over 450 festivals and organizations aligned with it, including Iceland Airwaves, this country's largest festival. In addition to a career development program for underrepresented talent, Keychange has a gender balance "pledge" that it encourages musical organizations to commit to. I am one of two Icelandic ambassadors for the initiative who, along with others from several countries, try to draw attention to gender disparity across the music industry and motivate consumers and others to demand change.

"But [gender equality in event lineups] should also apply to those small-town festivals," said Steiney. "If you see yet another ad where there are no women, it's just tiring to always tweet about it and draw attention to it. We need people to think really concretely and long-term about it. People who acknowledge that someone might sell fewer tickets this time, but they are doing it for the next generation. We just need to take more chances on unknown women to help even things out, because they are just as skilled as the men."

It would also allow more women to test their mettle as the Daughters have done with few regrets, regardless of internet trolls or occasional negative reviews.

"It's the most catharsis I find in my life," smiled Dísa, closing her eyes and leaning back into the sofa.

On an April day in 2019, I attended a performance of Mozart's Requiem at the Hof Cultural Centre in Akureyri, North Iceland. I sang with one of Iceland's leading amateur choirs when I was relatively new to the country, and I have always felt simultaneously soothed and uplifted in my spirit when I listen to choral music. What was noteworthy about this performance of the famous piece, though, was its conductor. Finland's Anna-Maria Helsing was her nation's first female conductor for a Finnish symphony orchestra. I chatted with her after the show (a perk of my position!) and mentioned how pleased I was to see a woman conducting a classical music performance, still a rarity.

She smiled and thanked me. "You know, I used to be frustrated that people only seemed to want to discuss my gender when they talked about me professionally," she told me. It was discouraging to her that this was the most notable takeaway for people and not her skill. "Then one day, I was flying, and the pilot started with the in-flight announcement. I was thrilled she was a woman! After that, it no longer bothered me that people wanted to recognize that I was a woman. I realized that we need to see women in these roles, and we're all happy for each other when we do."

A society that values the importance of cultural pursuits values nurturing its collective soul. When we neglect to enrich these myriad dimensions of what helps define us as human beings, we shortchange our full potential. Yet in many places, passions such as music, literature, and even sport are seen as extracurricular when it comes to how we prioritize our money and time in the fight for gender equality.

Not all these cultural activities are created equal, particularly for women who make their livings in these fields. But when we think about it, art, culture, and sport are all areas where many of us are consumers rather than creators. This is an opportunity to help shape the dialogue. Do we want to pay to see films where women's characters seem to exist only in relation to leading men and where they speak far less of the time? Do we want our children to collect playing cards for male sporting heroes and not female ones? Do we read the stories of people of a variety of gender identities, abilities, and backgrounds?

In Iceland, our long tradition of respect for and encouragement of the written word has largely flattened the playing field. In sport, Margrét Lára's chosen art, Icelandic women have made immense strides in very recent years, narrowing what has been one of the widest gender gaps. Yet the sheer vastness of that canyon means that even significant achievements leave gaping disparities. In music, we need to focus on more than lip service. Gender balance in festival lineups is important, but musical associations can't dictate people's practices and perceptions. In this field, the greatest change will come from that essential relationship between content creators and content consumers—musicians and their fans. That's daunting, because it leaves little room for legislation to bridge the gap, but also enormously hopeful, because it might just be happening on its own, especially with vocal role models like the Daughters of Reykjavik.

These fields cannot be left behind. They are perhaps also areas where, as individuals, we can do more to demand some tangible results, simply by supporting diversity in the arts and sports. If we can make a difference here, in these very public domains, we will be helping redefine society's messaging, both the overt and the subtle signaling through these channels, that women should keep quiet and passive. We owe it to humanity to encourage a diversity of voices when we nurture our souls. We need to tell women's stories, celebrate their victories, sing their songs. Perhaps, to paraphrase Oscar-winner Hildur Gudnadóttir, what we need to do is feel the equality bubble within us.

THE SPRAKKAR WHO
RALLIED A NATION

AS A GESTURE TOWARD RECOGNIZING equality, the United Nations dedicated the year 1975 to women. That year, women made up just 5 percent of Iceland's members of parliament. Women who worked outside the home earned 60 percent of what men earned.

To prove exactly how vital their contributions were, the women of Iceland decided to take a day off. Ninety percent of the nation's women are estimated to have taken part in the protest on October 24, 1975. Those women who worked at home or on the farm took leave from child care, cleaning, or food preparation that day. Those who worked outside the home did not show up to their jobs.

Elementary schools were closed. Preschools were closed. There was no telephone service. Bank managers filled in for female tellers at the banks. Fish factories closed; women usually processed the freshly caught fish. On radio programs and television broadcasts, children could be heard in the background as their fathers, now primary caregivers for the day, read the news. Flights were delayed. Hot dogs sold out in the stores as fathers struggled to prepare a semi-healthy dinner for little ones.

Twenty-five thousand women buoyantly gathered in the center of Reykjavík (that was over 10 percent of the entire population at that time). Young and old, they crowded onto a grassy hill near the prime minister's office to listen to impassioned speeches, poems, and songs, including the motto made famous during that event: "I dare, I can, I will."

Among the thousands of women in downtown Reykjavík that day was the artistic director of a local theater named Vigdís Finnbogadóttir, who had encouraged all her female employees to join her. On the other side of town, teenagers Hólmfrídur and Bjarney indulged in pancakes with whipped cream and jam when they returned from the protest with their mother. Hólmfrídur's daughter Ragnhildur, who founded the Icelandic Lava Show, recalled this anecdote because her grandfather was told he was under no circumstances to sample any of the treats; this was a reward for the ladies only.

It wasn't just city dwellers who took part. Fifty-three-year-old Margrét Jóhannsdóttir travelled with some girlfriends from her home in rural Vatnsleysuströnd, southwest Iceland. Her husband was unused to looking after everything at home, but he encouraged his wife to journey to the capital and take part in what he knew would be a historic event. Margrét's then thirteen-year-old daughter, Sigrún Símonardóttir, remembers the excitement with which her mother recounted events of that day upon her return and for several days afterward. Margrét's experiences were so detailed that it felt as if she, Sigrún, had taken part in person, Sigrún told me when we met forty-five years later at Bubba's house to talk about women's associations in Iceland.

The effect generated waves within society. Within a year, Iceland's parliament had passed a law guaranteeing equal rights between men and women. It even garnered headlines in foreign publications, making the front page of the *Times* in the UK and inspiring the National Organization of Women in the United States to call for a similar protest in that country.

But there was more. Iceland's women had dared. They had shown that they could and that they would. And soon, they reasoned, the country would be ready for a female head of state. That would come to pass five years later.[42]

9

NO WOMAN IS AN ISLAND

"Those People"

LOVE. NATURE. HORSES. EMPLOYMENT. STUDIES. Adventure. Security. The reasons immigrants have chosen to build a life tucked up under the Arctic Circle are almost as diverse as the individuals themselves. When I moved—for love—in 2003, my age and background were not so unusual as to raise eyebrows, but not so mundane as to avoid a barrage of questions on a regular basis. Why did I move to Iceland? Why did we choose this country and not Canada? When would I learn the language? And, the most sensitive of all for sufferers of small nation complex, how did I like Iceland? (I did! I do!)

When this island was settled in the late ninth century, there was no indigenous population to displace or exploit. For centuries, the inhabitants were an ethnic mix of Norse and Celt, with an occasional dash of stray Basque whaler, French sailor, or English merchant added for good measure. As recently as 1996, a mere 2 percent of the population were immigrants. In the next quarter century, with more open laws for European citizens and employment as well as increased economic prosperity in the country, this figure ballooned to 15.2 percent. This is a higher proportion of foreign-born residents than in the United States.[43] In fact, there are currently more residents with foreign passports in Iceland than there are senior citizens.*

---

* These figures exclude people like me who were born and raised abroad but who have earned Icelandic citizenship.

When I moved to Iceland almost two decades ago, I gravitated toward other immigrants to the country. I befriended recent arrivals and others trying to learn a new language and navigate living here as well as those old-timers, many of whom had earned almost legendary status among us for having survived, and often thrived, so long in this small nation. They shared insights on where to buy canned pumpkin, an elusive treat, and all the ways to decline the word "two" (it gives those of us learning the language bragging rights to know there are at least a couple dozen versions).

I was one of the large majority of immigrants who are Caucasian and, as such, did not attract stares in the way that visible minorities regularly did. But my given name is spelled with a *z*, which is not part of the Icelandic alphabet, so that letter gave my overseas origins away long before my accent did.

As an educated, heterosexual, cis white woman who spoke English as a first language and was married to an Icelandic man, I fell into the most privileged group of newcomers. Any "hurdles" I faced in my efforts to feel at home in the country were comparatively minor. Back then, on some job applications, I was asked not only for my own personal information but the names and national ID numbers of my parents (presumably so potential employers could increase the odds of finding a personal connection with the worthiest applicants). The law requiring new citizens to adopt an Icelandic name from an approved list had been quashed less than a decade earlier.[44] News outlets were almost exclusively in Icelandic, online banking and health care accessible only in that language. I was not allowed to donate blood because I could not understand the consent form, and the staff, who spoke perfect English, were not allowed to translate it for me.

In an effort to give strangers a heads-up that I was a novice in the language, I sometimes wore a black T-shirt I bought from the

Intercultural House, a now-defunct not-for-profit that offered services to new immigrants. To encourage locals to be patient with immigrants who were learning the language, they produced a series of shirts that were designed to turn the tables on phrases that had been used in a derogatory way toward immigrants. My shirt read in Icelandic: "I am one of 'Those People.'" And I was proud of it (the status and the shirt).

Two decades on, the situation is much improved for many immigrants but is also riddled with additional bureaucracy. Many services are now available in English and Polish, the latter being the language of by far the largest immigrant group in the country.* Many schools send notices to parents in multiple languages. There is a mosque in Reykjavík and a resident rabbi who leads services on Jewish holy days. Yet we all still make snap, unconscious judgments about those with "foreign" names, and people of color are subject to racial microaggressions on a daily basis.

My identities as a woman and as an immigrant are inextricable. My experience has been largely positive. Most people in this country would be pleased about that, it seems. A 2020 Gallup survey ranked Icelanders' tolerances to immigrants at 8.41 (out of a maximum of 9), second only to my home country, Canada, in the global rankings.[45]

But there is no cookie-cutter immigrant experience. For every woman like me who moves here with a built-in network of local in-laws and finds a job related to her education, there is another who is exploited, working for a pittance in unsafe conditions because she hasn't been made aware of her labor rights in this country. Asylum seekers arrive with few possessions, fleeing persecution and seeking peace and stability. There are women who live here for decades and speak the language flawlessly, and others who spend mere months or years on the island, cheerfully existing in a social bubble with other immigrants

---

* Polish citizens comprised 5.4 percent of Iceland's total population in 2020.

and rarely interacting with the locally born population. Some become lonely living in small, seemingly homogenous communities. Others make their dreams come true with new opportunities and directions. To paint all immigrants with the same brush, assigning them the same challenges and ambitions, benefits no one.

Yet women of foreign origin in Iceland undoubtedly face unique tests that those whose names end in -dóttir are less likely to encounter. We need to learn a new, arguably complicated, language. We do not have a built-in support network of childhood friends and our own families, nor do we always know where to look to seek support when we need it. We can face prejudice based on our countries of origin, our ethnicities, our accents, our religions. We are disproportionately represented at the capital's women's shelter and are less likely to be aware of the legal rights and protections available to us should we ever need them. Immigrant women in Iceland are more likely to be overqualified for the jobs they find than immigrant men and are more likely to work long shifts than locally born women.[46]

The #MeToo revolution reached Iceland too, and one of the most vocal groups were immigrants, who shocked native-born Icelanders with tales of sexual, physical, and psychological abuse that generated uncomfortable but necessary dialogue about how far we had yet to go to achieve gender equality.

While in Iceland, we are generally conscientious about considering gender parity for groups, companies, and media, we too often forget to factor ethnic diversity into the equation. We are reacting quickly to a tremendous increase in diversity. While most people see the positive side, many immigrant women, in particular, are left behind as our gender as a whole marches slowly but surely toward equality. How effectively we listen to the concerns of immigrant women will have an impact on our ultimate success.

The thirteen-hundred-kilometer (about eight-hundred-mile) Highway 1, Iceland's "Ring Road," circles the island. Fully paved only in 2019, numerous bridges on the road are still single lane. The Ring Road is popular with self-driving tourists who want to take a road trip with a view: black sand beaches and ocean on one side, glaciers, volcanoes, and mountainous interior on the other. Although the total driving time in good weather is only about eighteen hours, most give themselves at least a week to take in some of the sights.

About as far on the Ring Road as you can travel from Reykjavík, in the northeast of the country, is the turnoff to Road 85. A remote area removed from what is already the least travelled stretch of the Ring Road, this corner of the country has been least affected, for better and worse, by the tourism boom that began just after 2010.

Forty-five kilometers along Road 85 is the village of Vopnafjördur, population 659. The air here is the very definition of pristine. In winter, the northern lights dance brightly in the sky on cold, clear nights. In summer, whales frolic in the sea easily visible from the shore. Houses and cars are almost always kept unlocked. Hótel Tangi, one of the three restaurants in town (two of which shut down every winter), serves up a delicious "Vopna" burger and offers live music on occasion. By the Selá River, a ten-minute drive away, is one of the most exclusive lodges in the country, a hideaway for the world's rich and famous to escape for some solitude and wild salmon fishing (catch and release only). The local school, offering classes from Grade 1 to Grade 10, has seventy-eight students. In a good year, about nine children will start the first grade. At the time of writing, there were no children of the right age scheduled to enter their first year of school in September 2021.

Without extensive tourism to provide local income (aside from the foreign-owned and therefore controversial luxury fishing lodge), the community relies on a fish processing factory, fish catches, and the local farmers for its economy.

"You're at the end of the world here. You go out to sea and there's nothing else. The North Pole," Monserrat Arlette Moreno told me as she gestured out the large window of her farmhouse toward the slate-gray North Atlantic.

Arlette, as she is known, grew up in Mexico City. She has lived in eighteen different locations in Mexico and the United States, speaks Spanish and English fluently, and completed a certificate in business communication at Harvard. In the summer of 2020, she had been living for over a decade in Vopnafjördur, married to a local farmer whose family has been toiling this land for centuries. When I interviewed her, she was working at the community's home for the elderly and was active in the local women's association.

To be an immigrant in relatively cosmopolitan Reykjavík is a world of difference from the often overlooked many who live in the small communities that dot the country's coastline. In these more remote places, children run freely, the most hardened criminals are the teenagers breaking into the town pool after hours, and even those who grew up a mere fifty kilometers (about thirty miles) away are often considered outsiders. People from over twenty nationalities live in Vopnafjördur, and the foreign-born community, many of whom work jobs in fish processing, represent around one-quarter of the population. It is the influx of this foreign labor that has helped sustain the often-precarious economies of these towns, and their transformation to truly multicultural municipalities over roughly the past two decades is generally considered a positive development, though not without its challenges. These immigrants are frequently drawn to not only relatively well-paid jobs but also the clean and picturesque environment, the friendliness, safety, and accessibility within a village, and the social security net that the entire country provides.

I first met Arlette when she volunteered at the Iceland Writers Retreat in Reykjavík. She had secured funding from her local women's association to help her travel to the capital and stay at a hotel during the event. Warm and enthusiastic, Arlette is a natural people person, hardworking and welcoming. She even arrived with a handful of tourist brochures about the northeast of the country to share with our overseas attendees.

Yet when I visited her at the farm just outside Vopnafjördur one summer a couple of years later, she confessed to me, "Iceland has made me more introverted." She must have noticed I was surprised by this. "During many days since I've moved here," she explained, "I don't have any conversation with people other than my husband and my son." She sipped her tea. "At first that was difficult, and now it's habit."

Arlette falls into the category of individuals who moved to this country for love. She met her husband online.

"I knew nothing about Iceland except that it was far away," she told me. "So I thought we'll never actually meet each other, just be friends online.

"I had once told him I lived in a small town in Mexico, of about eight hundred thousand people," she continued, a fond smile on her face at the recollection. "And he said casually, 'Oh, here it's a little bit smaller.' When I first visited him, he suggested we go 'downtown' for the evening, so I got all dressed up. When we arrived, he told me that this was it, and I thought he was joking and started laughing. There is no bar, no disco, no movie theater."

Looking on the bright side, she quickly added, "But it's only a two-and-a-half-hour drive to Akureyri." (Akureyri, the largest community in the northern part of the country, has a population of around nineteen thousand.)

When deciding whether to make the leap of moving to a new country, most immigrants create some sort of metaphorical ledger, balancing anticipated sacrifices with expected returns. Arlette knew she was giving up professional opportunities and proximity to her family when she moved to Iceland. But she would be giving her daughter a chance to grow up in a clean, safe environment. "There are moments in life you have to choose between your children and your own ambitions," she admitted frankly.

It was a bittersweet but ultimately not difficult choice. Arlette made her move to Vopnafjördur in February, when the sun glances above the horizon for only seven hours a day. But she was welcomed into her new husband's family and spoken to only in Icelandic, which helped her pick up the language very quickly.

"I was invited to annual parties and [the pagan-inspired festival] *thorrablót*. My mother-in-law taught me how to make lamb soup, fish soup, Icelandic doughnuts," she recalled. "When my colleagues speak of foreigners in town, they aren't including me in that group, because I have this connection to a local family. If I had moved here and was married to another immigrant, I would not have been accepted in the same way."

Vopnafjördur may be one of the most isolated communities in the country, but it is located in a picturesque setting by the water. Arlette said there are about three extended families who live here with their children and their grandchildren, and they are the backbone of the community now.

"It's beautiful. It's safe. The air is clean. You get a good education," she said, and all those advantages made it worth sacrificing the benefits of life in a large city. "Especially for me. I haven't seen my family in Mexico in eleven years because it's so dangerous there." (She has seen them in the United States, though.) "For my children, it's been good growing up here." Arlette's husband works long hours every day of the year on the farm, but she said this is preferable to a career where many days in a row are spent away at sea.

"It's a very nice country. A very nice place to live. It's safe. But you have to be sure," she emphasized. "If you visit, it's going to be very beautiful, but if you are going to live here, you have to be sure that Icelandic people are ready to receive foreigners."

There is in theory a tolerant attitude toward newcomers, a curiosity about other cultures and traditions, and an appreciation for an immigrant's willingness to contribute to the economy. Even so, Arlette experienced many challenges, some of which one might encounter anywhere and others unique to living in a remote location.

Arlette suffered from postpartum depression after the birth of her son in 2010. She was given medication for depression, but it was only after six years of increasingly severe symptoms that a doctor in Akureyri took a blood test and diagnosed a thyroid disorder rather than a mental health condition.

Although Arlette's difficulties ended up being physical rather than mental, she asserted that "if you want to move to a remote place, you really have to take care of your mental health. I have talked to foreign women a lot here, and I would guess that about 70 or 75 percent take medicine for depression that they were not on before moving here." She is writing a book for immigrants on how to maintain strong mental health.

Arlette began working full-time soon after she moved to Vopnafjördur. A local woman noticed that she seemed isolated and offered her a job as an assistant to organize a festival for immigrants that was sponsored by the Red Cross. She taught Zumba for adults and dancing classes for children and then worked as a substitute English teacher at the local elementary school. She was never offered an opportunity to teach permanently, however, despite having a teaching qualification from the United States.*

"The principal was hiring young people with less education to teach," she told me. "I asked him why, and it turns out he had never read my CV where it detailed my experience." She now works as a home caregiver at the local nursing home and enjoys the personal contact and work.

Arlette added that she had been subjected to some stereotypes about immigrants. "People are so surprised that I am educated. They think we are just looking for jobs to clean…and those are the jobs that we get." Arlette also believed that nepotism was responsible for many of the most desirable positions going to the friends and relatives of local families.

During my conversation with Arlette, she appeared frequently torn between the undeniable difficulties of being Mexican in an extremely remote Icelandic village and her clear affection for the people and place to which she continued to adapt. "My life is finally good here. I don't have big problems. Every time I watch the news, the world is getting crazy. I think I made the right decision when I moved here. I feel blessed for many things."

But her pragmatism won her internal battle of minds. "It works in some ways, for some time, but not for the rest of my life."

Just two weeks after I spoke with Arlette in Vopnafjördur, the metaphorical balance sheet of her life shifted. Her daughter was now in university in the capital, and her ten-year-old son was becoming more independent, while her own professional and social opportunities stagnated. For the nineteenth time, Arlette moved, this time to Reykjavík

---

* Having a qualification from abroad does not guarantee relevant employment anywhere in the country unless it has been officially certified as of equivalent value to locally granted qualifications.

with her son, where she was closer to her daughter. Her husband remained on his family farm.

When Claudia Ashanie Wilson moved to Iceland from Jamaica in 2001, fewer than 6 percent of the resident population was born outside the country, and only a small number of them were visible minorities, like she was.

"People always wanted to tell me the story about the first time they met a Black person," she recalled. "They were trying to imply they were so cosmopolitan that they had met a Black person before me!"

Claudia was still a teenager when she moved to this country. The trip to the north was the first time she had stepped aboard an airplane. She grew up near Montego Bay, in a large extended family of her mother, siblings, grandparents, and various cousins who moved in and out "depending on the circumstances."

Despite the loving family who emphasized education over almost all else, "there was always a notion that life is better elsewhere," Claudia told me over a Senegalese dinner in Reykjavík (we immigrants like to support other immigrant enterprises).

Between mouthfuls of spicy jollof rice, Claudia told me that her first days in the brand-new country are still "crystal clear" in her mind. One that stands out in particular is her first Sunday in Iceland.

"I remember thinking it was weird that I was here in Iceland. I remember what I was wearing and what my bedroom was like and the pattern of the bedsheets on the bed. And I felt strongly that I would have a purpose here. I didn't know what it was at the time, but I trusted that one day I would find out."

The adolescent was at first hesitant to identify certain interactions with locals as racism. "I had to gain an understanding of my surroundings," she told me. "The more I saw, the more I started to question things."

For example, when she was a student completing courses at the local college, fellow classmates asked not to work with Claudia on a group project, even though she had been valedictorian of her class in Jamaica. "They said they were concerned my level of Icelandic could affect their work," she told me. In another course, Claudia was paired for a geography assignment with a slightly older student, a large, muscular man with many tattoos who perhaps also didn't conform to the norms of the college participants. It turns out he was an inmate from the nearby prison who was finally completing his college diploma. "We were actually the only two who did so well we did not need to take the final test," Claudia recalled with some fondness. "That emboldened me.

"Obviously, I've had encounters with people who are racist," Claudia admitted. "People did things that they didn't even realize were offensive, like ask to touch my skin or my hair. Clerks followed me around in stores, monitoring my every move." Given the opportunity, she said she would have focused more on cultural sensitivity to make people aware of the effect on her and others of these all too commonplace indignities, "but I was just a young girl living my life."

It is this intersectionality of race and gender that is of great professional and personal interest to Claudia today. After that experience in her first years in the country, she continued her studies. Many people don't have lofty expectations for immigrants, especially those from countries where simply the move to Iceland is considered to have been enough of an "achievement." But Claudia knew there was something else in store for her. She persisted and eventually became the first foreign-born woman to pass the bar exam in Iceland, a feat worthy of extra commendation because of the challenge of taking the exam in Icelandic.

Since qualifying as a practicing attorney in 2016, with an emphasis on human rights law, Claudia has acquired increasing national attention, from a fiery speech delivered to the crowd at the 2018 Women's Day Off (since the original 1975 success, these events have been held regularly, each one beginning a little later in the day as the gender wage gap narrows) to her reputation as a strong advocate for asylum seekers, women, and other vulnerable groups trying to navigate Iceland's bureaucratic system.

"I want to use my voice to raise attention to the issue of representation in different spheres of society. We cannot rely on just looking to gender equality on the basis of man and woman. For me, it's about including immigrant women in that conversation. If we ignore the fact that your immigrant status can also make you vulnerable, then we are creating problems and ignoring problems that may have simple solutions," she explained to me.

One of those challenges is the idea of being "othered." Claudia's now teenage twin boys are mixed race and regularly asked where they come from, although they were born in Reykjavík and Icelandic is their first language. Claudia herself also struggles with her desire to serve as a role model for women, for immigrants, for people of color, while also seeking to avoid becoming the "token" visible minority in public discussions that seek to pay lip service to diversity.

But in the end, it all comes down to helping people. "I have tried to figure out what I could bring to the table, not because I'm Black but because I have a different life experience. I think my only limitation is me. And no one can limit me, ever, unless I let them."

→»

I first met Rose in 2005.* In those days, it seemed that the same group of relatively recent immigrants to Iceland kept running into one another, our limited social circles overlapping. Many of my good friends were fellow newcomers to the island; we spoke English together and commiserated about both the good and the bad of our new lives in the country.

Rose and I were not close, but we had many mutual friends. We were both in our twenties, outgoing, and social. We had similar middle-class backgrounds, and I enjoyed speaking with her about England, her home country and the place where I had most recently lived. Although she had initially moved to Iceland for a year abroad as part of her university studies in anthropology, she soon settled down with an Icelandic man and had two sons with him. As a childless young woman myself, I admired her ability to raise two toddlers, work in an interesting job, and be an entertaining and lively companion when groups of us immigrants were out on the town. Rose was not one of the new arrivals who used every opportunity to complain about how Iceland was different from her home country, how the weather was bad, the selection of fresh produce abysmal, or the language too challenging to learn. She brought vigor and positivity to discussions—attitudes that are invaluable to surround oneself with during the sensitive early months and years of moving to a new and relatively isolated country.

After I began having children of my own and founded the Iceland Writers Retreat, I socialized less with this group of people I first knew in my adopted home. I lost touch with Rose. It was only in 2017 that her name appeared to me again, this time in a much different context. In a closed #MeToo-themed Facebook group for women of foreign

---

* Rose is a pseudonym.

origin in Iceland, Rose had published an articulate, impassioned plea to inspire women in abusive situations to find the courage to leave their abusers.

"Leaving is not easy," she wrote. "In fact, it is the second most difficult thing I have ever done in my life. The only thing more difficult was trying to stay in an abusive relationship."*

I was shocked. In her post, Rose referred to more than a decade of psychological abuse in her relationship, a situation that ended only after she called the women's shelter and took her children there for what ended up being a three-month stay. If her post was anything to go by, the always happy, fun-loving, energetic woman I knew at parties had been returning home to fear and trauma. My instinctive reaction was a cliché: I had no idea, and it can happen to anyone.

Domestic abuse can and does happen to anyone, irrespective of education, background, neighborhood, class. In Iceland, the country that is regularly dubbed the best place in the world to be a woman, half of the women murdered are killed by a male partner (that figure is 38 percent globally).[47] The nation has ratified the Istanbul Convention, which is designed to fight violence against women, yet reports of gender-based violence continue. While these statistics can be spun to argue that Iceland's women feel more comfortable reporting gender-based violence or that the country's legal definitions of domestic violence and assault are broader (there is a legal definition of psychological abuse, but it is not considered a valid reason for issuing injunctions in accusations of domestic abuse or in custody cases), the increasing reports of domestic violence remain a black spot in a nation that prides itself on gender equality.

Further, these increased incidences of gender-based violence

---

* This quote is reproduced with Rose's permission.

reporting do not result in a greater number of convictions. Only 11 percent of rape charges resulted in convictions in a 2008–2009 study (the newest figures available).[48] Sadly, this figure is high compared with other countries.[†]

Foreign-born women in Iceland are affected disproportionately by domestic violence. In 2020, 65 percent of the residents of the women's shelter were of foreign origin, a statistic that is also indicative of the limited support network such women have in Iceland. They also make up the large majority of those who eventually return to their abusers.

"As a woman in a foreign country, you are automatically disempowered," Rose told me when recalling her own ordeal. Foreign-born women don't generally have extended family and friends to whom they can turn—especially when escaping an Icelandic partner. Nor do they necessarily understand their legal rights and where to go when they do need help. Both of these factors can make foreign-born women targets of abusive men who may seek victims that do not know their rights or are otherwise easily exploited.

"I thought there was no direction I could turn," Rose said of her own situation.

In the years since she stayed at the women's shelter, Rose has been outspoken about women's rights in situations such as hers. Although she acknowledges broad societal trust in the police and individuals

---

† In early 2021, it was announced that a group of nine women, fed up with these dismal statistics concerning the perpetrators of sexual and domestic violence failing to be held accountable for their crimes, had taken the unprecedented step of taking their cases to the European Court of Human Rights. Supported by the Education and Counseling Center for Survivors of Sexual Abuse and Violence, the women claimed that the Icelandic state had failed to protect their human rights through their dealings with the police and that the accusations they made against their alleged abusers were not thoroughly examined or prosecuted. Organizers said the intention of the action was to draw attention to a systematic problem and have the Icelandic state answer for it in the international arena.

within the system who want to do the right thing, she feels, ironically, that it is Iceland's dedication to equality that has failed her.

"It was as if the equality pendulum swung away from logic," she told me. "During this time, I felt that the principle of equality was working against me."

After taking the giant step of packing a few belongings and moving to the women's shelter with her children, Rose began the process of legally separating from her partner. Then she tried to have her ex-partner expelled from the family home so she could return there to live with their two children.

"But the law said that he had an equal right to live there," she said. "When I called the police to ask how I could return with the children, they basically told me that if I went back and he hit me, then they could remove him, but otherwise, their hands were tied. Even our children's rights to live in their own home didn't trump his right to stay there."

The very system that is built, understandably, on equality as a guiding principle could fail women in situations like Rose's. According to her, the point is not to treat men unfairly but to prevent victims of violence and their children from becoming pawns in the system, as can happen if abusers launch numerous, costly appeals. Proving psychological abuse, in particular, can be overwhelmingly difficult.

In the end, Rose visited the police station in person and spoke with a female police officer who was sympathetic. "The officer just said, 'I have had enough of this shit. Give me until the end of the day,'" Rose recalled. "She went to the house and said something to him she maybe shouldn't have, and he was gone within twenty-four hours."

Rose's troubles did not end after selling the house and splitting the money. Rose was sent a large bill for outstanding taxes and was told that her ex would not be liable for them because he had invested his savings in his private business, rendering them out of the reach of tax collectors. She couldn't leave the country with her children because by default, she and her ex-partner had joint custody unless she could prove he was not able to care for them by undertaking a costly court case. This is a huge problem for women of foreign origin: in its fight for equality, Iceland's justice system does not often award sole custody to one parent. Although she understands the reasoning behind this, Rose told me she believes such a practice effectively imprisons foreign-born mothers who have escaped domestic abuse for up to eighteen years in the country, effectively cutting off the option for them to return to their native country, where they may have more support.

"My Icelandic friends were shocked about how difficult the situation was," Rose said. "And when I spoke to individuals within the system, they all wanted to help me and were equally frustrated by the situation. But it was like the computer said no. In the end, I had to rely on the shelter and a gutsy policewoman."

Rose had only good things to say about that women's shelter. "When a colleague first told me about it, I thought that it was not for me. I didn't want to waste their time," she said. But at her first meeting with the staff there, as she spilled out her story and her fears and her pain, the counsellor calmly asked her to "trust that your future self can deal with it."

Rose's experience in this realm was not entirely negative. There is also a general lack of stigma in Iceland when it comes to identifying as a survivor of domestic violence. "In the UK, I would probably have lost my job," Rose believed. "But my employer here gave me three months paid leave and helped with the costs of counselling and legal services."

Today, Rose has the same job that she loves, two happy teenage boys, and a new, loving partner. She remains active, however, in supporting other women, especially those of foreign origin, who have to navigate a daunting system and in calling out areas where she feels survivors of domestic violence are falling through the cracks of a system that should have been designed to protect them.

"Society has worked here because it's so small and almost everyone has a support network," she said. "So when you don't have that, it doesn't work."

I used to be regularly asked why my husband and I had chosen to make Iceland our joint home and not Canada. The answer, initially, was pragmatic: he had been missing enough of his daughter's childhood while he was studying in England (though he returned every summer to be with her). He would never continue that separation beyond what was necessary.

I was always a little surprised at the insecurity the question belied. Why *wouldn't* we want to make Iceland our home? It is safe, clean, open-minded, and socially responsible toward its citizens.

Achieving various unplanned milestones over months and years convinced me of the truth in a mantra I had used since moving here: I belonged. There was the first time I recognized someone as Gudni and I strolled down the street, and *I* had to introduce them to *Gudni* rather than the other way around. When I finally got a joke (in Icelandic) during the annual New Year's Eve satirical news roundup. Or the first of what would be many Björk sightings (the world-famous singer still lives in her hometown).

It took effort. Despite international work experience, a graduate degree from Oxford, and speaking English and French, when desperately seeking a job, I was turned down for interviews for global marketing roles for the sole reason (or so I was told) that my degree was not in marketing. I arrived at informal parties where the room fell silent as I, a stranger, entered and was greeted with stiff smiles and no words after introducing myself in faltering Icelandic. To this day, when Gudni and I host large receptions at the presidential residence, there is always at least one guest who speaks to me first in English and not Icelandic. (While their intentions may well be to put me at ease, this still belies assumptions they have made about my ability to speak Icelandic despite having lived here for almost two decades.)

I love living in Iceland, of course. I am grateful to have made it my home and the country where we are raising our family. Arlette, Claudia, and Rose have also built enriching, rewarding lives for themselves here.

Thirty years ago, women like us were not so commonplace in the capital and elsewhere. If asked, a majority of people in Iceland will say this is a positive development. I certainly do. But for us immigrants to make the most of our lives here and for our society to do its best by us, to the benefit of everyone in the country, we need to be aware of the challenges that women of foreign origin face. Challenges such as living in isolated locations without built-in support networks, tackling prejudice, and being aware of our rights to fair treatment in the eyes of the law. We are rightly proud of our approach to gender equality in Iceland. But one of the largest impediments to achieving it is by overlooking—I optimistically believe more by omission than design—to treat "those people," like me, Arlette, Claudia, and Rose, equally. Not just in policy but in practice. We should accord all our fellow humans respect and kindness, but it's important to make an extra effort when choosing whom to hire for a job or interview for a story or when making predetermined assumptions about our motivations, abilities, or experience— these moments make a big difference. Until we achieve this consistency, true gender equality will remain out of reach.

THE SPRAKKI WHO SHATTERED THE GLASS CEILING

AFTER THE STUNNING EFFECTIVENESS OF their national day off five years earlier, those behind Iceland's women's movement decided that society was ready for a female political leader. Fifty-year-old teacher and theater director Vigdís Finnbogadóttir was one of the country's most visible people who came to mind. She was highly educated, well versed in multiple languages, and as a theater director had plenty of experience dealing with the media.

After a few months of campaigning, Vigdís beat the (then) largest field of candidates for a presidential election and by the slimmest of margins—a mere 1.5 percent—becoming Iceland's fourth president. She was the world's first democratically elected female head of state, and she would hold the office for sixteen years, still the longest term for any elected female head of state.

Though rightly cited as a pivotal moment in Iceland's history, Vigdís's election was far from a foregone conclusion. As the campaign got underway, Vigdís faced increased scrutiny in an otherwise male field, despite the fact that Icelandic presidential campaigns are generally not vitriolic affairs. Her professional background and qualifications were not in doubt. Even the fact that she was a divorced, single mother of an adopted daughter did not incite the same level of gender-based patronizing criticism that it would no doubt have in other countries.

She was also a breast cancer survivor, cured after a mastectomy. She was asked if she thought it would be a disadvantage as president that she had only one breast. She would not be breastfeeding the nation as president, a confident Vigdís responded. There were other patriarchal concerns, letters to the editor, or earnest queries at campaign events.

Vigdís's election at the end of June 1980 made headlines around the world and catapulted Iceland onto the global stage. She had broken one glass ceiling, but the experience was only just beginning. At her inauguration on August 1 that year, she was one of only five women of the hundred or so people in attendance. When she took office, there were only three other female heads of state in the world, all of them unelected queens. (When she left office sixteen years later, that number had only increased by two.)

Vigdís was known as a warm and culturally minded president, one who maintained her neutrality in politics and acted as a unifying figure more than one with a dogma to promote.

But it was of course the fact of her gender, the fact that she was the first (and in Iceland, to date the only) woman in the role that has made her a role model to so many. When questioned about their role models, few Icelandic women who came of age in the 1980s and 1990s will neglect to name Vigdís. Female politicians who entered the public sphere after her tenure credit her election as a pivotal moment. She is a woman who led in a man's world and did so with aplomb, dignity, humor, intelligence, and warmth. To this day, Vigdís as a person and a president is almost beyond reproach in Icelandic discourse.

There are variations on the tale of young people who grew up with Vigdís as president, those children who are now adults, with their own families, who are running companies, sitting in parliament, teaching the youngest generation. They grew up thinking nothing was amiss about a divorced single mother as their head of state. And as the story goes, sometimes they would enquire innocently to their teachers or elders, "Can boys be presidents too?"[49]

10

POLITICS ON HER OWN TERMS

"I dare, I can, I will"

THE MOTTO OF THE PROTESTORS in the 1975 women's day off was *"Ég thori, get og vil"*: I dare, I can, I will. The number of Icelandic women who "dare" to seek elected office has increased since then, many of them of a generation that came of age during the sixteen-year period when Iceland had a female president. In 1982, emboldened by Vigdís's election, a group of women formed a Women's List party, a phenomenon unique in the Nordic countries and possibly the world. They ran candidates in municipal elections, advancing to the national stage the following year. Their efforts led to female representation in the Althing tripling from 5 percent to 15 percent in that 1983 election alone and influenced all major parties to increase the number of women on their tickets. By the time of the short-lived session of 2016–2017, Iceland in fact had the highest percentage of female members of parliament of any non-quota-regulated parliament in the world at 47.6 percent.[50]

Women are not merely prominent in national politics. At a municipal level, where individual appeal often counts for more than party platforms, role models are equally important, and sometimes, it takes those with experience in tapping at the glass ceiling to topple the status quo. Yet even well into the twenty-first century, success can require the same steely determination as the protestors of almost half a century ago. A recent scandal involving numerous parliamentarians, alcohol, misogyny, and a midrange Samsung sparked both outrage and cynical resignation about how far—or not—we had progressed as a tolerant society.

Student activism, especially at the University of Iceland, the country's largest and oldest such institution, is another popular stepping-stone for young women keen to dip their toes in the political waters of campaigning and network building. Women make up the majority of postsecondary students in Iceland and consequently a majority of its student governing body, some of whom garner national attention for their work. Yet despite this popular path to the national stage, women's political dominance at the university level does not translate to proportionally as many seats in the Althing. In 2020, the newly elected head of the University of Iceland's students' council broke barriers not for her gender but because she is the first individual of foreign origin in the role, and despite positive attention for the achievement, she too initially grappled with the all too recognizable sentiment that she wasn't convinced she was qualified enough to seek elected office.

As an immigrant myself, I can relate. I am actually the third Icelandic First Lady who was born and raised abroad. Since I never had to run for this unofficial position, my perspective as a woman in a somewhat political sphere is different from those of elected officials and those who have seen their names on a ballot, yet I have also taken on a role that carries with it certain assumptions, and I am working hard to try to make an old-fashioned title fit a modern country. We can all be role models. It's up to us whether our words and deeds are affirming and inclusive or insipid and cynically reinforcing an outdated norm.

"Now I need to wash my hair every day and look presentable," I lamented in my diary when my husband's presidential campaign kicked off in earnest in the spring of 2016. The curve from anonymous journalist to arguably the most famous immigrant in the country was steep and rapid. It did not take much grumbling to change my morning routine, and I was already adept at delivering speeches—albeit fewer off-the-cuff ones and certainly fewer in Icelandic—but my sartorial IQ was abysmally low.

I spent much of the campaign and the months that followed Gudni's inauguration fielding well-meaning advice and queries from numerous corners, almost all of which centered on traditional assumptions of where a dutiful First Lady ought to focus her attentions. I should choose some issues to support. I should have some easy, go-to outfits for such unofficial yet public tasks as dropping off the children at preschool. Would I hire an interior designer—at my own expense—to decide where all our furniture would be placed when we moved to the official residence and to generate a wish list of new furnishings now that our accommodation at Bessastadir would be significantly larger than our own home closer to the center of town?

On the day of Gudni's inauguration, it took a team of three at least half an hour to foist a *skautbúningur,* the most formal of traditional women's costumes in Iceland, over and around me. They fixed the elaborate headpiece in place using dozens of bobby pins, and I practiced sitting in a very upright position so the whole contraption would not knock me off balance and topple me over. Meanwhile, my husband donned his white tie and chain of office in a few minutes.

The final touches were the "orders." Without ceremony, someone from the office of the president (I assume, though I can't recall) handed each of us a velvet-lined box containing a large, star-shaped silver pin. The Order of the Falcon is the highest honor that can be granted an Icelandic citizen (or foreign citizen who has done much for the Icelandic nation). Twice a year, we host solemn ceremonies at Bessastadir at which active members of the community are presented with this award.

Recipients are individuals from all parts of the country and all walks of life who have demonstrated exceptional service in either their occupation or voluntary work. It's a touching service and visibly moving for many.

Duly, then, the Order of the Falcon was pinned to the chest of the incoming president of the republic, in advance of the good works on which he was about to embark in service of the nation. And one was pinned to mine, because I was his wife.

There is no handbook on how to be the spouse of a head of state. I have yet to see any sort of protocol guidelines or rule book on how I should behave, what I can and cannot take part in, whether I have any formal obligations (when we went on our first state visit, to Denmark, I googled how to curtsey). I am grateful that my father insisted I learn how to hold my cutlery properly, "because you never know when you'll dine next to kings and queens."

It is a tremendous honor to have the opportunity to serve in this capacity, one that I never imagined I would have. Yet being awarded the Order of the Falcon on that first day of Gudni's first term, simply for being a spouse, took with it certain assumptions about what a (usually) female partner of a head of state should do and say and how she should behave.

It was by no means prevalent, especially within Iceland, but there were undercurrents of small, persistent expectations that I play the role of genteel sidekick. We would arrive at a location, and the hosts spoke only to Gudni. Or he would show up to an event alone and be asked where I was, although nothing on the original invitation had mentioned me. On state visits, when partaking in what is usually known as "the spouse program," I was often invited to do something associated with traditionally female roles—visiting children or a healthcare facility or perhaps an art gallery.

Although I was hyperaware of the irony that attention was now on me for something my *husband* had achieved, I decided to satisfy myself that the challenge was not feeling guilty about *how* I got my bully pulpit but rather what I would do now that I had the opportunity to use—or squander—it. The president of Iceland is not a political role on a day-to-day basis, despite his or her veto power over legislation and possible influence in coalition government negotiations. His or her spouse is certainly not expected to stray into the political sphere. But I was convinced that my public persona—really the same as my private one—must inevitably reflect my values. I would be nonpartisan, but I would have opinions.

Rather than resign myself to the fact that these somewhat antediluvian expectations also exist in Iceland, meant to be a leader in gender equality, I chose instead to think, *If there is anywhere from which to challenge these outdated, gender-based assumptions, Iceland is it.*

Gradually, as I found my footing in the role, I began to choose activities that would help to confound the image that people might have of a First Lady. First and foremost, I talked. As much as possible. If I was invited to present an award, for instance, I always asked to say a few words first. I accepted as many invitations as I could to deliver opening remarks or other speeches at conferences, awards ceremonies, anniversaries. Not only did I try to project the image that women have voices to use but also that women with accents when they speak in Icelandic have voices to be heard too. I shared images of me standing in front of groups on social media, not merely smiling next to my husband. When we went on trips abroad, I asked that I have an opportunity to deliver my own speeches, if it was appropriate, or if that was not feasible that my visits did something that did not usually coincide with traditional perceptions. Consequently, I have visited, for example, start-ups and business incubators. More often than not, though, I simply don't travel with Gudni, with the exception of state visits or a trip where I feel like I can make a contribution other than that of arm candy.

Late in 2019, after seeing an image on Instagram that reduced spouses of G7 leaders to some sort of policy muses for their husbands, I was compelled to write a Facebook post about how offensive it was to dismiss these women as mere props for their spouses. They were no doubt more than this, I argued, as was I. "I am not my husband's handbag, to be snatched as he runs out the door and displayed silently by his side during public appearances," I wrote. The metaphor was clunky, but it caught on. I wrote an opinion piece for the *New York Times*, amplifying my message further.

True to the stereotype of my gender, the evening before the *NYT* story was scheduled to run, I was filled with unease. I had not told anyone in the president's office about the piece nor asked any permission about what a First Lady should or should not publish while her husband was in office. (The office helps me coordinate official events, but I work from my home, write my own speeches, and rely largely on intuition and the counsel of Gudni and close friends for what best to take part in.) What if I came across as spoiled, entitled, ungrateful? What if other First Ladies read the story and thought I was mocking them for criticizing some of their recent activities? Was I just asking the world of misogynistic internet trolls to have a go at me?

Reaction was overwhelmingly positive. All major Icelandic media outlets picked up the story, and "I'm not my husband's handbag" became a calling card of sorts for me—a meme of confident independence for my supporters and in a mocking way for my detractors. It seems a great many women, those married to diplomats or surgeons or ministers or politicians and many more, are very tired of being identified primarily as their husband's spouse, regardless of how proud they are of his achievements. Far from seeming out of touch and spoiled, what I wrote had struck a chord, and I heard from many people who were grateful that I had expressed the sentiment.

A few months later, I delivered a TEDx Talk on the same idea. And I could now show with my actions that I meant to speak up for gender equality and women's empowerment, that it was not merely a pet topic to keep me occupied as the president's wife.

In the international arena, I knew that this could have a positive impact too. If Iceland's First Lady speaks up for these issues and a majority of the population supports this, then Iceland must have a progressive approach to gender empowerment.

The opportunity to challenge preconceived gender roles has been one of my most rewarding experiences to date of being First Lady, and I believe that a majority of those in Icelandic society support what I am trying to do (there are no polls either way to indicate anything scientifically). I have an advantage, however, in that I am not linked with a political party and am only building on the reputation of previous First Ladies in Iceland, which have all generally been positive. Many women in this country, and others, who choose to step into the political spotlight plant themselves fearlessly in the firing line. In doing so, they make the path a little smoother for those who follow in their wake.

In a 2018 municipal race, one such woman garnered more national attention than she had anticipated and reshaped expectations within her community of what a mayor should look like.

"Local politics is so much more personal than national politics," Íris Róbertsdóttir, the first female mayor of the Westman Islands, told me at the outset of our conversation about her experience in upsetting the traditional balance of power in her community's governance.

"What is special about politics in Iceland is that you don't need to be rich to be successful," she said. "You have to work and fundraise and develop your network, especially if you want to go far, but Iceland is a land of opportunity, because we can do what we want."

The Westman Islands are a small archipelago situated just off the south coast of Iceland. The teardrop-shaped Heimaey ("Home Island") is home to all 4,370 Westman Islanders, most of whom work today in the tourism or fishing industries. Although only just over a mere four nautical miles from the "mainland," until 2010, Heimaey was reachable only via an expensive and weather-dependent propeller flight or a generally queasy, three-hour ferry journey in the North Atlantic. Even today, the smoother forty-five-minute ferry trip from a new but shallower harbor can often, especially in winter, be rescheduled into the three-hour (or more) trip when the seas command it.

Tiny Heimaey has been inhabited since the settlement of Iceland over one thousand years ago, and its residents have developed a reputation for directness, assuredness, and heartiness. Isolated from other Icelanders, they had to rely mostly on their own resources to survive.

Íris was just one year old when, in the early hours of January 23, 1973, the residents of Heimaey experienced a catastrophe. Those still awake were astonished when, without warning, a fissure opened in the ground near the old part of the town, spewing ash and lava high into the sky. Within minutes, the tiny community sprang into action. As sirens sounded throughout the night, residents hastily grabbed what little they could and made their way down to the harbor, where, by providence or luck, bad weather the night before had kept most of the fishing fleet in harbor. With little more than the clothes on their backs, in a mere six hours, fifty-three hundred people filled fishing boats large and small and headed in shock to the mainland. When they were finally able to return six months later, the community they knew had been profoundly changed. Of 1,350 homes, over 400 were submerged in lava, and another 400 were damaged or destroyed by ash.

Íris's mother was seven months pregnant. "My mother took me to the boat with just a bottle for milk and some extra diapers," she told me over coffee at a harbor restaurant next to her office in the town hall. "She thought we'd be circling a few hours around the harbor and then return." When they finally did later that summer, her family was one of only about two-thirds of the original population who decided to continue on at Heimaey. Her new sister, Hrönn, was the first baby to be baptized on the island after the eruption.

"I literally grew up in the shadow of a volcano," Íris stated. "I could see it from my bedroom window. When I first returned, I had nightmares that there would be another eruption."

Íris is of the generation of Icelandic women who came of age in the era of a female head of state. "Vigdís held the highest office in the land, which showed us that women could do everything," she told me. "There was also something charming about the fact that she was unmarried, alone. That was even more symbolic."

Long after its magma began cooling into jagged rocks on the island, the '73 eruption continued to shape the character of the people and therefore politics too. "When you enter politics here, a huge advantage is that you just know there are people who will help you along the way, just like we all stood together back then," Íris said. "What is special here is that we can be really cruel and blunt, really let ourselves be heard. But when there's a shock, in work or play, and when something goes well for us, like we win a sporting trophy, then this compassion and solidarity take over. We take it on together and get through it together. This is so important."

Íris was always drawn to politics. At age sixteen, she joined the Independence Party—by far the most popular party on the islands and one of Iceland's oldest overall. She would not run for office until she was in her late thirties, first on the national stage, where she represented the Southern Constituency for the Independence Party as a deputy member of parliament. Yet she became better known nationally during the 2018 municipal elections, when she broke from her beloved party to form a new one that unexpectedly prevailed at the polls, leaving Íris the first female mayor of her hometown.

"I won't say that it was all bad, because it wasn't," Íris insisted of the former Independence Party governing coalition that had been led by the same mayor for over a decade. "But you just need to change perspectives sometimes." With the exception of a four-year period at the beginning of this century, the Independence Party has controlled the majority of seats on the Westman Islands' town council since 1990, and it was the dominant political force in the decades before that. Unlike in national politics, however, where all a constituency's party members usually vote for the order of a list in the party primary, in the Westman Islands, a small committee determines the order of the list for the party.*

"I found out that you made the top spots on the list if you were one of a sort of clique, not necessarily because you were the best candidate," she told me.

But to Íris and her supporters, the status quo was no longer an option. She formed her own party list to compete against the Independence Party at the spring election.

"It wasn't that things were awful here, they weren't at all, but people

---

* Incidentally, this electoral system makes it arguably easier to achieve gender parity. For many individuals in the top tier of seats for a party, the real electoral battle happens in a party's primary months before a general election, and most, but not all, of the major parties have policies that require gender balance among the top names on party lists, which is then reflected in parliament after a general election.

wanted to have a choice. I had to leave my party. I still support it nationally. So do a lot of people who work with me now. But here in the
Westman Islands, people had had enough and wanted a change."

Icelandic political campaigns are not showy affairs. There are many
photo ops with babies, many handshakes, varying degrees of vitriol on
social media. But campaign placards and posters stuck in the front yard
are a rarity. Negative ads serve mostly to galvanize those who favor the
attacking candidate's policies to begin with but are seen with scorn by
the mainstream.

In a country with such a small population, the key to success in
any campaign is personal contact. Candidates pick up the phone, go to
workplaces, stop by nursing homes, walk in the neighborhoods (though
never "cold call" by knocking on doors). A firm handshake and direct
eye contact can be the difference between a guaranteed vote and a lost
one.

"I went to the fish processing plants, onto the fishing vessels, all the
'male' working places," Íris told me. "I was CFO of a fisheries company,
I taught math, I ran the sporting association; these are topics the men
on the island are used to and could relate to."

Only one poll was conducted before the election, about four weeks
in advance, which showed some support for her "For Heimaey" list but
not enough to indicate a majority. On election day, Íris estimated the
turnout was about 90 percent.[†]

As a woman, Íris was used to breaking barriers. She was the first
woman to chair the Independence Party on the islands and the first to
chair the ÍBV sports club. And she is quick to emphasize that she has
not seen her gender as a hindrance.

"I don't agree that it's unpleasant to be a woman in politics. It's

---

[†] It was actually 83.2 percent, significantly higher than that year's national municipal election
average of 67.6 percent.

just a lot of work to be in politics, regardless of your gender. But there is something still underlying, maybe with women ourselves, that the challenge is too big, that we overplan, that we don't trust ourselves. A former politician gave me the wise advice that I should never arrive at a campaign event and begin by saying I'm a good choice because I'm a young woman. Everyone can already see that. I need to tell them what I'm going to do if elected."

When she campaigned in the primary for national politics in 2009, Íris's two children were three and thirteen years old. Her husband was often away at sea, which is the reality for many wives of the islands.

"Yes, I was asked how I could manage it all," she admitted to me. "But it was always other women who asked me. I never got that question from a man. I answered that I was used to my husband being away and to handling everything by myself, and that would not change. Over the years, it's been an advantage that people have sometimes underestimated me."

On election night, May 26, 2018, the For Heimaey supporters gathered at the community center to watch the returns arrive. The final tally was three seats to the For Heimaey list, tied with the Independence Party's three. The left-leaning list, with its single seat, would become kingmakers for any coalition. After four days of negotiations, they agreed to work with the For Heimaey party if Íris served as mayor. The rift that was created with the Independence Party stalwarts will likely take years to heal, though.

"It wasn't just me. There was an underlying unhappiness," said Íris. There are about four large extended families on Heimaey who still will have nothing to do with her or her party. "I didn't just end up having them leave their jobs," she acknowledged. "It was their livelihoods too." Just as in sports, though, there are winners and losers. "But there wasn't room for more than one approach then. And I think it was healthy for us to go through this change. No one should be mayor forever. Some people were saying that it would be too hard for me to do this. But then the competitor in me came out."

It is refreshing that Íris's achievements during that election were considered nationally newsworthy more for toppling a dynasty than for her lack of a Y chromosome. But she has still become a local role model for the youngest Westman Islanders, just like she had growing up in Vigdís. "When I first started meeting kids, they used to ask me where the mayor was," Íris recalled. "If you don't have something in front of your own eyes, it's more unrealistic. As soon as you see it, then it's real."

She can now also use her platform to build visibility from within. Traditionally, there have been more men on the town's council. It's a volunteer job, and men find more time to do it. But the council under Íris has a majority of women. "It makes a difference to bring women to the table at all levels, not just nationally," she said.

She sipped her latté, glancing out the window as a sightseeing boat prepared to leave the harbor for closer glimpses at the puffins lining the cliffs across the bay. "We are dealing with the same challenges here as elsewhere in the world, you know," she added, lest I paint too rosy a picture. "Women are more hesitant about participating. Women everywhere are second-guessing themselves. That is universal."

Íris had some suggestions for women seeking to get involved. "The first step is to go to political meetings, get to know the issues, and be a part of something. We don't tend to ask questions at big meetings because we're so scared of saying something wrong. There is so much interesting and fun about politics, but we women are often more sensitive than men about the negative things," she told me. "A goal for us politicians is to make politics more accessible, so you don't need to worry whether your kids are reading something about you online. You don't need to work away late into the night. And we all have to work together to change this.

"I think that most women want to have an impact in our near environments. We just need to expand [that range]," she contended. "Nothing happens if you're complaining around the kitchen table at home. We have to be the change, not just talk about it."

If sure-footed Íris Róbertsdóttir represents how far we have travelled when it comes to women climbing the rocky slopes of politics, Isabel Alejandra Díaz, president of the student council at the University of Iceland, is indicative of a younger generation of up-and-coming politicians who remain focused on all the work we have left to do and on how much of this work should be within the confines of traditional political structures.

I met Isabel one afternoon over lunch with her and four other employees of the student council's rights office in their on-campus headquarters, which was festooned with placards and posters on climate change, rainbow flags, and pamphlets on student services. She told me first about her formative years in the Westfjords, having moved there in 2001 from El Salvador with her grandparents, who raised her.

The most sparsely populated region of an already sparsely populated country, the Westfjords jut off the northwest corner of the island, a sort of three-fingered claw grasping for Greenland. A series of tunnels carved deep into the mountains, many only a single lane with pull-offs for two-way traffic, connects otherwise remote villages to one another. Yet the north and west parts of the region remain accessible to each other only some months of the year by a dirt road that zigzags precariously between mountainside and deep, Arctic blue fjord.

Ísafjörður (pop. 2,600), the region's largest community and

Isabel's hometown, is accessible from Reykjavík either by a six-hour drive snaking fjords and bisecting mountains, or by a half-hour flight, weather permitting and during daylight hours only. The airport's short, mountainside runway would no longer be approved if something similar were built today. It is not uncommon for visitors to enjoy an unplanned extended stay when the harsh winter weather is unwilling to cooperate with flight schedules or road conditions.

"It's a dream to grow up in Ísafjördur. You can get everything you need. We have a school, healthcare center, a bank, grocery stores, two bakeries, several restaurants, a small movie theater," Isabel told me proudly.

Isabel had not really thought about entering politics when she was younger, although she was active in music, sports, and school clubs, and there was always a certain level of civic engagement simmering within most of those around her. "I think we [residents] all feel this social responsibility that you should have opinions on things in society. In Ísafjördur, everyone has opinions on everything, from whether we should build a new sports hall to whether we should sell an elderly care home. And we believe you really are obliged to have these views, because we are building this society together."

In 2017, Isabel left Ísafjördur to head to the capital and to university. With this strong sense of duty to be involved in her community, Isabel thrived at university and soon became interested in extracurricular life at the school. Members of Röskva, one of two university-based political parties, got in touch with her after reading some articles she had published, and she turned her energies to student governance more broadly.

Although she was already sharpening her political chops with an elected position on the University Council, Isabel was initially reluctant to run for head of the student council after her final year of studies in political science and Spanish (recently graduated students may also serve on this council). She wanted to focus on academics in the end rather than a campaign. And she was unsure of herself and why people would want to vote for her.

"That is just normal for women," she admitted. "We ask ourselves these questions. What reason do I have to be here? What do I have to offer? Men don't even consider that. They just say they are going to do something and go for it. We're always looking to check all the boxes first." Yet Isabel did check a lot of boxes, having already served two years on the Röskva board, producing a podcast for the group with over twenty episodes, and sitting on the affairs committee that dealt with everything from housing challenges to mental health services on campus.

"I found myself blossoming somehow," she remarked, seemingly still a little surprised by her own success at canvassing for votes. "I was really scared I would lose the election, but I did it, and afterward, I wondered why I had so little confidence in myself."

In the campaign, Isabel had to contact every Röskva member and put forward her case for why she should be elected. "You have to follow your own integrity and instinct and just do it. What's the worst that can happen? You don't get elected. I think having confidence helps you tremendously. If you're calling to promote yourself, you can't say 'I *think* I'd be good.'" She made a shy face but looked me in the eye. "You say, 'I *will* be good because I'm approachable, straight talking, objective, and hardworking.' You don't need to worry about what others think."

The group of five student leaders I met with that spring day readily acknowledged they exist in their own bubble. They are privileged young adults who know the importance of casting their ballots, of speaking up, of pushing against what they view as injustice. Some have heavy student loan debt, which is compounded here by inflation-indexed interest but in real terms significantly lower than what it can be in other countries.

Their energy and vacillation between optimism and pessimism (with an eventual settlement on the former) reminds me of my days in student government at the University of Toronto almost a quarter century ago.

Yet the "average" student life here in Reykjavík is much different from my experience. I spent four years living in a student residence, sharing a bathroom with others on my floor, waiting my turn for the laundry room in the basement, scrounging for abandoned milk crates outside the local Loblaws to use as my bookshelves and liquor cabinet. Mikael Berg Steingrímsson and Gudný Ljósbrá Hreinsdóttir, two of the other students at the lunch, live at their parents' houses in converted basement flats and commute to work each day from the suburbs in their own cars. The very limited and highly prized student housing at the university is composed of single apartments with their own bathrooms and kitchens. They are reserved for students who come from outside the capital region, such as Isabel, or perhaps have a young family of their own (the on-site preschool accepts toddlers as young as six months old, instead of the usual one or two years for most preschools in Reykjavík).

But as in all Nordic countries, in Iceland, education is seen as a right. Anyone who has earned a secondary school diploma can register to take courses at the University of Iceland (though some subjects, such as medicine, require further entrance limitations). There is no tuition aside from an annual 75,000 krónur (about U.S. $550) administration fee, and the amount of this fee is the subject of relentless discussion, often led by the student council representatives, including those with whom I spoke.

Pundits who follow student politics think Isabel could have a future in a more diverse Althing, a path several of her predecessors in Röskva have taken. But she has not expressed any public interest in running for further office. "I am of the belief that all we deal with in our society is po-litical, and that's why it's important to have an opinion, to use your vote, because we all have something to say," Isabel explained. "Sometimes students don't have this approach, and then something touches them or one of their friends, and they realize that student government can make a difference. In the end, everything is political."

The challenge for Iceland's idealistic, educated, woke youth, though, is that the best answers to the world's problems may not even lie with traditional party politics. A majority of those in the student council office that day were initially reluctant about running under a party label even at the university level, lest it pigeonhole them into a rigid party ideology, a longer commitment than any were willing to make.

They are, it seems, seeking other ways to exert their influence. "Young people now are maybe putting together a society or activism around an issue that they think is important, independent of what parliament is doing," asserted Helga Lind Mar, managing director of the council and one of the organizers of the country's popular annual Slut Walk. "They think the Althing is an institution where they can't have an impact. And there is so little taught about democracy in the schools that people don't really even know how to take part in the process."

Sara Thöll Finnbogadóttir, a political science student who is student loan officer on the council, agreed. "There is a different understanding of democracy now. Maybe some don't use their vote, but they join an organization or society where they think they'll have more of an impact."

In this world, beyond the very real self-doubt so many women must overcome to take the plunge into politics, complacency of a different sort is possibly the biggest risk to the momentum of reaching for gender equality. "The biggest challenge when we are in this position is that we stop holding ourselves accountable, as if we have arrived at the destination just because we are ahead of the others," Helga commented on Iceland's reputation as a global leader in the fight for gender equality.

"Not to detract from all the work of all the women who have fought for so much, but I think there has also been a lot of luck, not necessarily conscious decisions."

At this almost "entry level" into politics, there are in fact six women and one man employed at the student council's rights office and twelve women and five men on the current student council, although that is not hugely dissimilar to the division of the university's population as a whole, where roughly two-thirds of the students are women. It's hard to convince men to run, Isabel told me. "They see no role models, so that's a real challenge for us. Obviously, we want all perspectives."

Mikael, the solo man at the office, said he found it "very fun and no problem," and added, "I have also been on a committee with four men and one woman, and then my impression was more that the guys hung out together and left her out."

That female dominance is clearly not translating to the national stage, although as Isabel put it, women are being more "determined" about putting themselves forward. "When people are ranking the party lists, they think it's no problem to have two men leading the lists of two neighboring constituencies, but for some reason, it's considered too risky to have two women in those positions," she said. "But someone has to take that step. You have to break the precedent and take the risk. It's an investment not only in women but in society as a whole."

But if everything is political in some way and we all have an obligation to have opinions and to take a stand in one form or another, Isabel advised women to do as she has done in her life, to "follow your heart" and "throw yourself in the deep end."

"If you're thinking about making society and the world better, that is enough reason to do it," she said firmly. "You have a right to use your voice in the discussion. You have a right to be at the table."

⇥

While the faces of politics in Iceland are increasingly feminine, it will take more than positive statistics and general goodwill to create solid foundations for sustained equality.

On a winter's evening in November 2018, a group of six Icelandic politicians, including a former prime minister and a former foreign minister (who had helped to launch the United Nations' HeForShe gender equality campaign), took a break from an ongoing session of the Althing and strolled across the street to indulge in a few drinks at Klaustur, a watering hole popular with politicos. The bar was near empty (it being midafternoon on a weekday), and the group, which included one female parliamentarian, stayed several hours and consumed many drinks, their conversation becoming louder as the alcohol took effect.

Aside from their colleagues at the Althing, who may perhaps have noted their absence, this excursion may have gone unnoticed and unremarked were it not for the fact that one other patron, by her own admission too offended by the volume and content of the discussion to ignore it, decided to record the group of officials and release it to the Icelandic media.

In the recording, the group is heard discussing several of their female colleagues using language and tone that makes proverbial locker room talk sound as mild as Raffi lyrics. They ridiculed the looks of one, the attitude and behavior of another, and the disability of a third. One labelled a fellow parliamentarian a "raving mad cunt;" another dismissed a female cabinet minister as a "fucking bitch."

Íris Róbertsdóttir was also targeted by the carousing legislators, mocked for being "far less hot" over the last few years after one of the revelers suggested she could once have been elected solely for her looks.[51]

The affair dominated the headlines for several days. Public opinion was firmly against the parliamentarians, with demands they apologize and resign. Two of the group were kicked out of their party's caucus (whose chair was the subject of some of the vitriol). Fewer than half took leaves of absence of varying lengths. Yet as of the time of writing, all are still serving members of parliament. The two who were dismissed from their party are now members of the Centre Party, whose leader is the former prime minister and was also at Klaustur that day (and is, incidentally, the same prime minister who was implicated in the Panama Papers scandal of 2016). Some of the group also threatened legal action against the individual who recorded them, saying it violated their rights to privacy.

As president, my husband was asked to comment publicly on the scandal, and, using the diplomatic language necessary when it's important to remain impartial about political issues, he said that he was "astonished and dismayed by the vocabulary, disrespect, and self-exultation" that those in the recording displayed.[52]

Three years later, Klaustur-gate, as it was dubbed in English, remains raw in the collective consciousness, a festering sore that reminds Icelandic society in stark ways that this country is no gender paradise. It nourished a cynicism that real equality will be impossible to achieve and was acutely felt among those politically engaged in the young generation.

"Klaustur was such a setback. You were just, like, really? There is no hope," Isabel Díaz told me. "When this story broke, I just thought there is no chance I would ever want to go into parliament or the diplomatic service after this. I'll need to find role models and inspiration in other places."

It will take time for this wound to heal, for faith in the integrity of the system to be restored, for women to cultivate enough conviction that change will happen, albeit more slowly and less smoothly than they wish.

We look instead to the faces of politicians who elicit optimism, who spark hope. Íris and Isabel have each nudged the bar in their own way, the former for taking on the political establishment and the latter for increasing diversity at the university level. Both have acknowledged the ongoing need to encourage women to step forward, use their voices, and defy expectations. Just like the doggedness of the Westman Islanders after the eruption, they persist, despite self-doubt, entrenched traditions, and all the other challenges of claiming their space in a male-dominated environment. They join a growing group of Icelandic women from across the political spectrum who are all helping to normalize female voices in political dialogue in this country, from the local to the national level. (I have deliberately avoided speaking with current national politicians for this book due to my position as First Lady.) They have earned my respect for daring, for willing to stand for elected office and putting themselves in the public eye.

Growing up with strong female role models, in their own lives and in the public sphere, has had a nourishing effect on many of the nation's female leaders of today. In turn, they mirror our aspirations for gender equality, serving as role models for the power brokers of tomorrow.

"This country, a tough country, a volcanic country, with harsh nature, awful weather, we go out to sea, we are really that hardy, James-Bond-in-the-glacial-lagoon type, but we are also ready to elect a woman as president," Íris reminded me when we met. "This shows that when someone has something to give, then we are ready to listen—and that is special about Iceland."

11

WITHIN REACH

*It lies in the eyes upstairs**

ONE CLOUDY SEPTEMBER MORNING IN 2017, I found myself boarding an Icelandair flight to London to connect onward to Amman, capital city of Jordan. From there, I would take the ninety-minute highway ride through desert landscapes to near the border with Syria and the massive Zaatari refugee camp, the world's second largest.

With almost eighty thousand refugees of Syria's bloody civil war crammed into 5.3 km² (3.3 mi²), the UN-administered camp was built rapidly to meet an acute demand, beginning with collections of white canvas tents and ballooning into the not-so-temporary city I visited. It contains unpaved shopping streets, twenty-seven community centers, two hospitals, nine healthcare clinics, and eleven schools. As many as eight people lived in each of thousands of prefabricated 30 m² (98 ft²) shelters, sweltering in the desert summer heat and frigid in the drafty winters. Populated by Syrians who had often led comfortable, middle-class lives before the outbreak of war in 2011 and who had been forced to flee with little more than the clothes on their backs while experiencing loss and unspeakable traumas on the way, the people of Zaatari were 80 percent women and children. There were only five thousand jobs available for camp residents, and almost all of those went to the proportionally few men. Women were unable to leave their homes after dark for

---

* *Það liggur í augum uppi* means it's obvious.

fear of assault, while girls were married off to older men at an alarming rate (one in three women and girls living in Zaatari were married before the age of eighteen), where they would more than likely stop what little education they were receiving and soon become mothers.

Among eight UN agencies operating within the Zaatari bureaucracy was UN Women, which ran three so-called oases, safe spaces at different locations in the camp. They were places where women could gather to work on a cash-for-work basis, receive psychological counselling, find schooling and day care facilities for their children, and take courses themselves on everything from basic computer skills or hairstyling to language classes in English or Arabic. Just as importantly, the oases provided the women with a secure environment in which to commiserate and find refuge.

Along with UN Women Iceland staff, one of the Icelandic chapter's patrons, and a team from an Icelandic ad agency, I was there to take part in the filming of a series of videos about the women of Zaatari.[53] They would be the flagship of a fundraising campaign in Iceland that autumn to help UN Women open even more oases.

On the first day, after a general briefing by staff from the UN High Commission for Refugees on the camp as a whole, we visited one oasis, where about a dozen women sat in a cool building sewing, stitching, and creating handicrafts.* Their main task was to prepare kits for the mothers of the eighty or so babies who were born every week in the camp. The kits included warm fleece clothing and information on where to get vital vaccinations. With the scraps from the clothing they

---

* One exchange is seared in my mind from this briefing. Thinking of the ongoing and often controversial debates back in Europe about the flood of refugees from Syria and other conflicts and how many each country was willing to invite to live within their borders, I asked the woman from UNHCR if there were any resentments within the camp. When one family found out they were moving to, say, Germany or Canada or indeed Iceland, did the family next door feel any resentment toward those who were leaving to begin a new life? She shook her head. "So few families are approved to go," she told me. "It's just a drop in the bucket."

sewed, the women used a form of macrame to create wall hangings of various sizes.

The largest one caught my eye. About 6.9 feet by 4.3 feet, from a distance, it looked like some sort of tactile abstract artwork. It was only when you moved closer that you could glimpse the fabric tags from onesies or T-shirts originally tossed into some clothing recycling bin in a wealthy European country. Featuring a color palette of rose pink and browns, the tapestry depicts the scales of justice in rudimentary style on a background of multicolor stripes. Along the top was a phrase in Arabic: *Equality is my right.*

I bought that tapestry (it took up half my suitcase for the return journey to Iceland), and it hangs to this day on the wall of the entrance area to our private residence at Bessastadir, a daily reminder of one of the struggles that unites us all.

I had friendly encounters with several other women during my second day at the camp, when one of my roles for the video we were making was to interview a local teenager, Zaad al-Khair, about her experience working at the oasis. She had likely been selected for the video because she was articulate, charismatic, and warm.

Sitting in plastic chairs under a shaded open tent, cameras capturing our faces and reactions from several angles, Zaad and I spoke about her upbringing and her experience of the camps and of the good UN Women was doing for her and her friends. Zaad was excited; it was her nineteenth birthday in a couple of weeks, she told me. It would be the fifth she would celebrate in the camp, where she lived with her parents in one of the many small pre-fab shelters. One brother and sister were still in Syria, condition unknown, and another brother had been killed by the same bombing they had fled in 2012.

"Before he died, my brother said, 'Don't leave your education,'" Zaad told me. "When he died, I left my school [for] two years. But when

I remember his words, I start again thinking about my future, so that's the reason I went back to school. I think it will make him happy in the sky." She wiped away some tears and smiled at me. "When I cry, I see myself not strong. To complete my way, I have to be very strong. I want to make my brothers and my sister proud of me."[54]

Iceland does not have a monopoly on extraordinary women.

Before she was briefed about our meeting, I doubt Zaad and her friends knew much, if anything, about Iceland, the word perhaps conjuring images of a wealthy and probably cold nation somewhere up near the North Pole. Zaad likely didn't know how many years in a row Iceland has topped the Global Gender Gap Index—why would it matter to her?

UN Women and other female residents of the camp had helped Zaad find her voice, make a difference, nudge the bar, even in a location where conditions are far from ripe for equality. In the camp, attaining life's fundamentals of shelter, food, and security claim the lion's share of one's energies.

Returning to Iceland, I resolved that I wasn't going to be yet another VIP guest/refugee tourist who distracted hardworking and underpaid staff from the vital aspects of their jobs to escort people like me from photo op to photo op. How many such VIPs had witnessed, if only for the briefest of moments, the realities of life in Zaatari only to return to an indifferent, wealthy home country whose people would continue to murmur about life's unfairness while shrugging their shoulders about how they could help?

The resulting campaign that featured Zaad and several other women became UN Women Iceland's most successful to date and allowed the Iceland branch of the organization to open two new oases in the nearby Azraq refugee camp. It was gratifying to know what had happened to the funds raised, but I selfishly felt I had learned more during those days by hearing firsthand about the role women play. I had been moved by their strength and courage.

I see the "Equality is my right" tapestry every day. I speak often of that trip to Jordan and the inspiring women I met there. And I try to channel that energy into the work I do. The more *sprakkar* I meet, the more I see the world around me in sharper focus. In Iceland, where we have been so fortunate, how can we best achieve what we're aiming for? How can we reach everyone? And while this privilege gives us a strong launching pad to propel us far in the right direction, to continue on the same trajectory takes the cumulative, unrelenting efforts of us all. The passion of girls and women like Zaad is infectious, and the rest of us have an obligation to elevate *sprakkar* like her wherever we encounter them, including in our own backyards.

At the tail end of that annus horribilis 2020, Iceland marked another small milestone in its journey to gender parity. For the first time in its sixty-five-year history, Iceland's Association of Sports Journalists' annual awards for Athlete of the Year, Coach of the Year, and Team of the Year all went to women (all, incidentally, in the sport of soccer). Sara Björk Gunnarsdóttir, the Athlete of the Year, won the maximum number of points allowable by the journalists who determined the winner. The news was met with near universal praise for the women's achievements.

Less than a week later, on the first day of a new year, legislation took effect in Iceland that expands parental leave from nine months to a full year to be shared between both parents. Likewise, other new legislation enables individuals to identify their gender with the marker X (instead of male or female) on official documents. The new year ushered in above-inflation wage increases for all the country's lowest wage earners and a shorter working week for those employed by the state and municipalities.

The often plodding, sometimes precarious march toward gender equality in Iceland, and indeed elsewhere, follows a path cobbled with changes of all sizes. That path is also formed of binding, seismic developments such as gender quotas and affordable child care, which are themselves the products of decades of pressure and increasingly inclusive social attitudes. But it is no less the collective result of small, individual actions, of all the people of this country, of all genders.

Where Iceland stands today is not purely chance, though circumstances of history, geography, and luck have certainly played their part. Our smallness is a strength. In a global context, we are not a massive tanker of a nation but more a tiny speedboat. Change is easier to demand, to implement, and to measure, though it can still feel like it moves at a glacial pace. Our island's isolation and our natural surroundings, often perilous to this day, dictate that all human resources be used to their full potential. Icelandic children have been raised on stories of tenacious women from the ages, including Hallgerdur Long-Legs and other heroines from the sagas, Ólöf the Rich, a poor woman who saved a waterfall, and a cultural luminary who became a very special head of state. An open economy, functioning democratic institutions, comparatively limited disparity between rich and poor, and a well-educated, internationally minded, and tech-loving society more than compensate for the parochialism and dogmatism that can occasionally plague a small country.

In the global context, this means Iceland is a stage where we have a working mic, a vantage point from which we can deliver some of our lessons learned about how to get closer to gender equality.

And if one day Iceland no longer tops the Global Gender Gap Index? If we fall a few rungs in the rankings? If that is the result of another country or countries overtaking us and not of us falling asleep at the wheel, of becoming complacent, then all the better. We don't need to be the best in the world, per capita or otherwise. But we do need to share our success stories, learn from others how to improve areas that call for attention, and help everyone, not only women, strive to use their voices, their space.

"I'm a bit surprised you want to talk to me for a chapter on parenthood," former parliamentarian Unnur Brá Konrádsdóttir admitted to me in passing as we wrapped up our conversation, which centered on her experience breastfeeding her infant daughter in Iceland's parliament.

"I'm no superhero in that field," she continued casually as I packed up my notebook. "I'm just trying to do the best I can."

Her candor is familiar to many of us. Aren't we all just hoping to make it all work somehow?

We wear a lot of proverbial hats here, as is so popular to say in Iceland. The *sprakkar* I interviewed in this book epitomize this and the intersectionality of what striving for equality means. To achieve gender equality, we cannot leave anyone behind, including immigrant women, women of color, women with disabilities, and queer women. We need to work with the many male allies here, who also benefit from increased balance and who recognize that gender equality serves everyone, not one gender at the expense of another.

Though she was a bit surprised to hear it, Unnur Brá was the ideal woman to speak to about parenthood in Iceland, because she exemplifies what it means for so many of us. She is making use of family-centric government policies to piece together a productive, fulfilling life for herself and her family. It's not an Instagrammable image. I doubt—or I hope not at least!—that Unnur Brá's house is perfectly cleaned, that her kids are on a strict regimen of limited and exclusively age-appropriate access to screens. Despite best intentions, she has probably shown up to chair meetings less prepared than she had hoped or has answered a colleague's query with less patience than someone with fewer daily distractions might have.

To my mind, this is why she is a *sprakki*. We all cut corners here, rationalize there. Unnur Brá could equally have been interviewed in my politics chapter, no doubt sharing insights into what women in Iceland face when they seek high office in the country.

Had I switched Unnur to another place in this portrait, I could easily have filled the gap with Gudbjörg Gudmundsdóttir, executive vice president at Marel Fish. When she's not overseeing a profitable strategy and a huge, multinational team, working against the fact that mostly men clutch the private sector's pocketbook, she returns home to her two young daughters, whom she is raising on her own.

In her place to talk about working life in Iceland, Pink Iceland's Eva María Thórarinsdóttir Lange could have shared more details about her experience as an entrepreneur.

It goes on. Saga Gardarsdóttir doesn't just crack jokes about giving birth and raising a toddler. She also works in the arts scene in the country. Isabel Díaz from the University of Iceland has her own immigrant's story to share, and the close ties she has formed with other members of the student body at the university are another example of the importance of friendships and support in helping us learn to venture outside our comfort zones. Ugla Stefanía has learned to deftly navigate the all too often murky waters of the media in their work as a trans activist.

What unites all these people is that they use the space they deserve. They are not necessarily trying to implement a specifically feminist agenda; many of them would not call themselves feminists. Their achievements don't fit neatly into one societal silo. They have an interdependence on so many dimensions of society, their positive actions creating ripples and waves that resonate throughout this fortuitously small pond of a country, like the daily tremors and earthquakes that this island experiences at nature's hand.

The dozens of women I have introduced in this book represent a diversity of ages, locations, backgrounds, experiences, and personalities. Some are well-known faces in Iceland. Others have a limited following within a niche area but are fairly anonymous beyond that. They are exceptional women for various reasons, but they are also everyday women, women in whose experiences, dreams, and challenges we can see something of ourselves.

In Iceland, we also have plenty of more high-profile gender equality role models for current and future generations. At the time of writing, women were serving in the roles of prime minister; minister of justice; minister of education and culture; minister of tourism, industry, and innovation; chief medical officer; secretary general of parliament; chair of the board of the Icelandic Travel Industry Association; executive director of the Iceland Chamber of Commerce; managing director of the union of fishing vessel owners and companies; and president of the Icelandic Confederation of Labour, to name but a few. Abroad, Icelandic women have recently or are currently serving in roles such as director of the Organization for Security and Cooperation in Europe's Office for Democratic Institutions and Human Rights, chair of the board of Women Political Leaders, and CEO of the B Team, the global nonprofit founded by Richard Branson. Role models are perhaps the single most crucial component of this great recipe for equality—or at least the largest.

In a less visible way, so too are the women featured in this book. They are everyday role models, *sprakkar*, for us all. Their examples reinforce the idea that outstanding women are a universal phenomenon, not a uniquely Icelandic one, if only we can help one another shine and share the proverbial mic to have all our voices heard.

↠

The curly-haired single Viking dad I met at Oxford University at the tail end of the last millennium, who rolled his *r*'s and had a sharp, dry humor, was always compelling to me. Not because he's the risk-taking or flamboyant type; rather it was his quiet nature, his reluctance to seek the limelight at an institution full of overachievers, that I found intriguing.

Both Gudni and I rowed for our college at Oxford. We weren't particularly good, but gliding in unison through the River Isis as the sun peeked above the legendary spires of the ancient university seemed like a sort of "Oxford" thing to do. One fall evening, the joint women's and men's crews held a fundraising event—really, just another excuse for a party. Various members of the crews, almost exclusively male, as I recall, lined up Styrofoam coffee cups along a table in the residence where the event took place. Each was marked with the name of a crew member. The rest of us could pay one pound, for which we would receive five paper tickets. We would write our names on each ticket and place them in the Styrofoam cups of our choice. At the end of the evening, each cup holder would draw a name from his cup and take that person on a date.

I clearly remember having a two-pound coin with me and thinking that despite being a poor student, I would splurge for a good cause. I bought ten tickets and dutifully wrote my name on each one.

Then I gave fate a little push.

I put eight tickets in Gudni's cup. Though he was the only one I was really interested in enjoying a date with, I didn't want to drop all ten tickets in his cup. If the truth were ever revealed, I would seem like some sort of obsessed stalker! But this was, after all, my opportunity to get to know him better, so I didn't want to leave things entirely to chance.

Inevitably, of course, Gudni drew my name. And while the "dates" for most others involved a late-night kebab at the van parked outside the college gates, Gudni treated me to a three-course Italian dinner at Luna Caprese the next evening, bottle of red wine and all.

That brief moment of carpe diem would have repercussions far greater and longer-lasting than I could ever have anticipated (and certainly made for captivating fodder on the campaign trail in 2016), but can't the same be said of some of our best and most spontaneous life choices?

Stuffing the proverbial ballot box was one small step toward controlling my own destiny, a proactive moment about something I thought was important. More than two decades later, it's a philosophy I have tried to emulate as First Lady. I am not going to change the world on a large scale. But I can do my part to nudge things in the right direction.

They are all baby steps in the grand scheme of things. Does it really matter that a privileged woman says she doesn't want to be photographed only as the stereotypical female sidekick on a state visit? That she earns her own living as an entrepreneur and writer while serving in the volunteer capacity of First Lady? Or that she sometimes wears secondhand clothing to public events? I hope it all adds up to something.

As much as I espouse the importance of role models, I still suffer from a degree of imposter syndrome when it comes to being referred to as one myself.

Early in 2020, I was invited to attend a seminar at the University of Iceland on gender imbalance in management positions in the country. I didn't have a specific role to play at the session; the organizer asked me because she knew of my interest in the topic. It was intriguing, and the timing worked; I was already scheduled to be at the university that morning, speaking to a group of graduate students on gender, diversity, and inclusion in the workplace.

So after my short lecture and a dynamic Q and A with about two dozen students, I made my way over to the main hall for the event. The organizers had saved a seat for me in the front row, next to other high-profile guests.

It was a fascinating presentation, a summary of recent research on why there are so few women in the C-suite in Icelandic businesses and what policy makers and stakeholders can do to improve the situation. At the end, the official photographer assembled the glass-ceiling-shattering women who had attended the talk: Vigdís Finnbogadóttir, the world's first democratically elected female head of state; Jóhanna Sigurdardóttir, Iceland's first female prime minister and the world's first openly gay head of government; Agnes Sigurdardóttir, Iceland's first female bishop of the state church; Sigrídur Björk Gudjónsdóttir, first female head of the national police; and Bergthóra Thorkelsdóttir, first female head of the Icelandic Road and Coastal Administration. All are role models who had to fight public and private battles to reach the professional summits they had attained, who have helped pave the way for others to follow in their footsteps, who have inspired people of all genders and of all political affiliations.

Then the group asked me to join them.

Rather sheepishly, I stood and aligned myself in a row with the others. I have a lot of self-confidence, but I can recall few occasions when I have felt so utterly out of place, so undeserving of inclusion. I couldn't help but make a remark to that effect to Bishop Agnes, who was standing next to me, aware (too late) that it must have sounded like some sort of humble brag, the insecure person's stock comment from which to elicit some sort of sign of encouragement, of validation.

"No," Agnes told me firmly, putting both hands on my shoulders and looking at me in the eyes. "You most definitely should be here, especially after that important article you wrote," referring to my *New York Times* op-ed.

I have often reflected on that moment since. When does the energy we expend on self-doubt transfer to something more productive? When will I stop spending so much time questioning my legitimacy, my right to talk about gender equality when I have been primarily, or at least initially, recognized as someone's spouse?

Maybe it's just the uncomfortable feeling of truly starting to use my voice, to fully take up space. I am grateful each and every day to be able to serve as First Lady and thankful for the warm reception I have almost universally received in that capacity. So I continue to try and update the image of a female spouse of a male head of state, going in my husband's place to support the national men's team at the soccer World Cup in Moscow, serving as patron for organizations including the Alzheimer's Society, Pieta House suicide prevention, and even the National Culinary Team of Iceland (I confess I lobbied for that one!), and delivering keynote addresses at graduations, on panels, and at conference openings. I evolved from inadvertently calling myself lazy at our largest campaign event (I meant to say "thankful" and got a declension wrong in Icelandic) to being nominated by some media outlets for person of the year in 2019 after my op-ed in the *New York Times* clearly struck a chord with the progressive population.

What I should be doing is leaning in to that uncomfortable feeling. It's our inner voice's way of confirming we're on the right path, of reminding us that while it's healthy to avoid a Brobdingnagian ego, it's also vital to have the self-assurance to get over superficial qualms and make ourselves heard.

Now, rather than question whether I belong in a group photo, I ask myself: If I don't use this unique opportunity to speak up for issues I know are important, who else will? And how can I possibly expect others to take such risks if I don't? Writing this book while I am still serving as First Lady is another step in my efforts to push my own boundaries and society's expectations of my role. But having the freedom to do so is no less a testament to the state of gender equality in Iceland.

A mere six months after their conquest of the English Channel, four members of the Jellyfish swimming group were approached about a new physical challenge.[55] They joined seven other intrepids, including the first Icelandic woman to ascend Mount Everest, to fulfil a life-long ambition of cancer survivor Sirrý Ágústsdóttir to raise funds for two charities by crossing Vatnajökull Glacier on foot in June 2020. Europe's largest glacier had never before been fully traversed by a group composed exclusively of women. Over the course of nine days, the group, who dubbed themselves the Snowdrifters, encountered extreme cold, earthquakes, and cracks in the glacier, much of which sits atop active volcanoes, as they skied the 102.5-mile route, sleeping in tents under the midnight sun and pulling all their supplies on heavy pulks behind them. Their ultimate success encouraged Sirrý to plan a 2021 challenge: scaling the country's highest mountain with one hundred women.*

The Jellyfish, and their glacier-crossing incarnation the Snowdrifters, have used their enduring bonds of friendship to stretch their personal boundaries, to follow their dreams. They succeeded not because of legislation or societal will but by pushing themselves to their physical and mental limits and then a bit beyond. In doing so, they show that women too can test their physical limits and that these are worthy objectives.

---

* Sirrý achieved this ambition too, summitting Hvannadalshnjúkur in early May that year with 125 other women.

When I indulged in a Christmas buffet with her, television presenter Thóra Arnórsdóttir said we can't just send other countries a blueprint about how to achieve gender equality. But it's not rocket science either, and Iceland has certainly not patented a solution.

The people of Iceland are changing the world by bringing gender equality within reach. But the secrets to doing so, and even to trying to achieve it one day (an important, if utopian, target), are in the open domain. To translate an Icelandic idiom verbatim, they "lie in the eyes upstairs": they are actually obvious, in plain sight for us all to see if we take the time to look, to understand their significance and how we can use them to press forward, step by step.

In macro form, for entire communities, the secrets lie in letting go of the unrealistic "having it all" balancing act and in doing what we can with what we have, nursing babies at the pulpit if required or taping over our nipples when it's time to wean our child cold turkey. It means nourishing our arts, our culture, and our athletics, not by comparing women to men but by letting everyone's unique voices be heard. It's moving with the times, helping trans girls and women live the lives they know are right for them, and recognizing the unique challenges immigrants face and the valuable contributions they make. It's understanding, on both a national legal level and a personal moral one, that sexual and gender-based violence are never acceptable, under any circumstances, and that women who are victims of such assault are not to blame. It's hiring people like Marel's Gudbjörg and funding entrepreneurs like GeoSilica's Fida and giving them access to the same funds while also compensating our lowest paid workers, most of whom are women, fairly for their work. It's leaving no one behind, women, men, or non-binary people; native-born or immigrant; with or without disabilities, on our journey to parity so that all will benefit.

For those of us who don't determine policy, we bring gender

equality within reach by using our voices and making ourselves heard. Like Dóra the Fish Whisperer and Heida the farmer and sheep shearer, we follow our dreams, wherever they might take us. We volunteer with women's associations to help share skills, support, companionship, and altruism, all of which help sustain us when life hurls its worst. We speak out and let ourselves be seen and heard on television, on radio, in print, and on social media, amplifying one another's voices and not belittling them. We dare to step into the fray, to run for office at any level, to be role models.

It takes concerted, systematic, never-ending, exhausting, thankless effort. For just as easily as we move forward, a bolt from the blue, an unanticipated foe could knock us back—just as 2020 saw years of global progress in this field abate in the wake of the COVID-19 pandemic.[*] We must always remain vigilant, on alert. I acknowledge that it is a privilege to be able to channel energies to fighting for equality when so many don't have the money, the access, the voice, or simply the energy, even if they wished to. Those of us who are fortunate enough not to pay such a high price for using our voices, demanding our space, and filling it owe it to the others, and we need to make room for their voices too.

We all know *sprakkar*. They are in our families, our communities, our places of worship, our governments, our cultural institutions, and our schools. They don't need Iceland's unpredictable nature or saga protagonists or edgy rap music to shine. They only need us, and themselves, to elevate them, showcase them, teach others to be like them. If we help turn on their mics and let their voices be heard, we can elect more of them to public office, to help us forget about the impossible ledger of the balancing act, control society's pocketbook, permeate traditionally

---

[*] The 2021 Global Gender Gap Index quantified this in its findings that the pandemic had increased the time predicted to close the gender gap by an additional generation, or thirty-six years.

male domains, and advocate for further change. *Sprakkar* may be an Icelandic word, but it is not the exclusive domain of Nordic, privileged feminism. There are extraordinary women everywhere, across our beautiful planet. That's the secret.

Equality is my right. It's yours too.

ACKNOWLEDGMENTS

To walk with a book in one's belly

IT IS SAID IN ICELAND that everyone "walks with a book in their belly" (*"að ganga með bók í maganum"*), that we all have stories to share, experiences, wisdom, and adventure that we are waiting to birth.

The gestation of *Secrets of the Sprakkar* was not a long one. The spark was an idea to share with the world what it's like to live in a country where the aspiration to gender equality is a guiding principle. But it also quickly became my own love letter to Iceland and an opportunity to explore my experiences about being an immigrant, becoming a parent, incorporating a company, and unexpectedly but happily serving as First Lady. Combined, I hope to have shared some stories about Iceland but, more importantly, inspired others about what we can all be doing to fight for equality, empower one another, and make the most of unforeseen opportunities. Perhaps the kernel of this story was in my belly all along.

I must first and foremost thank everyone I interviewed for this book, for their candor, humor, and perspectives. I am grateful to each and every one of you for taking so much time to share your stories and experiences with me. I wanted to capture a diverse group of women, in age, background, location, and life experience, not necessarily the ones who were first to achieve something or who serve as official spokespeople for something else. There are ample other *sprakkar* in Iceland, of course, as there are in every community; I acknowledge that I cannot be all things to all people, and the viewpoints revealed here are by no means exhaustive.

I am grateful to Samantha Haywood, Anna Michels, Justin Stoller, Nita Pronovost, and the teams at Transatlantic Agency, Sourcebooks, and Simon & Schuster Canada, who guided me through the fascinating process of writing a book, from Sam's enthusiastic response to my very first email, to Anna's and Justin's sage editorial advice, all the way through final production, where Sabrina Baskey, Liz Kelsch, Ashlyn Keil, and Madeleine Brown with Sourcebooks, and Adria Iwasutiak, Jillian Levick, and Melanie Pedersen at Simon & Schuster Canada took over the reins to make sure the book reached the most readers. It has been a joy to work with all of you. Thanks also to Diana Gvozden, who helped find the Icelandic publisher for this manuscript.

Thanks to Jonas Moody, Erica Jacobs Green, Elizabeth Lay, Fridjón Fridjónsson, Ingibjörg Sólrún Gísladóttir, Katrín Jakobsdóttir, Krista Mahr, Paula Gould, Gudrún Nordal, Unnur Birna Karlsdóttir, Lára Magnúsardóttir, and Markús Thórhallsson, all of whom read over sections large and small of this book and provided valuable input. Thórdís Elva Thorvaldsdóttir spoke with me extensively and guided me to valuable research. Jonas earns a second thank you for introducing me to the obscure word, *sprakkar*.

A whole host of others answered queries large and small related to the mysterious (to me!) world of book writing, supplied answers to specific questions for this project, or put me in touch with people to interview. In alphabetical order the Icelandic way (i.e., by first name), they are: Alexander Elliott, Andrea Róbertsdóttir, Anne Giardini, Arndís Thorgeirsdóttir, Áslaug Arna Sigurbjörnsdóttir, Ásta Dís Óladóttir, Barbara Bruns Kristvinsson, Björk Óttarsdóttir, Bryndís Loftsdóttir, Claudia Casper, Dagur S. Dagbjartsson, Daníel J. Arnarsson, Edythe Mangindin, Gudrún Jónsdóttir, Gunnar Kristjánsson, Gunnlaugur

Karlsson, Hanna Birna Kristjánsdóttir, Heidar Ingi Svansson, Hulda Bjarnadóttir, Hulda Ragnheidur Árnadóttir, Jóhanna Katrín Fridriksdóttir (whom I don't know personally, but who told my friend Jonas about the existence of the word *sprakkar*), Jón Ingvar Kjaran, Katja Pantzar, Klara Bjartmarz, Kristín Bogadóttir, Kristín Brynjólfsdóttir and her family for hosting me and my family in Vopnafjördur, Kristín Vidarsdóttir and Lára Adalsteinsdóttir at Reykjavík UNESCO City of Literature for allowing me to conduct an interview at Gunnarshús, Kristinn Ingvarsson, Kristján Schram, Laura Murphy, Lilja Hrund Ava Lúdvíksdóttir, Líney Halldórsdóttir, Marcello Di Cintio, Margrét Steinarsdóttir, Maria Helena Sarabia, Marta Godadóttir, Oddný Arnarsdóttir, Ragnar Thorvardarson, Rán Tryggvadóttir, Randi Stebbins, Sema Erla Serdar, Sigrídur Björk Gudjónsdóttir, Sigrún Ingibjörg Gísladóttir, Sigthrúdur Ármann, Sigthrúdur Gudmunsdóttir, Sindri Sigurjónsson, Skarphédinn Gudmundsson, Sóley Tómasdóttir, Steinunn Gydu- og Gudjónsdóttir, Sue-Lyn Erbeck, Sveinn Valgeirsson, Sverrir Jakobsson, Tara Flynn, Thelma Kristín Kvaran, Thorsteinn V. Einarsson, Thórdur Snær Júlíusson, Thórhildur Sigurdardóttir, Una Sighvatsdóttir, Valgerdur Sigurdardóttir, Vidar Thorsteinsson. Thank you. Needless to say, all errors are my own, and any omissions in thanks above come with sincere apologies.

I would also like to acknowledge the hundreds of people who have taken part in the Iceland Writers Retreat over the years. I am so grateful for the faith you have shown in the endeavor and have learned a lot about the writing process from meeting all of you.

I had the tremendous fortune of growing up surrounded by *sprakkar*. My mum, my aunts, my grandmothers: I am grateful for all these strong, feminist role models. I have smart, fun, and supportive friends, whom I learn a lot from, who help ground me, and who tease me about my foibles to just the right degree. Thanks also go to the *sprakkar* in my family life in Iceland: my stepdaughter, Rut; my daughter, Edda Margrét; and my mother-in-law, Margrét Thorlacius.

The word *sprakkar* describes only women, but grammatically it is a masculine word. In addition to the *sprakkar*, Iceland would not be where it is today were it not also for men who recognize that gender equality benefits everyone, not one gender at the expense of another, and who respect, hear, and elevate the women around them. I believe that this is most men. As with female role models, I have been fortunate with the men in my life: those in my Canadian family growing up, and in my Icelandic family: my sons Duncan Tindur, Donald Gunnar, and Sæthór Peter. And, of course, my *r*-rolling, newspaper-article-clipping, funny, and kind husband, Gudni Thorlacius Jóhannesson. Thank you all.

APPENDIX 1: LIST OF INTERVIEWS

Chapter 2: Helping Parents Helps Us All

Saga Gardarsdóttir, August 24, 2020*
Unnur Brá Konrádsdóttir, August 21, 2020*

Chapter 3: The Strength in Sisterhood

Women's Associations (Gudbjörg Björgvinsdóttir,
Arnfrídur Jóhannsdóttir, Magnea Sigrún
Símonardóttir, Gudrún Sveinsdóttir, Rosemarie
Brynhildur Thorleifsdóttir), September 4, 2020*
Jellyfish (Birna Bragadóttir, Sigrún Th. Geirsdóttir, Sigurlaug
María Jónsdóttir, Brynhildur Ólafsdóttir, Halldóra Gyda
Matthíasdóttir Proppé, Thórey Vilhjálmsdóttir Proppé, Soffía
Sigurgeirsdóttir), August 21, 2020*

Chapter 4: Stigma-Free Sexuality

Ragnheidur Bjarman Eiríksdóttir, August 31, 2020
Eva María Thórarinsdóttir Lange, September 21, 2020
Ugla Stefanía Kristjönudóttir Jónsdóttir, August 21, 2020

Chapter 5: Claiming the Corporate Purse Strings

Ragnhildur Ágústsdóttir, October 12, 2020 (via Zoom)
Gudbjörg Heida Gudmundsdóttir, November 5, 2020 (via Teams)*
Fida Abu Libdeh, November 5, 2020 (via Zoom)*

Chapter 6: Being Seen and Heard in the Media

"Christmas buffet" discussion (Thóra Arnórsdóttir, Sólborg
Gudbrandsdóttir, Thorbjörg Marinósdóttir, Steinunn Ása
Thorvaldsdóttir), December 8, 2020*

Chapter 7: Finding Harmony in the Wild

Heida Gudný Ásgeirsdóttir, September 2, 2020*
Halldóra Kristín Unnarsdóttir, October 27, 2020*
Elín Matthildur Kristinsdóttir, November 14, 2020*

Chapter 8: Art as an Instrument of Equality

A tale of two writers (Kamilla Einarsdóttir and
Gerdur Kristný), December 2, 2020*
Margrét Lára Vidarsdóttir, December 2, 2020*
Daughters of Reykjavík (Thurídur Blær Jóhannsdóttir, Steiney
Skúladóttir, Thórdís Björk Thorfinnsdóttir), December 3, 2020*

Chapter 9: No Woman Is an Island

Monserrat Arlette Moreno, July 18, 2020
Claudia Ashanie Wilson, October 22, 2020
"Rose," October 24, 2020

Chapter 10: Politics on Her Own Terms

Íris Róbertsdóttir, May 21, 2020, and
March 8, 2021 (via phone)*
Isabel Alejandra Díaz, May 20, 2020, and March 8, 2021*
Sara Thöll Finnbogadóttir, Gudný Ljósbrá Hreinsdóttir, Helga
Lind Mar, Mikael Berg Steingrímsson, May 20, 2020*

Chapter 11: Within Reach

Unnur Brá Konrádsdóttir, August 21, 2020*

Quotes were sometimes condensed and edited for clarity. All interviews by author were conducted in person unless otherwise noted.

*Interview was conducted in Icelandic. Translations by author.

APPENDIX 2: FURTHER READING

ICELAND IS ONE OF THE world's most tech-savvy countries, and it's fairly straightforward to find a lot of information online. Almost all—if not all—government agencies, charities, and companies with an international focus will have a website with information in English. Much of the research I conducted was in Icelandic, but I have listed only English sources in the endnotes, unless the Icelandic source provides otherwise hard-to-find additional information.

If you're interested in keeping up-to-date with news about Iceland in general, there are now several online sources, including RÚV English (www.ruv.is/english), *Iceland Review* (www.icelandreview.com), the *Reykjavík Grapevine* (www.grapevine.is), and Iceland Monitor (www.icelandmonitor.mbl.is). Local writer Alda Sigmundsdóttir also posts regularly about current affairs in Iceland on Facebook (@aldasigmundsdottir) and Instagram (@alda.sigmunds). It was in fact a comment on one of her posts in April 2020 that sparked my idea for this book.

Those who wish to research more concrete information about the country are encouraged to begin with the Government of Iceland's website, www.government.is, where you can find information on all the various ministries and policies. The website for Statistics Iceland, www.statice.is, is very user-friendly and a great source for statistics of all sorts. Those wishing to visit the country in person can start their planning via www.visiticeland.com.

This is an excellent overview of the timeline and highlights of the gender equality fight in Iceland: https://www.stjornarradid.is/media /velferdarraduneyti-media/media/acrobat-skjol/jafnrettisstofa _stepping_stones.pdf. Iceland's Directorate of Equality has extensive additional information: https://www.jafnretti.is/en. Needless to say, there is a wealth of information on gender equality in general, much of which readers will already be familiar with. A few recent nonfiction books that have inspired me include *Shrewed* by Elizabeth Renzetti (House of Anansi Press, 2018), *The Moment of Lift* by Melinda Gates (Flatiron Books, 2019), pretty much everything by Roxane Gay, *Invisible Women: Exposing Data Bias in a World Designed for Men* by Caroline Criado Perez (Abrams, 2019), and *What Works: Gender Equality by Design* by Iris Bohnet (Belknap Press, 2016).

Books in English that I used in research and preparation for this book include *A History of Iceland* by Gudni Thorlacius Jóhannesson (Greenwood, 2013), which I must highly recommend because my husband wrote it. I also enjoyed *Saga Land* by Richard Fidler and Kári Gíslason (HarperCollins, 2017). Egill Bjarnason recently wrote a charming history of the country, *How Iceland Changed the World* (Penguin, 2021); it's worth reading. Gerdur Kristný's book *Bloodhoof* is available in English, translated by Rory McTurk (Arc, 2013). Kamilla Einarsdóttir's *The Kópavogur Chronicles* is to date only published in Icelandic. Additional books are mentioned in the endnotes. I would be remiss not to mention that many works by Icelandic authors have been translated into English (and many other languages); needless to say, reading the fiction, poetry, and memoirs of a country provides a special insight into its culture, and I highly recommend delving into the Icelandic literary oeuvre.

For further research on specific themes in these chapters, see the endnotes. Additionally and in the order in which these topics appear

in the book: Details on Iceland's parental leave scheme are here: https://
work.iceland.is/living/maternity-and-paternity-leave. See https://www
.pewresearch.org/fact-tank/2019/12/16/u-s-lacks-mandated-paid
-parental-leave/ for information in a global context. Trans activist
Ugla Stefanía writes a regular column in the UK's *Metro* newspaper.
The government's policy and information on climate change is here:
https://www.government.is/topics/environment-climate-and-nature
-protection/climate-change/. Andri Snær Magnason's book *On Time
and Water* (trans. Lytton Smith, Open Letter, 2021) discusses the
climate crisis, with a focus on Iceland, glaciers, and the sea. You can
find out all about Iceland's search and rescue crews on www.icesar
.com. The Daughters of Reykjavík are on www.rvkdtr.com. Residents
of Vopnafjördur are very welcoming to visitors; take a look at what
you can see and do on www.visitvopnafjordur.com/en. Stígamót, the
Education and Counseling Centre for Survivors of Sexual Abuse and
Violence, is available in six languages on www.stigamot.is. There is an
excellent documentary on the first Women's Day Off, *Women in Red
Stockings* (2009), directed by Halla Kristín Einarsdóttir and with English
subtitles, on Vimeo at https://vimeo.com/141731463. *The Sealwoman's
Gift* by Sally Magnusson (Hachette UK, 2018) is historical fiction based
on a pirate attack that took place on the Westman Islands in 1627 in
which hundreds of Icelanders were kidnapped and sold into slavery in
North Africa, another pivotal moment in the island's history.

These suggestions merely skim the surface. If you know someone
who lives in Iceland and need further information on something, try
asking that person. It really is a small place with few degrees of separation, and locals can usually provide smart advice on where to look. I
hope you enjoy learning about Iceland as much as I have over the past
nearly quarter century.

READING GROUP GUIDE

1. Iceland routinely ranks as one of "the best places in the world to be a woman." Where would you expect your own country to rank, and why? What differences and similarities stood out to you between Icelandic culture and your own?

2. What was the most surprising thing you learned about Icelandic culture?

3. Which of the interviewees did you find most relatable? Why did that person resonate with you?

4. Reid emphasizes that even Iceland is not perfect when it comes to gender equality. What would perfect gender equality look like to you? Do you have different ideas about it now than you did when you started reading?

5. Iceland provides generous parental leave for both men and women, and all citizens have access to health care. How do these assurances affect the decisions Icelandic parents make? Would such programs change your view toward having children one way or another?

6. Which of the featured *sprakkar*—from Hallgerdur Long-Legs to President Vigdís Finnbogadóttir—were your favorites? How did their stories change your understanding of the rest of the book?

7. Describe the role of *saumós* in Icelandic society. How does the advance of gender parity affect these gender-segregated spaces? Do you have a group that you consider your *saumó*?

8. Many cultures around the world are considering how to incorporate the names of new technologies into their languages. What are the benefits of developing a new word in one's native language as opposed to adopting a name from another? What else do Icelanders do to preserve their culture in the modern day?

9. When it comes to the comfort and safety of LGBTQIA+ people in Iceland, queer activist Eva Maria asserts, "People come here because society is so accepting, not just because the legislation exists." How can we foster an inclusive environment in our communities with and without legislative support?

10. In discussing compliance with mandated gender ratios for board members, entrepreneur Ragnhildur says, "Things are still moving too slowly." How do we speed up the tides of change?

11. Rose's story highlights some of the hidden pitfalls of "equitable" custody arrangements. What changes would you make to ensure that joint custody arrangements are safe for survivors of domestic abuse and their children?

12. According to Reid, Iceland's size is one of the factors that enables comparatively rapid changes to its social policies. What lessons can larger countries learn from Iceland's activists and policy makers? What lessons stood out to you personally?

13. As someone who found herself unexpectedly in the spotlight, Reid has tried to make the best of her platform. If you were in her shoes, what would you try to accomplish with your platform? How would you contend with the scrutiny from the media?

14. What are some ways you can get involved in your local community to promote gender equality? What can you encourage your government to do?

ENDNOTES

Chapter 1: An Immigrant in Iceland

1   According to "The Population Increased by 1,290 in the First Quarter of 2021," Statistics Iceland, May 4, 2021, https://statice.is/publications /news-archive/inhabitants/population-in-the-1st-quarter-2021/.

2   As shown in the Society at a Glance 2019 report for OECD social indicators   (https://www.oecd.org/publications/society-at-a-glance-19991290 .htm).

3   Iceland actually became a sovereign country in 1918, but its head of state was the king of Denmark until Iceland claimed full independence in 1944.

4   See, for example, Andre P. Audette, "Gender Equality Supports Happiness and Well-Being," Gender Policy Report, September 13, 2019, https:// genderpolicyreport.umn.edu/gender-equality-supports-happiness/.

5   "Global Gender Gap Report," World Economic Forum, March 30, 2021, https://www.weforum.org/reports/global-gender-gap -report-2022/.

6   For an excellent overview of this situation and the Nordics in general as compared to other nations, see "The Nordic Gender Effect at Work," Nordic Council of Ministers, August 20, 2018, https://www.norden.org/en /publication/nordic-gender-effect-work-0.

Chapter 2: Helping Parents Helps Us All

7   Parents can also agree upon additional payments beyond the legal pre-scribed minimum and can make arrangements for direct payments of

these additional funds. For more information, see https://www.tr.is/en /child-support.

8   See, for example, Jacqueline Howard, "The Least and Most Dangerous Countries to Be a Newborn," CNN, February 20, 2018, https:// edition.cnn.com/2018/02/20/health/unicef-newborn-deaths-by-country -study/index.html; Nanna Árnadóttir, "Iceland Has a Low Rate of C-Sections," *Reykjavík Grapevine*, January 18, 2016, https://grapevine.is /news/2016/01/18/iceland-has-lowest-rate-of-c-sections/.

9   For data on fathers and paternity leave, see, for example, Ásdís A. Arnalds, Gudný Björk Eydal, and Ingólfur V. Gíslason, "Equal Rights to Paid Parental Leave and Caring Fathers: The Case of Iceland," *Icelandic Review of Politics and Administration* 9, no. 2 (December 2019): 323–344, http://dx.doi.org/10.13177/irpa.a.2013.9.2.4; Arna Ólafsson and Herdís Steingrímsdóttir. "How Does Daddy at Home Affect Marital Stability," *Economic Journal* 130, no. 629 (July 2020): 1471–1500, https:// doi.org/10.1093/ej/ueaa009. See also "The Nordic Gender Effect at Work," which states that Icelandic fathers take the highest share of their leave of all the Nordic countries.

10 Studies vary on the results, but see, for example, "Gender Equality in Iceland," https://www.stjornarradid.is/media/velferdarraduneyti-media/media /acrobat-skjol/jafnrettisstofa_stepping_stones.pdf; "Iceland Leads the Way to Women's Equality in the Workplace," *Economist*, March 4, 2020, https:// www.economist.com/graphic-detail/2020/03/04/iceland-leads-the-way -to-womens-equality-in-the-workplace; Esteban Ortiz-Ospina, Sandra Tzvetkova, and Max Roser, "Women's Employment," Our World in Data, March 2018, https://ourworldindata.org/female-labor-supply.

11 Ninety-five percent of all three- to five-year olds in Iceland are enrolled in child care (stat from 2016). See "The Nordic Gender Effect at Work."

12 See, for example, Thoroddur Bjarnason and Andrea Hjálmsdóttir, "Egalitarian Attitudes Towards the Division of Household Labor Among

Adolescents in Iceland," *Sex Roles* 59, no. 1 (July 2008): 49–60, https://doi.org/10.1007/s11199-008-9428-0.

The Saga-Era Sprakki Who Defied Convention

13   All quotes from *Njáls Saga* in this section are from the Penguin Classics edition (2001), trans. Robert Cook.

14   Hallgerdur Long-Legs: The sagas are Iceland's most well-known and important contribution to global literature. Written between the twelfth and fourteenth centuries loosely about events that took place from the island's settlement until about the eleventh century, Iceland's sagas are gripping (though often meandering) yarns of family feuds, fierce battles, tragic romances, and adventurous travel. Themes of honor, vengeance, and armed conflict permeate the sagas and provide an insight into the values and way of life of the first generations of inhabitants of what has become Iceland. While the authors of most of the sagas are unknown, modern scholarship indicates that most were likely written by men and told from a male perspective. In *Njáls Saga*, for example, of the 650 named characters, only 100 are women.

Chapter 3: The Strength in Sisterhood

15   Richard Kenny, "How One Country Persuaded Teens to Give Up Drink and Drugs," BBC News, November 15, 2017, https://www.bbc.com/news/av/stories-41973296.

16   The documents are unclear on whether the same two farms had both electricity and telephones, though it's likely this was the case.

17   *Gengnar Slóðir: Samband sunnlenskra kvenna fimmtíu ára 1928–1978* (Samband sunnlenskra kvenna, 1978), 175, translation by Jonas Moody.

Chapter 4: Stigma-Free Sexuality

18   The national curriculum can be accessed in English at https://www.government.is/topics/education/curriculum/. An overview of the sex

education provisions under the auspices of the health care service is here: https://www.heilsugaeslan.is/um-hh/frettasafn/stok-frett/2018/02/14 /Kynfraedsla-i-skolum/. In late 2020, the Ministry of Education, Science and Culture formed a committee to improve sex education at the primary and secondary school levels in Iceland.

19   Gréta Sigrídur Einarsdóttir, "Digital Sexual Violence Now Punishable by up to Four Years in Prison," *Iceland Review*, February 18, 2021, https://www .icelandreview.com/politics/digital-sexual-violence-now-punishable-by -up-to-four-years-in-prison/.

20   "BBC 100 Women 2019: Who Is on the List This Year?," BBC, October 16, 2019, https://www.bbc.com/news/world-50042279.

21   Owl Fisher, "Too Many of Us Young Trans People Are Crying Out for Help. Will You Listen?," *Guardian*, March 28, 2018, https://www.theguardian .com/commentisfree/2018/mar/28/trans-young-people-suicide-support -mental-health.

22   Vala Hafstad, "Big-Breasted Jesus Causes Controversy," Iceland Monitor, September 14, 2020, https://icelandmonitor.mbl.is/news/culture_and _living/2020/09/14/big_breasted_jesus_causes_controversy/.

The No-Holds-Barred Sprakki of the Middle Ages

23   Ólöf the Rich: Ólöf the Rich is best known through her words upon receiving news of her husband's death, and the phrase about avenging it is now a saying that means "Don't get mad, get even." It is a symbol of female determination that harkens to the strong women from the sagas. Her tenacity and bravery are undisputed, but many of the details surrounding the murder of her husband, Björn, her subsequent actions, their travels, her visit to the king, and of course the legend around her deathbed wish remain mere conjecture and legend.

Chapter 5: Claiming the Corporate Purse Strings

24 Ortiz-Ospina, Tzvetkova, and Roser, "Women's Employment."

25 The top eight hundred is determined by Credit Info, an Icelandic company, and is similar to a Fortune 500 ranking, although turnover is not the only ranking. See https://www.creditinfo.is/um-creditinfo/frett .aspx?NewsID=81 (Icelandic only).

26 Sundiatu Dixon-Fyle, Kevin Dolan, Vivian Hunt, and Sara Prince, "Diversity Wins: How Inclusion Matters," McKinsey & Company, May 19, 2020, https://www.mckinsey.com/featured-insights/diversity-and-inclusion /diversity-wins-how-inclusion-matters/.

27 For details on the equal pay certification, see "Equal Pay Certification," Directorate of Equality Iceland, https://www.jafnretti.is/en/vinnumarkadur /equal-pay-certification/equal-pay-certification.

28 In November, 2011, the government of Iceland recognized an independent and sovereign State of Palestine within the pre-1967 Six Day War borders.

29 See "Direct Use of Geothermal Resources," National Energy Authority, https://nea.is/geothermal/direct-utilization/nr/91.

Chapter 6: Being Seen and Heard in the Media

30 Sólborg's Instagram page was called Fávitar ("Idiots") and had 32,200 followers. Shortly after this interview, she announced she would be pursuing other projects and would no longer be updating the page regularly, so when this book is published, the number of followers may have decreased.

31 Christian Mogensen and Stine Helding Rand, "The Angry Internet: A Threat to Gender Equality, Democracy, and Well-Being," Centre for Digital Youth Care, November 2020, https://cfdp.dk/wp-content/uploads/2020/11 /CFDP_the_angry_internet_ISSUE.pdf.

The Undaunted Sprakki Who Fought for Nature

32 Sigrídur of Brattholt: Sigrídur's accomplishments occurred only just before living memory. Her reputation and life have not been subjected to centuries of exaggeration and outright fictionalization, as have those of Hallgerdur Long-Legs and Ólöf the Rich, but her renowned victory of saving a waterfall solely by her own dogged persistence and physical endurance is almost certainly hyperbole. Gullfoss was preserved because of the economic inviability of the development plans and not Sigrídur's protests. And she almost certainly rode a horse—or at least walked with proper footwear—to the capital.

Chapter 7: Finding Harmony in the Wild

33 For information on the effect of climate change on women, see, for example, Mary Robinson, *Climate Justice: Hope, Resilience, and the Fight for a Sustainable Future* (London: Bloomsbury, 2019).

34 Steinunn Sigurdardóttir, *Heida: A Shepherd at the Edge of the World*, trans. Philip Roughton (London: John Murray, 2019).

35 "Áætlun um öryggi sjófarenda, 2019–2033" [Strategy for safety of seafarers, 2019–2033], Government of Iceland, https://www.stjornarradid.is /library/02-Rit—skyrslur-og-skrar/Áætlun%20um%20öryggi%20 sjófarenda%202019.pdf (Icelandic only).

36 Historian Thórunn Magnúsdóttir found around four thousand registered seawomen from 1891 to 1981, and more recent studies indicate that many more women were at sea during this time than legend has led us to believe. See, for example, Margaret Willson, *Seawomen of Iceland: Survival on the Edge* (Seattle: University of Washington Press, 2016).

Chapter 8: Art as an Instrument of Equality

37 The national basketball teams have no bonuses, but men's and women's team members receive the same per diems.

38 It is not housed in the home of a former writer, but a "women's book lounge museum about Icelandic women writers" called Konubókastofa is located in the village of Eyrarbakki. www.konubokastofa.is.

39 Gerdur Kristný, *Bloodhoof*, trans. Rory McTurk (Todmorden, UK: Arc, 2012): 40.

40 Kamilla Einarsdóttir, *Kópavogskrónika* [The Kópavogur chronicles] (Reykjavík: Bjartur, 2018), translation by Jonas Moody: 58.

41 Additional grants were awarded in the summer of 2020 and early 2021 in the wake of the COVID-19 pandemic.

The Sprakkar Who Rallied a Nation

42 The Women's Day Off: The idea for the women's day off originated with the Red Stockings, a radical (for the times) feminist group that was inspired by an American organization of the same time. The concept initially was to strike to protest wage inequality and other unfair practices, but organizers felt that the term "strike" would discourage people from taking part. It would instead be a "day off." After all, what employer would not permit his or her employee to take a day off? Many men, it should be noted, were very encouraging of the protest. Despite the impact of the event on society on that day and in subsequent years, at the time of writing forty-five years later, the gender pay gap still has yet to be eliminated, and every few years on October 24, Iceland's women leave work early at the time they have been paid as much as they should be. On the first day off, that was 2:05 p.m.; in 2016, it was 2:38 p.m., and 3:01 p.m. in 2020.

Chapter 9: No Woman Is an Island

43 For figures in the United States, see Phillip Connor and Abby Budiman, "Immigrant Share in U.S. Nears Record High but Remains Below That of Many Other Countries," Pew Research Center, January 30, 2019, https://www.pewresearch.org/fact-tank/2019/01/30/immigrant-share-in-u-s

-nears-record-high-but-remains-below-that-of-many-other-countries/. For Icelandic figures, visit www.statice.is.

44 You can search the list here (in Icelandic but intuitive to use) to see if your name would make the cut: https://vefur.island.is/mannanofn/leit-ad-nafni/.

45 Iona Rangeley-Wilson, "Icelander's [sic] Immigration Tolerance Increasing," *Reykjavík Grapevine*, September 24, 2020, https://grapevine.is /news/2020/09/24/icelanders-immigration-tolerance-increasing/.

46 Unnur Dís Skaptadóttir and Kristín Loftsdóttir, "Konur af erlendrum uppruna. Hvar kreppir að?" ["Women of foreign origin: Where do the constraints lie?"], University of Iceland, 2019, https://www.stjornarradid .is/lisalib/getfile.aspx?itemid=c6482f7c-570d-11ea-945f-005056bc4d74 (Icelandic only).

47 Sigrún Sif Jóelsdóttir and Grant Wyeth, "The Misogynist Violence of Iceland's Feminist Paradise," *Foreign Policy*, July 15, 2020, https:// foreignpolicy.com/2020/07/15/the-misogynist-violence-of-icelands -feminist-paradise/.

48 Hildur Fjóla Antonsdóttir and Thorbjörg Sigrídur Gunnlaugsdóttir, "Tilkynntar nauðganir til lögreglu á árunum 2008 og 2009: Um afbrotið nauðgun, sakborning, brotaþola og málsmeðferð," ["Incidents of rape reported to police in 2008 and 2009"], University of Iceland, October 2013, https://edda.hi.is/wp-content/uploads/2014/04/Einkenni-og-meðferð -nauðgunarmála-október-2013.pdf (Icelandic only).

The Sprakki Who Shattered the Glass Ceiling

49 Vigdís Finnbogadóttir: Vigdís admitted years later in her memoirs that she herself was skeptical about whether she was "up for the job"; the self-doubt, she said, was so prevalent among women of her generation. A telegram signed by all members of the fishing vessel *Gudbjartur* imploring her to run indicated that her support was broader than merely among the capital's chattering classes. Once elected, Vigdís made the most of

the attention her election garnered on the global stage. She undertook twenty state visits abroad during her tenure. The delegations on such visits were also much larger than they had been, comprising not only politicians but also leading business and cultural figures who would promote the image of a progressive and forward-thinking nation. In 1986, she hosted the historic Reykjavík Summit between Ronald Reagan and Mikhail Gorbachev, an occasion often credited as signifying the beginning of the end of the Cold War. Vigdís also championed the protection of the Icelandic language, and on visits to various communities around the country, she began a tradition of planting three trees, not only to defend against erosion but also to leave lasting memories of the occasion behind.

Chapter 10: Politics on Her Own Terms

50   Recent rankings on the number of women in national parliaments can be found here: https://data.ipu.org/women-ranking/?month=9&year=2021.

51   For English stories on the scandal, see Anna Andersen, "'Finally, a Body Worthy of My Dick': Inside the Sexist Political Scandal Rocking Iceland," Nylon, March 28, 2019, https://www.nylon.com/political-scandal -iceland-sexism-metoo; Jelena Ćirić, "In Focus: The Klaustur Scandal," *Iceland Review*, February 8, 2019, https://www.icelandreview.com /politics/in-focus-the-klaustur-scandal/. A defense from one of the individuals involved (in Icelandic) is "Ekki í stjórnmálum til að vera vinsæll," ["Not in politics to be popular"], *Morgunblaðið*, April 8, 2019, https:// www.mbl.is/frettir/innlent/2019/08/04/ekki_oedlilegt_ad_tonninn_se _grimmari/.

52   Jóhann Bjarni Kolbeinsson, "Forseti Íslands: 'Auðvitað ofbauð mér,'" ["The president of Iceland: 'Of course I was shocked'"), RÚV, December 2, 2018, https://www.ruv.is/frett/forseti-islands-audvitad-ofbaud-mer.

Chapter 11: Within Reach

53   Funding for the expenses of the trip was covered by Iceland's Gender Equality Fund and the private pharmaceutical firm Alvogen AlvoTech.

54   The interview can be seen here: "Konur í Zaatari þrá nýtt upphaf," ["Women in Zaatari want a new beginning"], UN Women Iceland, https://unwomen.is/herferdir-verkefni/konur-zaatari-thra-nytt-upphaf/ (Icelandic voiceovers but interview is in English).

55   The four Jellyfish who took part in this adventure were Brynhildur Ólafsdóttir, Birna Bragadóttir, Soffía S. Sigurgeirsdóttir, and Thórey Vilhjálmsdóttir Proppé.

INDEX

ABOUT THE AUTHOR

© Kristín Bogadóttir

Eliza Reid is a journalist, editor, and cofounder of the annual Iceland Writers Retreat. Eliza grew up on a hobby farm near Ottawa, Canada, and moved to Iceland in 2003, five years after winning a student raffle for a date with the man who later became her husband. That husband, Gudni Th. Jóhannesson, took office as president of Iceland on August 1, 2016, and Eliza became the country's First Lady. In that capacity, she has been active in promoting gender equality, entrepreneurship and innovation, tourism and sustainability, and the country's writers and rich literary heritage. Being the spouse of the head of state is an immense privilege, full of surreal and wonderful experiences. Eliza has been candid about the role, which is an unofficial position with no job description, penning a lauded op-ed in the *New York Times* and delivering a TEDx Talk on the topic. This is her first book.